The Celebrated

Mrs Oldfield

The Life and Art of
an Augustan Actress

Joanne Lafler

Southern Illinois University Press
Carbondale and Edwardsville

92 91 90 89   4 3 2 1

Library of Congress Cataloging-in-Publication Data

Lafler, Joanne
    The celebrated Mrs. Oldfield: the life and art of an Augustan
actress / Joanne Lafler.
        p. cm.
    Bibliography: p.
    Includes index.
        1. Oldfield, Anne, 1683–1730. 2. Actors—Great Britain—
Biography. 3. Theater—Great Britain—History—18th century.
I. Title.
PN2598.O5L34   1989
792'.028'0924—dc19
[B]   88-34654
ISBN 0-8093-1485-1   CIP

Frontispiece: The youthful Anne Oldfield. Portrait attributed to Jonathan
        Richardson. Courtesy of the Garrick Club.

For my parents
Sol and Dorothy Wolffson
in loving memory

Contents

Illustrations on pages 73–82.

Preface

Anne Oldfield began her career nearly forty years after the first women began to perform professionally on the English stage, but she is the first English actress whose life and career can be examined in some detail. During her lifetime, the first theatrical biographies were published. Incomplete, inaccurate, often sensational, they are at least a starting point for the work of the modern biographer. They are also an index of popularity or notoriety.

Anne Oldfield was the subject of two early biographies: *Authentick Memoirs of the Life of that Celebrated Actress, Mrs. Ann* [sic] *Oldfield* (London, 1730) and *Faithful Memoirs of the Life, Amours and Performances of that justly Celebrated, and Most Eminent Actress of her Time, Mrs. Anne Oldfield* (London, 1731). *Authentick Memoirs,* rushed into publication less than a week after her death, is the work of an anonymous author who attempted to discover something about the actress's origins and early life but knew almost nothing about the history of the stage or her early theatrical career. *Faithful Memoirs,* by "William Egerton, Esq."—a pseudonym for the bookseller, Edmund Curll—is much more reliable about Mrs. Oldfield's stage career, but it is a typical product of Grub Street, a magpie's nest of excerpts from earlier published works, letters from contributors, and lucubrations on related subjects. Curll dedicated the book to Margaret Saunders, an actress whom Mrs. Oldfield had taken into her household and who was therefore hardly an unbiased source of information. In his *History of the English Stage,* published in 1741, Curll included a statement from Mrs. Saunders that corrected details about John Vanbrugh's patronage of Mrs. Oldfield and the age of young Arthur Maynwaring. In using material from *Authentick Memoirs* and *Faithful Memoirs,* I have tried to be careful to indicate items for which there is no independent evidence.

The invaluable source for Mrs. Oldfield's professional life, and indeed, for any study of early eighteenth-century theater, is Colley Cibber's autobiography, *An Apology for the Life of Mr. Colley Cibber,* written in 1740. Cibber was Anne Oldfield's colleague from the beginning of her career in 1699 until her death in 1730. I am mindful that he was often sloppy about dates and that he had his prejudices and passions. He plainly adored Mrs. Oldfield, as well he might, for she performed brilliantly in many of his own plays and acted with him in countless others. Aside from his admiration of her acting, he seems to have gotten on with her very well in professional dealings, and in his autobiography he left a picture of her common sense, good humor, and artistic dedication that may be a shade too perfect but offers a pleasant contrast to the barbs that were sometimes hurled at her by unhappy rivals. Snob that he was, he also admired, and perhaps envied, her success in the social world. Partly because he liked her so much, I tend to like him and must remind myself that others did not.

The standard modern biography, *Gay Was the Pit: The Life and Times of Anne Oldfield* (London: Max Reinhardt, 1957), by Robert Gore-Brown, has been a frustrating source. The author did considerable research, but he failed to document any of it. Annotating his text occupied the better part of my first summer's research in London. Without his valuable clues I would never have stumbled upon important material in the British Library manuscript collection, the Garrick Club, and so on. But he also tended to be creative in the use of his sources, to put thoughts and feelings into the minds of his characters, and to invent scenes, such as the one in which Anne and her lover stand hand in hand in the wings, listening to a love song from *Sir Courtly Nice.* In addition to setting the record straight—or at least straighter—I have tried to rescue Mrs. Oldfield from the excesses of the quaint tradition of theatrical biography in which Gore-Brown was writing. Without intending to, he often belittled his subject. *Gay Was the Pit* preserves the legend that the actress herself probably helped to create, of a "gay, thoughtless creature" not unlike the heroines she played. That acting could be a serious business for a woman is a notion too often ignored in popular theatrical biography.

It is a pleasure to acknowledge the institutions and individuals who have aided me in the research and writing of this book. The staffs of the Harvard Theatre Collection, the Yale School of Drama, and the Folger Shakespeare Library helped me to make the most of the very short time I was able to spend on these important collections. Roy H. Fry and Brother Michael Grace of the Loyola University of Chicago Library responded patiently to my queries about the "Richard Savage" letter.

During two research trips to England, I received valuable assistance from Betty Beasley and Patricia Lumsden at the Garrick Club, and from the staffs of the Enthoven Collection at the Victoria and Albert Museum and the Westminster City Library. I am grateful for the help of Clyve Jones, of the Institute of Historical Research in the University of London, and Frances Harris, who led me, literally, to important materials that she was indexing in the Duchess of Marlborough's papers in the British Library; to Victor Belcher and John Green-acombe, editors in the Survey of London project, who shared notes and unpublished material about Mrs. Oldfield's house in Mayfair and helped me to find the deed for her property on Southampton Street; and to William James Taylor and Norman Keen, of British Alcan, who provided me with information and pictorial material about Mrs. Oldfield's younger son's estate, Chalfont Park.

A number of scholars in eighteenth-century theater and related areas of history have been generous in sharing material and answering questions. In 1978, Edward A. Langhans invited me to look through his notes and his then-unpublished entry on the life of Mrs. Oldfield for the *Biographical Dictionary*. He has since answered numerous questions. My debt to the scholarship of Robert D. Hume and Judith Milhous is obvious. Kalman A. Burnim showed and discussed with me his work on Mrs. Oldfield's iconography for the *Biographical Dictionary*. Catherine Howells read and made helpful comments on my chapter on Arthur Maynwaring. Norma Perry shared some ideas about Hariett Churchill. Shirley Strum Kenny responded to queries about the work of George Farquhar and made many valuable comments. Errors in the use of this material are, of course, my responsibility. Dunbar Ogden, who first encouraged me to explore the relationship of actors, texts, and theatrical tradition, has continued to be a source of encouragement and inspiration.

Because this study was accomplished without grants to cover travel expenses, I am especially indebted to the friends who provided hospitality as well as encouragement during my research trips: Sonya Caston-Chassell, Sue and Dan Gutterman, Lee Hutchinson, Anita King, Joan and Stephen Mason, Walt McKibben, Elizabeth Spillius, and my sister Davida Higgin and her family.

Closer to home, I am grateful to Marian Ury and Georgia Wright, who read the manuscript and made many thoughtful suggestions, and to my colleagues in the Institute for Historical Study, a haven for independent scholars in the San Francisco Bay area.

I also owe a debt of gratitude to Robert S. Phillips, editorial director of Southern Illinois University Press, who offered encouragement and support when it mattered most.

My family was closely involved in this project at every step. My daughter Ruth not only found a copy of *The Lovely Wanton* on a rack of historical romances in a Berkeley pharmacy, thereby sparking my curiosity about the later history of Mrs. Oldfield's legend, but applied her considerable copyediting skills to an early draft of the manuscript. My daughter Janet accepted Anne Oldfield as a part of her youth—the invisible lady at the dinner table—and once noted, without apparent irony, that she probably knew more about the subject than most college professors. Sometime later she pointed out that what I was getting at in one passage was a classical distinction between power and authority.

My husband has supported me in every sense of that overused word. He never counted the cost. He read every word more than once and made constructive comments. He created the software for my word processor and held my hand when it behaved badly. And he found endlessly persuasive ways of saying, "Finish the book!"

The Celebrated Mrs Oldfield

I

Origins

Next to the actor's art itself, nothing is more perishable than celebrity. At the time of her death in 1730, Anne Oldfield was known not only to every theatergoer in London but to the larger reading public. Stories of her luxurious style of life and socially prominent friends, gossip about her lovers, and rumors about the extent of her wealth were widely reported. Long after her death, whenever her name was mentioned it was inevitably as "the celebrated Mrs. Oldfield." Today her name is known chiefly to a handful of specialists in eighteenth-century theater. Her grave in the south aisle of Westminster Abbey is unremarked and unremarkable. In the dim light, one can hardly make out the worn inscription, which reveals only her name and the year of her death. There is nothing to indicate who she was or how she came to be buried in England's national shrine, among soldiers, statesmen, and poets.

If her lover Charles Churchill had had his way, a monument would have been erected near her place of burial, and the passerby would know at least that Anne Oldfield had been honored for her contribution to the English stage. But Churchill's request was denied. Despite her eminence, a lingering prejudice attached to her profession. And despite the propriety with which she conducted her private life, she was still the unmarried mother of two illegitimate sons. Perhaps the question to ask is not *why* she was buried in Westminster Abbey, but how it ever happened at all.

Only a handful of actresses have dominated the stage so completely. Throughout most of the eighteenth century, she had no peer in the portrayal of the aristocratic young ladies who were a principal ingredient of comedy—vain, headstrong creatures who contrived to be at once maddening and charming. From the time she became a star, in her early twenties, aspiring playwrights automatically thought in terms of "Oldfield roles." Memories of her Lady Betty Modish and Lady Townly haunted her successors for several generations. Even in tragedy, which she professed to dislike, she left her mark upon an impressive repertoire and created a new kind of heroine, the stalwart, saintly patriot. During her thirty-year career she appeared in over one hundred roles, of which nearly seventy were original. But history has been unkind to the age whose taste and values she represented so perfectly. Comedies that reflected the narrow world of fashionable society—"the Town"—and tragedies in the correct French manner, very much to the liking of Augustan spectators, sat poorly with Victorian audiences. In our own time, except for Farquhar's *Recruiting Officer* and *The Beaux' Stratagem,* virtually none of the plays in which she starred are performed; many of them are read today only as "landmarks" of eighteenth-century drama in anthologies—perhaps the worst fate that can befall once-popular works.

Her beauty was legendary in her own time and for generations afterward, prompting one author to write, more than one hundred years after her death: "I imagine Anne Oldfield, though descriptions of her give us no idea of such majesty as Mrs. Siddons, to have been otherwise the most beautiful woman that ever trod the English stage."[1] We must take this largely on faith. The best artists of the time painted her, but their work tells us little except that she had brown hair, blue or gray eyes, a fair complexion, a long but well-shaped nose, a small, full-lipped mouth, and that in later years she grew distinctly plump, in the manner of her contemporary, Queen Caroline. Sir Godfrey Kneller's portrait of her lover Arthur Maynwaring captures his personality so brilliantly that even the casual viewer has a distinct impression of the man. Kneller's portrait of Anne is disappointingly lifeless and conventional. (Styles of female beauty do not "travel" well to later eras.) Only the portraitist Jonathan Richardson succeeded in conveying something of the charm, elegance, and "large, speaking eyes" upon which admirers remarked.

Recapturing her impact on the stage, from fragmentary evidence, is a bit like restoring a mosaic from which one can finally step back and perceive—or at least guess at—the whole. Only with David Garrick, who made his debut eleven years after her death, do we begin to get detailed descriptions of what actors looked like and did. Before then, we must settle for general impressions of appearance and manner—as, for example, that Anne Oldfield was "of superior Height, but with a lovely Proportion," and that her voice was "Sweet, Strong, Piercing and Melodious; her Pronunciation Voluble, Distinct and Musical."[2] In the late 1720s, when she was still at the height of her artistic and personal powers, young Charles Macklin and even younger Tom Davies saw her perform. Their comments, both as eyewitnesses and as transmitters of theatrical tradition, are especially valuable in providing some badly needed detail. Davies, for example, noted her trick of half-shutting her eyes "when she intended to give effect to some brilliant or gay thought." Macklin testified to her great energy and liveliness and left behind a brilliant account of her incomparable Lady Townly.[3] For the most part, however, we must rely upon the more general comments of her colleagues and admirers, and upon play texts, in which hints of her distinctive manner can sometimes be detected in the speech rhythms and phrases of the characters that were written for her.

As the memories of eighteenth-century audiences grew dim, the actress began to fade from view. But if her art was eventually forgotten, her legend has stubbornly persisted. In 1744, Samuel Johnson made her a heroine (of sorts) in his biography of the poet Richard Savage. In 1750, the first allusion to her romance with George Farquhar appeared in print. Such stories, accepted uncritically by later biographers and critics, were spun into more elaborate myths. Since the publication of *The Palmy Days of Nance Oldfield* in 1898, her legend has surfaced in a lively, if unreliable biography—*Gay Was the Pit: The Life and Times of Anne Oldfield*—and in two romantic novels.[4] She herself contributed to the process of mythmaking, for she was undoubtedly the source of stories about her mother's genteel origins, her father's commission in the Horse Guards, her stagestruck childhood, and her fairy-tale discovery by George Farquhar. She must also have encouraged what we might call the ultimate legend, that Lady Betty Modish was her creation—perhaps her very self. At the same time, either by omission or design she left behind not a single letter, not even a hastily scribbled note, that might reveal her motives or feelings.[5] Indeed, like many public figures she may have consciously constructed a public image, "the celebrated Mrs. Oldfield," for the purpose of protecting her privacy.

The lives of actresses have always exercised a fascination for readers, simultaneously evoking feelings of envy and moral superiority. Every girl has probably entertained something like the Cinderella fantasy. The notion of achieving success almost by accident is charming. The idea of a woman working actively for success in a competitive world has another, darker fascination, giving rise to the popular archetype of the scheming, amoral vixen. Part of the enduring appeal of Anne Oldfield's story lies in the combination of these elements. In trying to make sense of a life lived so publicly, we can hardly discount such legends. True or not, they tell us what people wanted to believe about her and how she became the first stage star in the modern sense—the embodiment of ambivalent fantasies of success.

The story of Anne Oldfield's origins and early life derives from the two admittedly unreliable biographical memoirs published soon after her death: *Authentick Memoirs* (1730) and *Faithful Memoirs* (1731). The accounts are at best sketchy, and in some instances the two versions do not agree. She herself, telling different stories as the spirit moved her, must have been responsible for some of the discrepancies. Yet the accounts of her childhood reveal important themes and patterns.

Parish records indicate a number of Oldfields in Yorkshire and Essex, but without much more information about her grandparents it is impossible to trace the family origins any further than Pall Mall in the late seventeenth century. The many quaint spellings of the actress's surname in cast lists and other theatrical documents suggest that the family name must have been pronounced "O-feel," or "Ole-feel," a circumstance that led wits of the period to call her "Ophelia," although the Shakespeare heroine was a role she never played.[6]

There is some independent evidence to support the story that Anne's paternal grandfather was a tavern keeper in Pall Mall, a point that the two early biographies treat quite differently. *Faithful Memoirs* dismisses him in a single phrase: "Her Grandfather was a Vintner, but on her Mother's side she was well Descended."[7] *Authentick Memoirs* discusses at some length the honest, reputable, hardworking Oldfield and his success story, recounting how, after he completed his apprenticeship, he was able to purchase his own tavern, "The George." Eighteenth-century readers would have known exactly where to find the tavern: on the north side of Pall Mall, "over-against the *Cocoa Tree*,"[8] for the Cocoa Tree was a favorite resort of Tory wits in the first half of the century. Poor rate books for the Pall Mall district of the parish of St. Martin-in-the-Fields indicate that a George Oldfield was a ratepayer on the north side of Pall Mall as far back as 1670, and newspaper clippings from the 1670s testify to the existence of a tavern called "The George" in Pall Mall.[9] To be sure, there is nothing specific to connect Anne with these Oldfields or with the George Tavern on Pall Mall, but the story of the vintner Oldfield in *Authentick Memoirs* at least has some substance.

The rest of the story is on decidedly shaky ground. We are told that at his death Oldfield left his property—estimated in *Authentick Memoirs* as worth between sixty and seventy pounds a year—to his younger son, Anne's father.[10] According to the rate books, Oldfield's widow, not his son, was the nominal tenant of the Pall Mall property, a fact not inconsistent with the story that Anne's father inherited the property. (The paying of rates indicated tenancy, not necessarily ownership.) Unfortunately, the rate books are missing or incomplete after 1682, and no Oldfields are listed as ratepayers on Pall Mall after the street became part of the new parish of St. James Piccadilly in 1685. Therefore, even if we knew his Christian name, it is impossible to trace the whereabouts of Anne's father at the time of his marriage or at the birth of his daughter.

Anne was probably responsible for the characterization of her mother as a gentlewoman, but nothing is known about her mother's family. We know only that her mother, who outlived her and is mentioned in her will, was named Anne. Also mentioned in the will is an aunt, Jane Gourlaw. It is likely, therefore, that Anne's mother is the Anne Gourlaw who, on November 7, 1681, married a William Oldfield in the tiny parish church of St. Mary le Bone.[11]

The date and place of Anne's birth cannot be documented. If, as the early accounts of her life agree, she was born in Pall Mall in 1683, she was not baptised in the parish church, St. Martin-in-the-Fields, or in any of the neighboring churches.[12] The absence of a baptismal record is not unusual for the period. The births of many eminent personages of the eighteenth century cannot be accounted for, since parish records are not always complete and children might be born elsewhere than under the family roof.

That her father lived extravagantly and aspired to a more glamorous life than that of a tradesman's son is a theme of both versions of her childhood. *Authentick Memoirs* says that he first mortgaged, then sold the Pall Mall property to his elder brother, the proceeds of which enabled him to buy a position in the Horse Guards.[13] Yet it is unlikely that he held a commission. The Horse Guards and the Life Guards, as royal bodyguards, chose their officers from among the elite. Even the noncommissioned troopers, or "Private Gentlemen," tended to be the sons of gentry, not of tavern keepers.[14]

England was at peace during Anne's infancy, and the life of a Guardsman would be easygoing, if not very remunerative. The lowest-ranking officers, cornets, received a per diem allowance of fourteen shillings. A trooper received only two shillings sixpence a day, out of which he paid for his horse's forage.[15] By way of judging buying power, it is worth noting that the price of admission to the theater at this time was four shillings for a box, two shillings sixpence for the pit, one shilling sixpence for the middle gallery, and one shilling for the upper gallery. "Advanced prices," for new or spectacular productions, were, respectively, five shillings, four shillings, two shillings sixpence, and one shilling sixpence.[16] A reasonably good seat at Drury Lane cost approximately one day's pay for a trooper. It is easy to understand why few tradesmen's sons sought a career in the Guards, especially those who had families to support. The assumption was that even a trooper had an independent income.

Anne's father is said to have died "not many Years after" the time he joined the Guards, and both memoirs agree that Mrs. Oldfield and her daughter were left very badly off. But here the two accounts begin to diverge. *Faithful Memoirs* says nothing of Anne's education, merely noting that in their straitened circumstances mother and daughter went to live with Mrs. Oldfield's sister, a Mrs. Voss, who kept the Mitre Tavern not far away from Pall Mall, in St. James's Market.[17] According to this account, Anne was apprenticed to a local sempstress—not a mantua-maker, who sewed fine gowns and dresses, but a maker of shirts and underlinens. Yet Anne had at least learned to read, for "her Genius for the Stage was predominant, as appeared by her continual reading and repeating Parts of Plays."[18]

Authentick Memoirs, returning to the theme of the honest, reputable Oldfields, tells not of the aunt and her tavern, or of Mrs. Wooten the sempstress, but of Anne's father's brother, who saw to it that she was sent to school to learn "all the Accomplishments suitable to her Sex." She was not in school very long, however, "before she discovered such an invincible Inclination to become an Actress upon the Stage, that no Persuasions, Admonitions, or even Threatnings of her Parents and Friends (who were all to the last Degree averse to her engaging in

such a Profession) cou'd deter her from it."[19] How old Anne is supposed to have been when she set her heart upon a stage career, against
such strong family opposition, is not indicated. Presumably she would
have started school when she was seven or eight years old, a rather
young age at which to develop so invincible an inclination.

The anonymous author of *Authentick Memoirs* to the contrary, such
formal education as she received must have been sketchy, even by the
standards of female education in the late seventeenth century. Her
signature on legal documents—the only extant examples of her handwriting—is clear, but the letters are awkwardly formed, almost child-
ish. Poor handwriting need not, of course, reflect upon her intelligence
or on her ability to read.

There are two quite different versions of her passage to adulthood
in the late 1690s. *Authentick Memoirs* indicates that Anne continued to
live with, or at least under the care of, her paternal uncle. The third
edition, "with Large Additions and Amendments," offers a mildly
scandalous anecdote. "Her Uncle, in order to keep her from going
Abroad after she had got a little Learning, made her his Bar-Keeper,
in which Place she continued not long before she enamour'd the Heart
of a Gentleman who frequented the House; and soon after she left her
Uncle and went and lived with the said Gentleman."[20]

The far more romantic story told in *Faithful Memoirs* and, in a slightly
different version, by the Drury Lane prompter, Chetwood, is surely
the gospel as Anne wished it to be known. It tells of the young
playwright George Farquhar, who, dining one day at the Mitre Tavern, overheard someone in a room "behind the Bar" reading a play
aloud with "such just vivacity, and Humour of the Characters, as gave
him infinite Surprize, and Satisfaction." Curious about the reader's
identity, but loath to appear rudely inquisitive, Farquhar "made Pretence to go into the Room, where he was struck dumb for some Time,
with her Figure and blooming Beauty; but was more astonish'd at her
Discourse, and sprightly Wit."[21] The embarrassed girl could not be
persuaded to continue reading, but she consented to an interview
with John Vanbrugh, an established playwright with contacts at both
London theaters. After the interview, having discovered her predilec-
tion for comedy, Vanbrugh introduced her to Christopher Rich, manager of Drury Lane, who agreed to take her on at a salary of fifteen
shillings per week.[22] Anne evidently enjoyed telling the story of her
meeting with Vanbrugh, remembering it as an accomplished perfor-

mance. During the first part of the interview, she feigned indifference to the playwright's suggestion that she consider a theatrical career, although, as she told Chetwood, "*I long'd to be at it, and only wanted a little decent Intreaties.*"[23]

She was admitted to Drury Lane in the spring of 1699, when she was barely sixteen,[24] but she must have been a well-developed, mature sixteen. When her name first appeared in a cast list, early in 1700, it was preceded not by "Miss" (a term reserved for young girls, girlish-looking adolescents, and kept mistresses), but by "Mrs.," an honorific that designated women clearly of marriageable age, whether they were married or not. Her girlhood had come to a dramatically satisfying conclusion.

Very likely she and her mother moved out of Piccadilly, taking lodgings closer to Drury Lane. According to the third edition of *Authentick Memoirs* her mother had become a mantua-maker to support herself and her child after her husband's death, and "upon her Daughter's admittance into the Playhouse she was recommended to be a Maker of Habits for the Actresses,"[25] a position she retained until Anne was able to support her.

Anne's story follows a pattern familiar in stories of the lives of actresses: the exchange of a life of genteel poverty for a déclassé and risky, but far more remunerative and exciting, life in the theater.[26] What else were her choices? Marriage was always a possibility, but unless she were extraordinarily lucky it was unlikely to improve her social condition or financial circumstances. Practicing a genteel trade, such as mantua-making, was not a particularly attractive prospect. If we are to believe the two memoirs, she had been stagestruck from early childhood, but even if her vocation had not been so strong, given the alternatives her decision is hardly surprising.

2
Apprenticeship

*W*hatever dreams of glory Anne many have entertained after the excitement of her discovery at the Mitre Tavern, reality was to prove disappointing. For a year after she was taken on at Drury Lane, she remained "almost a Mute and unheeded."[1] But it should not be imagined that she was simply swallowed up behind the scenes. The months of silence were the beginning of her theatrical education.

We know very little about the experiences or training of young players at this time. Colley Cibber served a probationary period of nine months at Drury Lane in 1690, during which he received no salary but had "the Joy and Privilege of every Day seeing Plays for nothing."[2] In each company, a senior actor was responsible for directing rehearsals and sometimes for instructing young actors but, since he was also very busy with his own acting and rehearsing, such instruction would necessarily be perfunctory. For the most part, a novice was expected to watch and to listen and to make him or herself generally useful by playing walk-ons and the small speaking roles that were too inconsequential to appear in cast lists.[3]

The variety of the annual repertory was itself the best school imaginable. At the turn of the eighteenth century, the two London companies produced about sixty different plays each season: a mixture of tragedy, comedy, farce, and opera. Between the time Anne was taken on in the spring of 1699 and the first appearance of her name in a cast list in the spring of 1700, fifteen plays are known to have been performed at Drury Lane. This number represented a small portion of the total. Scanty information about the theatrical calendar, before the advent of regular newspaper advertising in about 1705, makes it impossible to reconstruct the complete repertory.[4] The fifteen plays included a popular new dramatic opera, *The Island Princess;* two new comedies, *Love Without Interest* and George Farquhar's enormously successful *The Constant Couple;* two new tragedies, *The Rise and Fall of Massaniello* and *Achilles;* and Cibber's adaptation of *Richard III.* The rest were stock pieces—four comedies and five tragedies that belonged to the company's standard repertory. Although very incomplete, the record of productions indicates the variety of offerings.[5]

In addition to some direct tutelage and the opportunity to appear onstage in small or nonspeaking roles in new plays, part of a new player's education involved the close study of an established actor. The demands of the repertory system tended to discourage originality and versatility; one often sees an actor described, with approbation, as "an exact copy" of a predecessor. Cibber tells us that he played Richard III as he imagined it would have been performed by Samuel Sandford, a Restoration actor noted for his portrayal of heavy villains. Robert Wilks was described by the prompter John Downes as "the finisht Copy of his Famous Predecessor, Mr. *Charles Hart.*"[6] Actors developed a "line" or specialty, amassing over the years a body of roles with common characteristics whose "ownership" was recognized by custom, if not by law. Since veteran actors snapped up most of the roles, it was difficult for younger players to acquire their own professional capital. An important part in a successful new play was a great prize, for as long as the play remained in the company's repertory the role would be played by the original actor—if he or she were present and still wished to play it. Younger players could look forward to adding to their small personal repertoires chiefly through the death or retirement of their elders, although a senior player might also "resign" roles to younger colleagues to make room for newer acquisitions.

If Anne had begun her career in the days of the United Company, when Drury Lane, as the only theatrical company in London, was top-heavy with experienced actors, she might have remained unheeded for much more than a year. But in March 1695 a group of leading actors, outraged by the managerial practices of the new proprietor, Christopher Rich, had walked out, obtaining a license to form their own company at a theater in Lincoln's Inn Fields.[7] The opportunity to work for their own benefit rather than Rich's had lured away most of Drury Lane's veteran actors, including the popular and respected Thomas Betterton and the actresses Elizabeth Barry and Anne Bracegirdle. Their departure left a vacuum at Drury Lane that was not easily filled;

a few years later, an inexperienced but talented newcomer would find it relatively easy to get established. The existence of rival companies also meant that playwrights had a better opportunity to have their work produced, and the increase in new productions after 1695 meant more parts for aspiring novices. Although competition between the two companies was often financially devastating for both, from Anne's point of view conditions could not have been better.

In 1699, the Drury Lane company consisted of about forty permanent members—actors, actresses, singers, dancers—not counting the musicians, the backstage personnel, the treasurer, and the proprietor himself, Christopher Rich.

The autocratic Rich was a lawyer and businessman with no previous involvement in theater until he purchased a majority interest in the patent in 1693.[8] Openly contemptuous of actors, indifferent to anything but profits and the pleasures of machiavellian manipulation, Rich was up to one of his favorite tricks at the time Anne joined the company—playing off two leading actors against each other, the better to maintain control over his underpaid, potentially rebellious players. His approach to theatrical management, according to Cibber, was forthright and quite original. Instead of paying his daily overhead— salaries, incidental expenses, building rent, investors' shares, and the like—and then taking the remainder for his profits, he took a fixed amount for his profits right off the top each day and then made good his obligations as best he could. Since his fellow investors were prominent, and in some cases powerful men, their share of the profits was usually paid, but actors and tradesmen could be put off somehow, with a pat on the back, a few glasses of wine, or a well-timed act of generosity.[9]

The chief actors were Robert Wilks, George Powell, John Mills, and Colley Cibber, and the comedians William Bullock, Benjamin Johnson, Henry Norris, and Will Pinkethman; the leading actresses were Susannah Verbruggen and Jane Rogers. The personalities and acting styles of these players—many of whom would be Anne's colleagues for the next thirty years—left their mark upon new plays and revivals at Drury Lane in the early eighteenth century. The tall, slim, elegant Wilks, who was to become Anne's costar, played certain tragic roles with considerable success, generally tender lovers and husbands, but his true bent was for the fine gentleman in comedy, which he endowed with vivacity and charm. He had become a star on the Dublin stage after a brief, unsuccessful attempt to establish himself in the United Company at Drury Lane in 1693. When he returned to Drury Lane in 1698 he was a popular, self-assured veteran. Partly to undercut George Powell, Rich appointed Wilks chief actor. The two leading men struck sparks immediately.[10]

The company should have been big enough for both of them, for they were performers of quite different types. Powell, fiery and impassioned, had a genius for tragedy and an unfortunate proclivity for the bottle. He was often capable of brilliance, especially when he played characters close to his own nature—violent lovers, or heroic libertines such as Polydore in *The Orphan* and Lothario (a role he originated) in *The Fair Penitent,* but his conduct was often unprofessional. Cibber admired Powell greatly but felt that he wasted his potential through drunken excesses and indifference. When the veiled hostility between Wilks and Powell finally erupted, the tragedian "cock'd his Hat, and in his Passion walk'd off" to Lincoln's Inn Fields.[11]

Reading between the lines of Cibber's account of the clash, it seems clear that Cibber was also badly hurt by Wilks's rapid advancement. Throughout their long association, including their partnership as actor-managers of Drury Lane, the Wilks-Cibber relationship was never easy. There were fundamental differences in personal as well as acting styles. Wilks, often peremptory and hotheaded, was demanding of himself and others. No one could fault his dedication to his craft. To the end of his career he maintained a daunting workload, combining acting, management, and directing rehearsals. Offstage he was reputed to be a devoted husband and loyal, generous friend—perhaps too loyal, his enemies would say, for he liked to promote his favorites.

Comparing the two actors, Richard Steele wrote in the *Tatler:* "Wilks has a singular talent in representing the graces of nature; Cibber the deformity in the affectation of them. Were I a writer of plays I should never employ either of them in parts which had not their bent this way."[12] Cibber was unfortunate, by his own admission, in having a weak voice and "an uninform'd meagre Person . . . with a dismal pale Complexion."[13] His overripe approach to the playing of villains, modeled on Samuel Sandford, tended toward caricature. To one critic, his Richard III resembled nothing so much as "the distorted heavings of an unjointed caterpillar."[14] Cibber was far more successful in comedy, playing outrageously affected fops, including some that he wrote for himself. For in addition to his acting career he was the author of a number of popular comedies: *Love's Last Shift, The Careless Husband, Love Makes a Man, The Double Gallant; or, The Sick Lady's Cure,* and *The Provok'd Husband.* As an actor, author, and manager he was perhaps the most influential theatrical figure of Anne's lifetime, but he did not wear fame and importance gracefully. There are many stories about his high-handed treatment of writers, his vanity, and his pettiness.[15]

An actor whose reputation barely outlived him, John Mills was tall and strong, with large features and a voice that was "manly and powerful, but not flexible."[16] Generally a player of second-rank characters in comedy and tragedy, he also came into possession of several leading roles, including Macbeth, partly because no one else wished to play them, partly through his diligence, and partly—Cibber claimed—because Wilks promoted him.

If, after the departure of Powell, the company was deficient in gifted tragic actors, it had a fine stock of comedians, each of whom had a distinctive personality and style of playing. William Bullock was Falstaffian in size, and indeed was a famous Falstaff, as well as being the originator of Sir Tunbelly Clumsy in *The Relapse.* Both he and the rubbery-faced Will Pinkethman were inveterate ad-libbers, the despair of playwrights as they were the delight of spectators. Benjamin Johnson was, appropriately, admired for his portrayals of characters in Ben Jonson's comedies: Wasp, in *Bartholomew Fair,* Corbaccio in *Volpone,* and Morose in *Epicoene; or, The Silent Woman.* Tom Davies noted approvingly that he was one of the few actors who entered into his parts so fully that he was never out of character.[17]

Small, sprightly Henry Norris specialized in comical servants, earning such fame as the servant Dicky in *The Constant Couple* that he was afterward known as "Dicky" Norris. Another of his popular roles was the cuckolded husband, Barnaby Brittle, in *The Amorous Widow; or, The Wanton Wife.* Anne, who eventually played the role of Mrs. Brittle, once remarked that Norris had "such a diminuative form, and so sneaking a look, that he seems formed on purpose for horns, and I make him a cuckold always with a hearty good will."[18]

In 1699, Jane Rogers owned many of the principal roles in tragedy as well as her line of virtuous heroines in comedy. Like Anne she was tall and "finely shaped," but there the resemblance ended, for she was neither strikingly beautiful nor charismatic. Very little is known about her work other than the roles she played. An anonymous memoir of Wilks, published shortly after his death in 1732, tells the story of his amorous pursuit of the actress, and how, eventually, he triumphed over "a Virtue which had been proof against the Temptations of the most accomplished young Noblemen, and large Settlements."[19] The result was a child, Jane, probably born in 1700. According to this account, the affair ended bitterly for Mrs. Rogers, which may explain why, when Wilks later sided with Anne in a dispute between the two women, Rogers was particularly resentful. She is said to have been responsible for rumors that Anne owed several plum roles to the granting of sexual favors to Wilks.[20]

Drury Lane was not blessed with many fine actresses, but the principal comedienne, Susannah Verbruggen, was one of the company's greatest assets.[21] She was plump and lively, able to play the witty sophisticate and willing to stoop to low comedy even if it involved "defacing her fair Form to come heartily into it."[22] Cibber cherished the memory of her portrayal of the "female fop," Melantha, in Dryden's *Marriage à la Mode,* describing in rare detail a scene in which she "played" her lover like a practiced angler.

> She reads the Letter . . . with a careless, dropping Lip and an erected Brow, humming it hastily over. . . . crack! she crumbles it at once into her Palm and pours upon him her whole Artillery of Airs, Eyes, and Motion; down goes her dainty, diving Body to the Ground, as if she were sinking under the conscious Load of her own Attractions; then launches into a Flood of Fine Language and Compliment, still playing her Chest forward in fifty Falls and Risings, like a Swan upon waving Water.[23]

Anne clearly made Verbruggen her model, eventually surpassing her in fame, if not in affectionate regard.

Acting of this kind depended in large part upon the intimate relationship of actors and audience. The Theatre Royal in Drury Lane, where Anne spent most of her professional life, had little in common with its mammoth modern descendant. The seating capacity was perhaps six hundred, although for special occasions, such as benefits, many more patrons could be accommodated on the stage itself, or shoehorned into the backless benches in the pit and in the galleries.[24] A significant change in the actor-audience relationship occurred shortly before Anne was hired at Drury Lane, when Rich, to increase seating capacity, shortened the deep forestage and replaced the two lower proscenium doors with stage boxes. The effect of these changes was to move the actors farther upstage, from which position "the minutist Motion of a Feature" and "the weakest Utterance" could no longer be easily perceived by specators seated toward the back.[25] That, at least, was Cibber's complaint. But the extent to which this development affected the style of playing is not clear.[26]

Despite Rich's alterations, actors enjoyed a far more intimate relationship with spectators at Drury Lane during Anne Oldfield's time than they do in modern playhouses. Entrances and exits were still made chiefly through the remaining proscenium doors, and stage directions suggest that much of the action continued to be played on the forestage. It is also significant that the actors were not separated from the audience by a wall of darkness. Since the auditorium was lighted by hundreds of candles in sconces around the perimeter, it could not be darkened when the play began. Members of the audience were therefore continually visible to each other and to the performers (a situation that contributed not only to greater intimacy but to casual socializing and occasional rowdiness). Spectators became much more conscious participants in the stage action, "eavesdropping" on the frequent asides, "seeing through" the disguises and deceptions that were common components of the plays, catching a performer's eye as he or she did something particularly outrageous. In the scene that Cibber describes, Verbruggen was able to draw the audience into the game she was playing on her lover.

Under such conditions, actors depended greatly upon their own skills and resources to achieve rapport with the audience. No amount of charm and beauty could make up for the confidence that came from experience.

Drury Lane was a home for Anne in more than a figurative sense. The ever-changing repertory required that actors put in long hours at the theater. Performances began at five-thirty or six o'clock each Monday through Saturday (excepting Lent) throughout a season that lasted from mid-September to early or mid-June. Since new works were brought out frequently and usually ran for only three to six nights, there would often be a rehearsal call for the morning. Although most actors had lodgings within an easy walking distance of the theater, many probably found it more convenient to stay there until it was time to dress and make up for the evening performance. A small room called the "settle" or "green room" provided a place for the actors to rest when not onstage during a performance or a rehearsal. The actor and bookseller Tom Davies recalled that "from time out of mind until about the year 1740" many of the actors relaxed in the green room after they had finished dinner at about two in the afternoon.[27] Living and working in close proximity, they resembled a large, sometimes jealous and competitive, extended family.

Anne's first full season at Drury Lane opened in the fall of 1699 with the usual run of repertory pieces. According to *Faithful Memoirs,* the offerings included John Dryden's *Secret Love; or, The Maiden Queen,* which had been written for the large number of attractive young actresses at Drury Lane more than twenty years earlier. The characters of Florimell and the maiden queen presumably belonged to Susannah Verbruggen and Jane Rogers, but the romantic Candiope, "a princess of the Blood" and the queen's rival in love, is supposed to have belonged to the popular young singer-actress Letitia Cross who had, some months earlier, "made an Excursion into France, with a certain Baronet." The role of Candiope then fell to Anne, who had not yet played a major speaking role.[28]

As welcome as the part might have been in her first year at Drury Lane, she had little affinity for weeping princesses. *Secret Love* combined a lighthearted subplot about two high-spirited, sophisticated lovers with the serious story of two women in love with, and loved by, the same man. The main plot, in the tradition of tragicomedy, contained scenes of pathos, noble internal conflict, and even nobler renunciation. It was played, as it was written, in the artificial tragic style of the time, which few actors performed successfully.

From prescriptive discussions, such as Charles Gildon's in *The Life of Mr. Thomas Betterton,* we know that in tragic acting great attention was given to facial expression, and above all to "the actions of the hands, more copious and various than all the other parts of the body."[29] Movements tended to be deliberate and formal. The unnatural vocal delivery, called "toning," which at its worst produced a monotonous singsong, served to remove tragic acting even further from the realm of nature. But it is difficult to imagine how else much of the popular tragedy of the time might have been spoken. The metrically smooth blank verse, the rhymed couplets that marked the end of a scene or an act, and the long, aria-like speeches would be difficult to recite in a less artificial, elevated fashion.

The difference between the gifted and the mediocre tragic actor was not a matter of style—all actors learned and practiced the same conventions—but of mastery. Within the limitations of any set of conventions there is the possibility for a masterful performer to create shadings and variations that command the spectator's attention. All ballet dancers use the same positions, steps, and pantomimic gestures; the virtuoso makes them look easy and natural, in the sense that they appear unforced, spontaneous, fluid. Augustan tragic acting was in part a display of virtuosity.

As a mature actress, Anne possessed the skill and the magical presence to animate the most wooden of tragic heroines, but as a beginner she could probably do very little with Candiope. Equally forgettable was her first role in a new play, Silvia in John Oldmixon's opera *The Grove; or, Love's Paradise,* which opened—and soon closed—in the spring of 1700. There is no evidence that Anne could sing—none of the roles in her established repertoire required singing—but Silvia was one of several speaking parts in this production. Expensive scenic display was usually reserved for opera, and *The Grove* was no exception. The scenery and machines included a flying cupid in act 3.[30] Silvia, a "Roman lady," had little to do but sympathize with the heroine (played by Jane Rogers) and make an occasional announcement or observation.

Later in the spring of 1700, Anne at last had an opportunity to show what she could do in a role of some substance—Alinda, heroine of *The Pilgrim,* which Vanbrugh adapted from a romantic comedy by John Fletcher. Interest in the production was stirred by the press, which noted that Dryden, the aging poet laureate, had written not only the prologue and epilogue but a secular masque for the finale. The male roles were all strongly cast, with Powell as the noble outlaw, Roderigo, Wilks as Pedro (a young nobleman turned pilgrim), and Cibber, Norris, and Pinkethman in small but colorful roles in the madhouse scenes. Clearly, Vanbrugh had decided that it was time to promote his young protégée, and he was in a position to do so. As the author of two successful comedies, *The Relapse* and *The Provok'd Wife,* and the newly appointed architect of Castle Howard, he was a figure of considerable influence with powerful patrons of his own. As the author, he would have the right to cast the actress of his choice, and in *The Pilgrim* he had found the appropriate vehicle.

Cibber, who found Anne shy and diffident, with little to recommend her but youth and beauty, observed that the "gentle character" of

Alinda was ideally suited to Anne's inexperience and lack of confidence.[31] But the maidenly, very "Fletcherian" heroine was no passive damsel in distress. Opposing her father's wish that she marry Roderigo, she flees in boy's clothing, following Pedro, the man she wants to marry. A scene in a lunatic asylum, in which Alinda is disguised as one of the inmates, introduced a touch of broad comedy. Altogether, we are told, Anne's beauty, freshness, and energy "charm'd the Play into a Run of many succeeding Nights."[32] Best of all, from her standpoint, *The Pilgrim* became a popular stock piece; the part of Alinda would be hers as long as she cared to play it.

Anne's name appeared in a newspaper advertisement for the first time on July 6, 1700, when the *Post Boy* announced a performance of *The Pilgrim* "for the Benefit of Mrs. Oldfield." There were benefits of many kinds throughout a theatrical season—especially for playwrights, who received, in lieu of royalties, the proceeds (less operating expenses) of the third night of a premiere run, and the sixth, if the play were particularly successful. Actors' benefits had become increasingly common at the turn of the century, owing in part to financial hard times which often resulted in the abatement of salaries.[33] Special tickets were printed for these occasions, to be sold at taverns or coffeehouses or by the actors in person, "waiting upon" aristocratic patrons in their homes. For their labors, they were often rewarded with donations of a guinea or more per ticket. Popular or persistent performers stood to gain as much in one night as they earned in the entire year. It was unusual, however, for junior players to have solo benefits. That Anne was singled out in this fashion may indicate the author's satisfaction with her performance—or his interest in her welfare, as her patron at Drury Lane.[34] To be sure, at this time of year there would not be many fashionable spectators, and Anne probably did not know many people to whom she could sell tickets; but whether or not she made much money, she had clearly made her mark.

Plays as successful as *The Pilgrim* were rare. In her second year, Anne was to appear in five premieres, but of those only one outlived the season. Most died after the fourth or fifth night, and with them died her hopes of adding to her tiny repertoire. In new plays, she was cast consistently in second leads and even in an occasional leading role. She would be given several prologues to speak and one epilogue, a sign that her ability to charm audiences was already recognized, and the Duke of Bedford—Drury Lane's landlord by virtue of his possession of a vast estate in the parish of St. Paul, Covent Garden—is said to have persuaded Rich to raise Anne's salary from fifteen to twenty shillings per week.[35] She was faring no worse than many successful actors in the early years of their careers. Still, the great number of false starts must have been discouraging.

Aurelia, the tragic heroine of Susanna Centlivre's *Perjur'd Husband; or, The Adventures of Venice,* came her way in the fall of 1700 largely by default. The part was probably intended for Jane Rogers, who might have made something noble and touching out of it. But, possibly because it was the work of a novice—and a female—the play was cast without any actors of the rank of Rogers, Wilks, or Susannah Verbruggen. It was left to seventeen-year-old Anne to enact the torments of a Venetian gentlewoman, betrothed in infancy to a man she does not love, and fatally attracted to a nobleman who (unknown to her) is already married.

In the next few months she appeared in three new pieces. It may be symptomatic of the times that these plays were presented for whatever novelty value they possessed—as the work of ladies, for example, or of a very young man. When Anne spoke the prologue for *The Perjur'd Husband,* she invoked a chivalric response: "Humbly she sues, and 'tis not for your Glory/ T'insult a Lady—when she falls before ye."[36] With war against France in the air in 1701, plays and prologues began to capitalize on patriotic sentiment, but whatever the basis of appeal, very little seemed to work. Play after play failed, with and without Anne Oldfield. These were trying times for would-be playwrights as well as for the theater.

In addition to the often self-destructive competition between Drury Lane and Lincoln's Inn Fields, there were increasingly shrill attacks from moralists, many of whom had no sincere interest in theatrical reform and would have preferred that the English stage disappear altogether. Actors could be hauled into court for uttering "Abominable, Impious, Lewd and Immoral Expressions."[37] In the spring of 1701 Anne—misnamed "Mariah Oldfield"—was among a group of Drury Lane actors charged with performing "obscene and profane comedies," *Volpone, Sir Courtly Nice,* and *The Humour of the Age*—two of which were often-performed stock pieces.[38] *The Humour of the Age,* the only play of the three in which we know that Anne appeared, is inoffensive enough to the modern reader. To condemn it because of words and phrases taken out of context, which apparently was the case, was certainly harassment. The charges were finally dropped, but the real threat to the theater lay not so much in any particular legal action as in the ever-present fear of censorship and the inconsistency with which the law was applied.

Despite the dubious motives of some critics, the desire for moral reform seems to have been genuine enough. There was, however, a great deal of confusion about means and ends and self-consciousness about moral positions, none of which was healthy for drama. Many of the plays in which Anne appeared were products of this uncertainty. In *The Humour of the Age,* she played Miranda, a cast-off mistress who has contrived to marry a greedy, lecherous, and thoroughly dishonest old justice of the peace and cuckold him as soon as possible. At the end, however, Miranda is so stunned by the revelation of the heroine's virtue that she vows to live strictly ever after, to "strive to love even Impotence itself, and make a more virtuous Wife than many that marry unspotted."[39] The strained morality of this speech is difficult to take seriously, although it was evidently intended seriously.

In Elkanah Settle's opera, *The Virgin Prophetess; or, The Fate of Troy,* the love of Paris and Helen is officially condemned through the pronouncements of Cassandra (the virgin prophetess of the title), and mightily celebrated with lavish spectacle, music, and song. As Helen, another nonsinging role, Anne made her first entrance in a spectacular "discovery," as the shutters toward the front of the scenic area opened to reveal

> the Town of Troy, with a magnificent Chariot twenty Foot high, drawn by two White Elephants, placed in the Depth of the Prospect [far upstage], between two Triumphal Columns; the one bearing the Statue of Pallas, and the other of Diana, and fronting the Audience. In the Chariot are seated Paris and Helen; in the two front Entryes on each Side of the Stage, advanced before the side Wings, are four more White Elephants, bearing, each a Castle on their Backs, with a Rich Canopy over each Castle, and in each three Women; on the Necks of all the Elephants a Negro Guide. Each of these Paintings Twenty two foot high.[40]

The effect is suggestive of a glossy Hollywood biblical epic, with Anne as the embodiment of lust and sensuality. Morality was satisfied by Helen's fiery death at the end, but audiences were not. Despite its exploitation of a popular formula, *The Virgin Prophetess* was an expensive flop.

During the season of 1700–1701 Drury Lane produced two plays by Catherine Trotter (later Cockburn), which failed to please audiences despite their reforming character. In *Love at a Loss; or, The Most Votes Carry It,* Trotter departed slightly from the formula in which the rake is reformed by the love of a good woman, and the coquette brought to heel by a devoted lover, by having Beaumine ("a Gay Roving Spark") marry Lesbia, the woman he has ruined.[41] In a subplot, Anne played a naïve young woman, Lucilia, whose flirtation with a nasty fop teaches her to tread the prudent, as well as virtuous, path. Trotter's *Unhappy Penitent* is a pseudohistorical tragedy set in France during the reign of Charles VIII in which Anne had the role of the resident moralist, Ann of Brittanie, a character so priggish and unattractive as to be a poor representative of virtue. The most that can be said of Anne's second season is that she appeared in a considerable variety of roles.

Richard Steele's *Funeral; or, Grief a la Mode,* which premiered in December 1701, was the company's first big success since *The Constant Couple* and *The Pilgrim.*[42] *The Funeral* was also the first dramatic work of the man who, more than any other, became a successful reformer of "immorality and profaneness" in English drama. Unlike many first plays, it is a work of great liveliness and originality. One of Steele's satiric targets was the funeral business of the early 1700s, and his opening scene, an exposé of undertaking practices, is as funny and telling today as when it was first written. But his principal concern was hypocrisy in genteel society, embodied in the character of Lady Brumpton.

In the first production of *The Funeral,* and for some time afterward, Anne played the role of Lady Sharlot, the younger, less sophisticated, more serious of two sisters who are wards of Lord Brumpton and live in his household. The encounter between the prim Lady Sharlot and her bashful lover, Lord Hardy, in the second act, was probably Anne's first opportunity to play a richly comic scene in which humor arises from character.

> *Lady Sharlot. (Aside)* Now is the tender Moment now approaching. There he is. (*They approach and salute each other Trembling.*) Your Lordship will please to sit; (*After a very*

long pause, stoln Glances, and irresolute Gesture.) Your Lord-
ship I think has travell'd those parts of *Italy* where the
Armies Are—
Lord Hardy.   Yes Madam—
Lady Sharlot.   I think I have Letters from You Dated *Mantua.*
Lord Hardy.   I hope you have, Madam, and that their purpose—
Lady Sharlot.   My Lord?— (*Looking serious and confus'd.*)
Lord Hardy.   Was not your Ladiship going to say something?
Lady Sharlot.   I only attended to what your Lordship was going
to say—that is my Lord—But you were I believe going to
say something of that Garden of the World *Italy*—I am
very sorry your Misfortunes in *England* are such as may
make you Justly regret your leaving that place.[43]

The tentative courtship proceeds awkwardly through the entire scene,
as both lovers are too shy and well-bred to get to the point.

In his first play, Steele demonstrated a sureness of intention and
technique, endowing even his exemplary characters with a distinctive
charm. In the last act, Lady Sharlot, having made her escape from the
Brumpton household (where her virtue is in danger), leaps out of a
coffin, bursts into passionate blank verse (having found her tongue
with a vengeance) and is happily united with Lord Hardy. The business
of her emergence from the coffin came in for censure from a critic who
objected to its lack of propriety,[44] but audiences were enthusiastic, and
for Anne it was a marvelous chance to parody high tragedy, a practice
that became one of the hallmarks of her mature comic style.

Amid preparations for war, William III died on March 8, 1702. This
blow, from which the country quickly recovered, was nearly fatal for
the theaters. Closed until April 23 for the traditional period of national
mourning, and reopening just in time to close again for the May Fair
recess,[45] the playhouses drew only small audiences for the rest of the
season. It was reported that "the poor players" were ready to starve,
and—no doubt facetiously—that "One cannot pass by the Play-house
now when it is dark but you are sure to be stripped."[46]

Before disaster overtook the theaters, Anne appeared in Vanbrugh's
False Friend, an adaptation of *Le Traître Puni* by Alain-René Lesage.
The role of the cynical maidservant Jacinta was probably conceived as
a vehicle for her. She was given an amusing epilogue to speak—her
first—and Vanbrugh enlarged the character of Jacinta from his source,

adding a lengthy scene of sustained witty repartee for her in the fourth
act. In the scene that Vanbrugh interpolated into act 4, Jacinta chides
earnest Don Guzman, who has stoutly maintained his innocence of the
attempted rape of Leonora, her mistress:

> You'd make one mad with your Impossibles and your Innocence,
> and your Humilities. 'Sdeath, Sir d'you think a Woman makes no
> distinction between the Assaults of a Man she likes and one she
> doesn't? My Lady hates *Don John,* and if she Thought 'twas he
> had done this Job, she'd hang him for't in her own Garters; She
> likes you, and if you shou'd do such an other, you might still die
> in your Bed like a Bishop, for her.[47]

Jacinta speaks not out of knowledge of her mistress, but "the world,"
whose cynical values do not prevail in the play.

The run of *The False Friend* had to be cut short after the fourth night,
when Cibber, playing Don John, was injured,[48] so there is no way of
knowing whether Vanbrugh's mixture of cynicism and moralizing
was well received. But Anne must have been pleased with her part,
for when the play was revived in 1710, she once more played the witty
maidservant, although she had long since been accustomed to playing
leading roles.

After the coronation of Queen Anne on April 23, 1702, the season
trickled to a dismal close. Each house presented one new play; more
often than not, the theaters seem to have been dark. This raises the
question of what the actors did for money, since they were paid only
while the playhouses were operating. Owing to the shortness of the
season, many of them did not even get their benefits. A few leading
players who had financial cushions could afford to rest. Others may
have turned to strolling or to working the fairs.

In Anne's case, there is an additional mystery: she seems to have
dropped out of sight for more than a year. There are no records of her
appearance at Drury Lane from late January or early February 1702,
when *The False Friend* probably closed, until March 11, 1703, when she
acted in Tom Durfey's *Old Mode and the New*. To be sure, incomplete
theatrical records do not tell the whole story. There may be many
unrecorded performances of stock pieces in which Anne played. But
she was not cast in any of the five new plays brought out at Drury
Lane between November 1702 and early March 1703. During this

time, the company boasted a new face, advertised in the *Daily Courant* on November 13, 1702, as "Mrs Hooke, the new Actress lately come from Dublin."[49] The young actress appeared in a number of new plays from mid-November through February, taking roles that might well have gone to Anne. We cannot be sure what her sudden prominence in the Drury Lane company signifies; evidently she was a temporary replacement.

If so, where was Anne? The first thought that comes to mind in the case of an otherwise healthy, young, and ambitious actress is pregnancy. One possible alternative to acting in the provinces or taking up an even less glamorous trade, when the theaters were closed in the spring of 1702, was finding solace in the arms of a lover. But if she did become pregnant in 1702, either the child was not carried to full term or it died at birth or soon after, for nothing was ever said about the matter.

It would be interesting to know how Anne managed to avoid frequent pregnancy, since she was—in the clinical phrase of our time—"sexually active" throughout most of her adult life, and birth control methods were not very reliable.[50] Many actresses were not successful in preventing pregnancy. There were those, as one wag noted, who "Trade like our *East-India* Ships, they take in their Lading in the beginning of Winter, and having calculated the Voyage for Nine Months, it falls out very opportunely for 'em to unlade again in the long Vacation."[51] Others simply brazened it out onstage, assisted by loose gowns and wide petticoats, a great deal of nerve, and the audience's goodwill. Those whose husbands, lovers, or families would have been shamed by the public display of pregnancy, or were able to afford a brief retirement, absented themselves from the stage—and so may Anne have done in the winter of 1702–3.

At any rate, she reappeared in late February 1703, when rehearsals for *The Old Mode and the New* must have begun. She had roles in all but one of the new plays brought out by Drury Lane that spring, and probably also appeared in performances of *The Funeral, The Humour of the Age,* and *The Pilgrim* in May, June, and July. But the failure rate of new plays continued to be high,[52] and although Anne seems to have regained—if she ever lost—her position in the company, prospects were discouraging.

Compared to Lady Sharlot and Jacinta, her roles this season were unworthy of her maturing comic gifts. As Lucia in *The Old Mode and the New,* she was no more than a conventional foil to the hoydenish Gatty. As another Lucia, in the subplot of Richard Estcourt's *Fair Example; or, The Modish Citizens,* she played a young wife of exemplary virtue, given to occasional bursts of blank verse. In *Love's Contrivance; or, Le Medecin Malgre Lui,* Susanna Centlivre's adaptation of parts of three Molière comedies, Anne had the more interesting role of Belliza. But the courtship of the witty lovers, Belliza and Octavio, is subsidiary to the main plot, which concerns Lucinda's attempt to thwart her tyrannical father. After a successful initial run, the play was often performed in a shortened version that emphasized the broadly comic characters played by Bullock, Johnson, and Norris.[53]

In four seasons at Drury Lane, Anne had known a few successes, endured many disappointments, and made some small progress. Then, in the summer of 1703, her fortunes changed suddenly. When the company completed its regular season and left for Bath to perform before the vacationing queen and her court, Susannah Verbruggen was left behind in London. From Cibber we know that she was mortally ill; from Tom Davies, that she died in childbed. Only thirty-seven years old, she was buried in St. Martin-in-the-Fields on September 2, 1703.[54]

In the "female scramble" for Verbruggen's parts that summer in Bath, one important character fell to Anne. Leonora in John Crowne's *Sir Courtly Nice* is a lively young woman kept in virtual captivity by her brother, who wants her to marry the foppish Sir Courtly instead of young Farewell, whom she loves. Cibber, having seen no evidence that Anne was equal to the task, was loath to rehearse the scenes that he, as Sir Courtly, would be playing with her. She, for her part, responded to his ill-concealed disdain with pretended indifference, muttering her lines "in a sort of mifty manner." And so their rehearsal was conducted, with little satisfaction to either. But on the night of the performance, it was quite another matter. Coming to life before an audience, she showed Cibber how wrong he had been, triumphing over "the Error of my Judgment, by the (almost) Amazement that her unexpected Performance awak'd me to; so forward and sudden a Step into Nature I had never seen." Her success was all the more commendable, he added, because it "proceeded from her own Understanding, untaught and unassisted by any one more experienc'd Actor."[55]

Her "overnight success," as Cibber tells it, is a wonderful story, but why did it take him so long to awaken? After all, he had acted opposite her on numerous occasions, notably as Lord Hardy in *The Funeral*. Had she shown so little promise? Or had she, perhaps, shown signs of developing in a different direction? Unfortunately, Cibber, in his eagerness to place himself at the center of the story, omits such details. But a revelation of some kind clearly took place that night. Perhaps, despite the important roles Anne had already played, it was not until that night that she made the "Step into Nature" that distinguishes the true artist from the diligent student. In any case, she had seized the opportunity and made the most of it.

3
Whig and Lover

Arthur Maynwaring was too poor to keep a mistress. Too poor, that is, to take a young actress from the stage and set her up for life with a handsome allowance, perhaps even holding out a promise of marriage. The practice was not as common in the early 1700s as it had been in Charles II's time, when actresses were a tantalizing new phenomenon and courtiers happily prowled behind the scenes of the London playhouses. In the infancy of a new profession, a pretty young actress had to consider whether entry into the *demimonde* might be preferable to a less certain, less profitable, and only slightly more respectable career on the stage. But by the turn of the eighteenth century, the theater was no longer the plaything of courtiers. Neither William III nor Queen Anne had much interest in the theater, the Whig magnates of the period seemed more interested in breeding and racing horses than in bedding actresses, and theater audiences contained an increasing number of middle-class spectators. By the early 1700s, also, a young actress could look forward to some degree of financial security in her profession. She would not receive a salary equal to that of her male counterparts,[1] but she could expect to earn a respectable wage of thirty to forty pounds per year, in addition to which there would be the proceeds of her benefit. If she set her sights upon stardom, the rewards would be even greater. Elizabeth Barry and Anne Bracegirdle were earning more than one hundred pounds per season in good times.

There was the case of the popular young singer-actress Mary Ann Campion, who left the stage in about 1703, having "so captivated the most noble William Duke of Devonshire. . . . that he took her off the stage and established her on his country estate."[2] But even if Anne had been willing to accept a similar arrangement, Arthur Maynwaring was in no position to offer it. Partly out of necessity, then, Anne did not become Maynwaring's kept mistress but continued to earn her living. Their relationship, unorthodox in this respect, ran counter to the customs and prejudices of several decades. For it was one thing to live openly together, since neither was married, but it was quite another for a man of Maynwaring's social class not only to tolerate but to abet his mistress's stage career.

The social code that governed the domestic relations of actresses was not clear-cut. We know that few actresses married outside of their profession and that, with few exceptions, those who made socially advantageous marriages retired from the stage. The Restoration actress Mary Lee became Lady Slingsby by virtue of her marriage to a baronet in 1680 and acted for about five more years as Lady Slingsby, but nothing is known about the marriage or her reasons for continuing her career. The charming actress Elizabeth Bowtell continued to act occasionally after her marriage to the son of a landed gentleman, but the marriage also seems to have been occasional, for a contemporary satire describes her as "Chestnut-man'd Boutel, whom all the Town F—ks."[3] Secret marriage was a possible resort and a subject for constant speculation. Anne Bracegirdle was, for a while, rumored to be secretly married to William Congreve. Anne Oldfield would not be immune from rumors of marriage.[4]

Where extramarital liaisons are concerned, it is more difficult to gauge the force of custom and prejudice, for such relationships could vary from brief flings to quasi-marriages. Charles II and his courtiers took both casual and serious actress-mistresses, and those of long standing almost always retired from the stage. A famous exception was the affair between Elizabeth Barry and the Earl of Rochester in the 1670s. Like Arthur Maynwaring, Rochester actively promoted his mistress's career; according to legend, he wagered that he could train her to be an accomplished actress within six months. But unlike Maynwaring he regretted his success, which made Barry independent of him and gave her scope to test the power of her attractions on other lovers. In any case, the affair, which produced a daughter in 1677, did not seem destined for permanence, for neither Rochester (who was married) nor Barry was inclined to fidelity.[5]

For Anne and Maynwaring, in 1703 or thereabouts, the decision to live together openly while she continued her career would not be taken lightly. Although a veil of sentiment has been drawn over the affair by her biographers, it constituted a risk for both of them, personally and professionally. On how they first met, and the early course of their relationship, there has been considerable speculation and inevitable romanticizing. They could have met at almost any time after 1700, most likely through Vanbrugh and the Kit-Cat Club. Since about the turn of the century, Maynwaring had been a member of the Kit-Cat, the most important of the men's clubs that developed in the late seventeenth century out of informal gatherings in coffeehouses and taverns.[6] Like all such clubs, the Kit-Cat was given to general conviviality; members consumed great quantities of wine and spirits and raised to a minor art the custom of composing witty verse toasts to famous beauties, whose names were inscribed on the drinking glasses. But they also took themselves seriously as a force in the social, cultural, and political life of the time. Their common bond was enthusiasm for the Whig cause, which Maynwaring embraced with all the ardor of a recent convert.

He had been born into an ancient family of landed gentry in Ightfield, Shropshire, in 1668. On his mother's side, he was distantly related to the Whig nobility, but a maternal uncle to whom he was especially close was a confirmed Jacobite who had refused to swear the oath of allegiance to William III and Mary, in 1689, and remained loyal to the deposed king, James II. Maynwaring matriculated at Christ Church College, Oxford, in November 1683,[7] but left after several years without taking a degree, a common circumstance for a young man whose family intended him for the law rather than the clergy. After leaving Oxford, he lived for a few years with his Jacobite uncle, whose views he fervently shared. Some letters in the British Library, identified as Maynwaring's, reveal his partisan view of the last few years of James II's reign.[8] To these must be added some satirical poems on the Glorious Revolution and William III, also the product of the "State of Political Darkness" in which he lived until his conversion to the cause of liberty, toleration, and the Protestant succession.[9]

When he was about twenty-one he came to London to read law. But he had little inclination for his studies, which are said to have undermined his always-precarious health, and soon found that he preferred the company of "Men of the first Character for Rank and Wit," some of whom practiced arts and letters in a gentlemanly way. He continued his law studies at a leisurely pace for four or five years until his father died, in about 1693, leaving him an estate heavily in debt, but also relieving him of parental pressure to pursue a career.

Over the next few years, he enjoyed the life of a gentleman who had no taste for the few respectable careers open to him—the military, the clergy, or the bar. He would have liked to sell the Ightfield estate outright, and eventually did so, but bowing to pressure from friends decided to mortgage it further, raising five thousand pounds on which to keep himself for a while.[10] In 1697, he traveled to France, where he was befriended by the poet Boileau-Despréaux and had an opportunity to refine his interest in literature. But as a gentleman he could not, of course, become a professional writer.

Sometime before the trip to France, he had shaken off his youthful Jacobitism, and not long after his return to England he joined the Kit-Cat Club. Through a Kit-Cat member, the Duke of Somerset, he was preferred to his first government post, commissioner of customs, in 1701, at an annual salary of twelve hundred pounds. Later, through the Lord Treasurer Sidney Godolphin, father of Kit-Cat member Francis Godolphin, he obtained the far more remunerative sinecure (also in the customs office) of Auditor of the Imprests, a lifetime grant directly from the monarch, which was not subject to the vicissitudes of party influence.[11] The auditorship was said to be worth two thousand pounds a year "in a time of good Business," and John Oldmixon reports that Godolphin obtained it for Maynwaring by paying off the current proprietor, Brook Bridges, to the tune of "several thousand pounds" of his own money.[12] Although there is little doubt that Maynwaring's loyalty to Godolphin arose from strongly shared convictions, his enemies naturally maintained that it had been purchased.

Kit-Cats took their role as patrons of the arts seriously enough to attend the theater en masse either for a worthy cause, such as support of Thomas Betterton when his company was foundering, or for a production of the work of one of their literary members, who included Congreve, Addison, Vanbrugh, and Steele.[13] It seems likely that Vanbrugh would have introduced his young protégée to his fellow Kit-Cats as early as the spring of 1700, when she was appearing in *The Pilgrim*.[14] Oldmixon's observation, that Maynwaring loved her "with a Passion, that could hardly have been stronger, had it been both her and his first Love,"[15] is tactful in the extreme. Fifteen years Anne's senior, worldly, and well connected, Maynwaring may be presumed to have had any number of romantic attachments before he met her.

As for Anne, since everyone agrees that she was exceptionally beautiful, there would have been no shortage of willing lovers during her early years at Drury Lane.

The significant fact is that, having found one another, Anne and Maynwaring wished to look no further. Their affair ended only with his death in 1712. In due course, it became formalized, if not by law, then at least by custom. She came "under his protection." The coy-sounding phrase is not without significance. The first generation of English actresses had been fair game for predatory gentlemen, against whose sometimes unwelcome attentions they had little protection. When Rebecca Marshall, a leading actress at Drury Lane in the early Restoration, dared to complain to the authorities about two different men who affronted her, the second—a courtier named Sir Hugh Middleton—hired a thug who waylaid her on the way home from the playhouse one night and smeared her with excrement.[16] Susannah Verbruggen's first husband, the actor William Mountfort, was killed during the bungled attempt of a would-be lover to abduct Anne Bracegirdle. Maynwaring's social position protected Anne Oldfield from violence, if not from slander. And as long as she remained faithful, she could expect him to acknowledge offspring of their union, if any, and otherwise look after her.

In connection with the formalizing of their relationship, there is a story that illustrates the mixture of gossip and sentimentality so often found in popular biographies of stage personalities. Before she became Maynwaring's mistress, she is supposed to have been approached by the Duke of Bedford, who offered to settle six hundred pounds per year on her for life. When Maynwaring called on her, the story continues, she confessed her feelings for him but told him that "he was an unlucky fellow," for something had happened the day before, "which must postpone their intended happiness." When he pressed her to know the cause, she would not tell him till some days later, "when she had returned the settlement to the Duke, and acquitted herself in all those points which trenched on her independence."[17] Bedford was, of course, the "landlord" of Drury Lane and not unfamiliar with theatrical matters and personalities. The story that Anne's salary was raised to twenty shillings per week at his instigation has already been mentioned. But it would have been an enormous leap from that small expression of interest to a "settlement" of six hundred pounds per year.[18]

If not money, Maynwaring had something equally important to offer. Oldmixon tells us that he took a keen interest in her acting career and that it was "doubtless owing in great Measure to his Instructions, that she became so admirable a *Player*." In addition, he wrote prologues and epilogues for her, "and would always hear her speak them in private, before she spoke them in publick."[19] In short, Maynwaring became for her something that the Duke of Bedford could never be— a mentor and artistic partner. A young actress would be foolish indeed not to be excited and flattered by the interest of a man known for his sharp wit and literary gifts.

The business of writing prologues and epilogues and rehearsing her in them was particularly significant. The tradition of the lightly mocking, mildly indecent epilogue, often appended to a tragedy, goes back to the period when playwrights began to capitalize on the popularity and undoubted sexual charms of actresses such as Nell Gwynn. These exercises were, in effect, mini-performances in which the actress, still dressed as the character she had just finished playing, stepped forward to address the audience as "herself." In one of the best-known instances, at the end of Dryden's *Tyrannick Love,* Gwynn leapt from the arms of the actor who was carrying her supposed corpse offstage, crying: "Hold, are you mad? You damn'd confounded Dog!/ I am to rise, and speak the Epilogue." (The "ghost of poor departed Nelly" then proceeded to commiserate with the audience, complaining about the "damned dull poet, who could prove/ So senseless to make Nelly die for love.")[20] With Maynwaring's help, Anne was to become one of the most sought-after speakers of epilogues in her time.[21]

Little is known about their domestic arrangements. Maynwaring's will describes him as a resident of the parish of St. Margaret, Westminster. Oldmixon says that he bought a house for his unmarried sister, Grissel, to whom he left "the management of his domestic affairs,"[22] but it must be doubted that he spent much time with his sister. To judge from his correspondence with the Duchess of Marlborough, his many activities did not allow him to spend a great deal of time with Anne. During the theatrical season, her work occupied most evenings, and also much of the day when rehearsals were called. He inhabited the masculine social world of coffeehouses, taverns, and the government in Whitehall. There is one reference to a holiday they spent together in Windsor in 1704.[23]

In 1705, Maynwaring became active in politics, as a member of

Parliament for the borough of Preston, a seat that was in the gift of the Earl of Derby.[24] Within a year, he was drawn into the Marlborough-Godolphin orbit, becoming an unpaid political advisor—or, as he called himself, "secretary"—to the redoubtable Sarah Churchill, duchess of Marlborough. The attractive, intelligent, and ambitious duchess was famous for her hot temper. During her long lifetime she managed to quarrel with nearly everyone: her devoted husband, her children and grandchildren, two famous architects, and, most spectacularly, Queen Anne. The duchess's fall from power in the royal household coincided with events of greater political import: the dismissal of the Whig ministry in 1710, the end of Sidney Godolphin's political career, and the dismissal of the Duke of Marlborough as Captain General at the end of 1711. For five years, Maynwaring labored faithfully in the cause of the Marlboroughs and his patrons in the "Whig Junto." He wrote to Sarah Churchill two or three times a week, sometimes in a playful or philosophical vein, and at other times with suggestions and moral support that some commentators have found more harmful than helpful, since they served to encourage her self-destructive outspokenness.[25] He always had a tendency to be carried away by causes, and like Jonathan Swift, with whom he crossed journalistic swords, he was a good hater.

Oldmixon observes that in his relationship with Anne, Maynwaring sought a respite from the cares and duties of political life. But the relationship itself put him at some risk: friends "of both Sexes" and of the "highest Rank" disapproved of it and urged him to break it off. These "friends" were almost certainly the Duke and Duchess of Marlborough and Whig political leaders. Part of the concern was economic, for while he was not keeping a mistress, in the strictest sense, he must have contributed to Anne's support. "It cannot be deny'd but this *Amour* was Expensive to him"—thus, Oldmixon—"And that this is not the only Instance of his Errors in Oeconomy."[26] Maynwaring seems to have had a more than usual gentlemanly disdain for money, which he spent freely.

When his influential friends attempted to break off the affair, Anne is supposed to have urged him, "for his own *Honour* and *Interest*," to end it, "which Frankness and Friendship of hers, did, as he often confessed, engage him to her the more firmly, and all his Friends at last, gave over importuning him to leave her. They saw she gain'd more and more upon him. . . . "[27] His open liaison with an actress was undoubtedly harmful to his political career, which was not distinguished.[28] There is, however, a suggestive pattern in his relationships with Anne and Sarah Churchill. Theatricality, both onstage and off, seems to have attracted him, but his chosen role was to stand in the wings, offering advice and encouragement. (Even when he entered the political fray directly, as a propagandist in the Whig cause, he managed officially to preserve his anonymity, though his identity was probably known.) In these relationships he should not be seen as a puppet master or callous manipulator so much as an interpreter and coach.

Since Anne and Maynwaring were both free to marry, it is natural to wonder why they did not. If this were an isolated instance there would be little basis for speculation. But after Maynwaring's death, Anne lived out of wedlock for the rest of her life with another unmarried man, and so it seems that the decision not to marry was at least partly hers. She would certainly have been expected to give up her career in the event of marriage to a man as prominent as Maynwaring. Although evidence about her attitude toward her professional life is only indirect, the weight of the evidence—including her brief absences from the stage after childbirth and her continuing to perform actively long after it was economically necessary—suggests that her career mattered greatly to her. Maynwaring had his own reasons for wishing to remain single, yet emotionally and financially committed. By the time he inherited the family estate in 1693, it was all but worthless; when he finally sold it outright, he had no further responsibility to the Maynwaring family line. Given the family's propensity for squandering money, it might have been positively embarrassing to produce a legitimate son. If he and Anne could enjoy a relationship as settled and mutually agreeable as marriage without going through the legal and sacramental motions, why not? It would have been no more respectable to marry an actress than to live with her; indeed, marriage might have been even more frowned upon.

Maynwaring cannot have been an easy person to live with. There was his moodiness, which became more pronounced toward the end of his life, when illness and the failure of his causes took their toll. At the best of times there was his caustic wit, of which even his social superiors among the Kit-Cats stood in awe.[29] Anne could have found a more genial, easygoing lover; in Charles Churchill, with whom she spent the last fifteen years of her life, apparently she did. But Maynwaring was the indispensable love of her youth and first flowering.

4
Lady Betty

*T*he Oldfield legend leaps from Anne's success in *Sir Courtly Nice* at Bath in the summer of 1703 to her appearance in *The Careless Husband* in December 1704, in which Colley Cibber is supposed to have drawn her "*real Character* under the *imaginary one* of Lady *Betty Modish.*"[1] Cibber himself contributed to the legend by asserting that the success of the play owed a great deal to Anne's "personal manner of conversing"—that, indeed, "many Sentiments in the Character . . . I may almost say, were originally her own, or only dress'd with a little more Care, than when they negligently fell, from her own lively Humour."[2] But she was not Cibber's original inspiration.

He had started to work on *The Careless Husband* sometime before the death of Susannah Verbruggen but left off after completing only two acts, "in despair of having Justice done to the Character of Lady *Betty Modish,* by any one Woman then among us; Mrs. *Verbruggen* being now in a very declining state of Health, and Mrs. *Bracegirdle* out of my Reach, and engag'd in another company."[3]

While Cibber was pondering the fate of Lady Betty Modish, John Vanbrugh was developing a proposal which, if realized, would have brought Anne Bracegirdle within Cibber's reach. Vanbrugh intended to build a new theater on the west side of the Haymarket, near Pall Mall, for his own company—an amalgam of most of the players from Lincoln's Inn Fields and nine actors from Drury Lane.[4] In the summer of 1703, he obtained a lease for the land for the theater and presented the Lord Chamberlain with a list of actors for the amalgamated company. Anne Oldfield and Jane Rogers were the only Drury Lane players on the women's roster, which was headed by Elizabeth Barry and Anne Bracegirdle. Although the salary indicated in Vanbrugh's proposal was much more than she had been making at Drury Lane, Anne did not stand to benefit from the move. She had just begun to demonstrate her powers, and she was no match, in experience, number of roles, or personal following, for Anne Bracegirdle. In the amalgamated company, she could have expected few major new roles, including Lady Betty. It was lucky for her, then, that delays in the completion of the Haymarket theater prevented the realization of Vanbrugh's plans until the fall of 1706. She needed the opportunity to solidify her position and establish her line in comedy, and the season of 1703–4 provided just that.

When the company returned from Bath in the fall of 1703, a number of Susannah Verbruggen's roles seem to have become Anne's, including Narcissa in Cibber's *Love's Last Shift*, Hellena in Aphra Behn's *Rover*, Florella in William Mountfort's *Greenwich Park*, Elvira in Dryden's *Spanish Fryar*, Celia in Jonson's *Volpone*, and Lady Lurewell in Farquhar's *Constant Couple*.[5] Near the beginning of the season, Drury Lane revived Thomas Shadwell's *Squire of Alsatia*, with Anne as Teresia, the more lively of a pair of young cousins. The revival proved as successful as the original production in 1688, playing for a total of thirteen performances during the season and becoming a valuable addition to the company's repertory. Robert Wilks played the popular character of the reformed rake, Belfond Jr., and Will Pinkethman had a richly comic role as the "rigid, morose, most sordidly covetous, clownish, obstinate, positive and forward" Sir William Belfond. The play was also popular for its broadly comic scenes of London lowlife, "Alsatia" being the slang designation for the Whitefriars district, which was famous until the late seventeenth century as a sanctuary for debtors and other criminals. Anne abandoned Teresia some years later in favor of her growing repertoire of sophisticated ladies, but the role was a valuable addition at this stage in her career.

The Lying Lover; or, The Ladies Friendship premiered in the fall of 1703, with Anne as Victoria, one of the ladies. The great success of *The Funeral* stirred interest in Steele's new play, but *The Lying Lover* was a disappointment.[6] Motivated by an incident in his own past, Steele attempted to use a comic vehicle, Pierre Corneille's *Le Menteur*, to strip the "vice" of dueling from "the gay Habit in which it has too long appear'd, and cloath it in its native Dress of Shame, Contempt, and Dishonour."[7] Three years earlier he had nearly killed a man in a duel, reluctantly undertaken in defense of a lady's honor. The experience left him with an understandable aversion to the practice which, although officially condemned, was still a common resort in "affairs of honor." Unfortunately, the abrupt shift in tone from the bantering and sexual rivalry of the first three acts of *The Lying Lover* to the supposed death of Lovemore, and young Bookwit's penitence, had the effect of attaching a lead weight to a bubble.

In the character of Victoria, Anne had an excellent opportunity to refine her comic art. One particularly delightful moment was the scene in act 3 in which Victoria and Penelope, as "dear friends" engaged in a deadly sex war over young Bookwit, disarray and disfigure each other with powder and face patches, all the while pretending great solicitude.

Anne's next new role was Mary, Queen of Scots in the premiere performance of *The Albion Queens* by John Banks. The play had been written twenty years earlier and published as *The Island Queens,* but the religious conflict that centered upon Protestant Elizabeth and Catholic Mary proved uncomfortably timely in the latter days of Charles II's reign, and the play was not produced. In 1704, retitled and with alterations by the author, it was officially found to be "an innocent Piece."[8]

With its nonhistorical scenes between the two queens and the sentimentalized treatment of the Duke of Norfolk's love for Mary, *The Albion Queens* owes more to the conventions of historical romance than to history. Both women are portrayed as victims of circumstances beyond their control. Elizabeth is the tool of manipulative courtiers, especially the evil Davison. Mary, rejecting apostasy, accepts the death of a Catholic martyr. In roles such as this, Anne would eventually find her line in tragedy. (In 1715, she played Lady Jane Gray, conceived by the author, Nicholas Rowe, as a Protestant martyr who chooses death rather than conversion to Catholicism.) The Scottish queen was very much in Jane Rogers's virtuous and long-suffering manner; that the role was offered to Anne was perhaps a straw in the wind—an indication of her new importance at Drury Lane.[9]

On March 20, 1704, Anne's rank in the company was unquestionably demonstrated when she entered into a verbal five-year contract with Christopher Rich for a salary of fifty shillings per week. This amount, Rich would later assert, was the highest that any actress in the Drury Lane company was paid.[10] Anne now claimed not only some of Susannah Verbruggen's roles, but her status as principal comedienne.

Before the beginning of the new season, Cibber completed *The Careless Husband,* having found his Lady Betty.[11] Premiering on December 7, 1704, the play ran for nine consecutive performances, and a total of sixteen for the season. Its long-term success was even more significant. Until Anne's death in 1730, with only one exception, the play was performed at least twice each season; generally it was performed three or four times. Cibber was gracious in assigning a large share of the success to Anne. But it was he who, with his finger on the public pulse, correctly guessed that a stylish comedy in which an erring husband and an arrant coquette are reformed by a patient wife and an honorable lover would succeed with contemporary audiences. The formula was realized far more successfully this time than in his first comedy, *Love's Last Shift,* in which the libertine's last-minute reformation was so unconvincing that Vanbrugh had been prompted to write *The Relapse* as a sequel.

Lady Betty Modish became for Anne, as Sir Harry Wildair was for Wilks, a "defining" character, shaped by her and in turn shaping the course of her career. No other actress would play the role during her lifetime. Since the character was so strongly associated with Anne, it is a pity that we do not have an account of her performance. But a fair amount is known about how coquettes were played and about Anne's comic style, and from this knowledge we may, in part, recover her Lady Betty.

Coquettes were a major ingredient in the comedy of manners. They had in common a certain liveliness, wit, and affectation, and a determination to hold their lovers at bay before the betrothal that always concluded the comedy of sexual pursuit and conquest. Sparring with their lovers, they often feigned indifference and sometimes even took a cruel delight in provoking jealousy. Virginal, yet wise in the ways of the world, they knew better than to yield to their lovers' importunities and often professed distaste for ties of any kind. In *Love's Last Shift,* Narcissa shows her true coquettish colors in her treatment of her lover, Young Worthy, whose proof of her love is that "She will suffer no Body but herself to speak ill of me, is always uneasy until I am sent for, never pleas'd when I am with her, and still jealous when I leave her." Narcissa's professed distaste for physical love is likewise typical: "Oh, Insolence! D'ye think I can be mov'd to love a Man, to kiss, and toy with him, and so forth?"[12] (By intonation and facial expression,

the actress who spoke these lines underscored the unmistakable significance of "and so forth.") The experienced player of coquettes knew,
of course, how to convey her real attraction to her lover even as
she tormented him, thus preparing the way for their eventual union.
Altogether, she had at her command an extensive vocabulary of sighs,
shrugs, pouts, titters, gasps, ogles, eye rollings, and flounces. She
knew how to manipulate, and upon occasion, break, a fan, how to
chatter nonstop, or pause significantly.

Any given coquette possessed distinctive attributes, depending upon
the skillfulness of the playwright and the personality of the actress who
played and had perhaps inspired the character. In addition to Narcissa,
Millamant in Congreve's *Way of the World* pointed the way to Lady
Betty. Cibber especially praised Anne Bracegirdle's portrayal of Millamant, in which "all the Faults, Follies, and Affectations of that agreeable Tyrant, were venially melted down into so many Charms, and
Attractions of a conscious Beauty"[13]—a woman, that is, who delights
in the power of her attractiveness. Cibber even borrowed a phrase
from the magnificent description that introduces Millamant in act 2—
"Here she comes, i'faith, full sail, with her fan spread and her streamers
out, and a shoal of fools for tenders"—for his prologue to *The Careless
Husband,* which begins: "Of all the various Vices of the age,/ And
Shoals of Fools exposed upon the Stage. . . ."[14] In Bracegirdle's Millamant he found the model for a heroine who could be at once exasperat-
ing and charming. The term "venially" is a key. Despite Lady Betty's
narcissism and her cruelty to the devoted Lord Morelove, there is no
real harm in her. Her cruelty is the natural consequence of her artificial
position, not ingrained in her character. The satisfaction afforded at
the end, of seeing her tamed by the love of a good man, would be
hollow if she were not fundamentally appealing.

In Lady Betty's first appearance—virtually an eruption—we see her
energy, shallowness, and good nature in equal parts. Where Millamant
is almost maddeningly self-possessed, Lady Betty positively fizzes,
engulfing her friend Lady Easy in a torrent of trivia:

Oh! my Dear! I am overjoy'd to see you! I am strangely happy to
day; I have just receiv'd my new Scarf from *London,* and you are
most critically come to give me your Opinion of it. . . . 'Tis all
Extravagance both in Mode and Fancy; my Dear, I believe there's

Six Thousand Yards of Edging in it—Then such an enchanting
Slope from the Elbow—something so New, so Lively, so Noble,
so Coquet and Charming—but you shall see it, my Dear.[15]

In playing Lady Betty, Anne would draw upon other characters she
had been playing, upon her study of other actresses, and upon her own
ear. We know that she could be a devastating mimic. The story is told
that in a famous scene in *Rule a Wife and Have a Wife,* she responded
to Wilks "with an archness of countenance and half-shut eye . . . in a
tone of voice so exactly in imitation of his, that the theatre was in a
tumult of applause."[16] But mimicry was only a tool, not an end in
itself. A skillful performer knew how to push "nature" to the brink of
excess; as Lady Betty, Anne became at once the epitome of a fine lady
and a satire upon her.

Descending from a long line of coquettes, inspired in part by Anne
Bracegirdle's Millamant, Lady Betty Modish nevertheless belonged to
Anne Oldfield by virtue of the engaging and distinctive energy that
bears down all opposition until the eleventh hour. Forty-five years old
when she played a very similar character, Lady Townly in *The Provok'd
Husband,* Anne still rushed onto the stage "with the full consciousness
of youth, beauty, and attraction" that electrified the theater.[17]

As if one extraordinary new role were not enough that season, there
was Biddy Tipkin in Steele's *Tender Husband,* which premiered at
Drury Lane on April 23, 1705. Superficially, the two heroines could
not be more unlike: one, a peer's daughter who has misspent her life
in the thoughtless pursuit of pleasure; the other, the niece of a London
banker who compensates for her unglamorous origins by indulging in
harmless fantasy and overindulging in romantic fiction. Yet both are
outrageous versions of femininity; both require a style of playing that
can make their affectations appealing.

Biddy's romanticism, however foolish, poses an alternative to the
crassness of an all too believable society in which children are sold in
marriage without regard for their feelings, a woman's chief attraction
is her dowry, and fortune hunting is the accepted occupation of an
impoverished gentleman. The "tender husband" of the title admits that
he has remarried for money and enlists the aid of his ex-mistress in
curing his new wife of her extravagance. His brother, Captain Clerimont (in the tradition of the landless younger brother), determines to
marry wealthily and is prepared to love Biddy Tipkin sight unseen

when he hears that she has ten thousand pounds per year in money, five thousand in jewels, and one thousand in land. Humphrey Gubbin's father, Sir Harry, comes to London "to dispose of an Hundred Head of Cattle, and my son."[18]

Steele—who was not above matrimonial adventuring—acknowledged his fundamental sympathy for Biddy by preserving her innocence. Unlike Lady Betty, she is not "cured" of her folly, but remains convinced to the end that Captain Clerimont is her dashing cavalier. There is, of course, much fun at Biddy's expense. Her forthright aunt dismisses Biddy's detestation of her Christian name as "meer Vapours." Biddy, however, is insistant:

> No, the Heroine has always something soft and engaging in Her Name—Something that gives us a notion of the sweetness of her Beauty and Behaviour. A Name that glides through half a dozen Tender Syllables, as *Elismonda, Clidamira, Deidamia,* that runs upon the Vowels off the Tongue, not hissing through one's Teeth, or breaking them with Consonants—'Tis strange Rudeness those Familiar Names they give us, when there is *Aurelia, Sacharissa, Gloriana,* for People of Condition; and *Celia, Chloris, Corinna, Mapsa* for their Maids, and those of Lower Rank.[19]

Anne had clearly acquired the vocal virtuosity that such speeches require.

The Tender Husband, an undervalued play that could be performed as successfully on the contemporary stage as the comedies of Richard Sheridan, became one of Drury Lane's most popular stock pieces, offered every season throughout Anne's lifetime.[20] But Biddy Tipkin has been overshadowed by Lady Betty, in part because Cibber, not Steele, was mainly responsible for telling the story of Anne's professional life. Anne's biographers added to the legend that Lady Betty was a portrait of Anne herself. A story that she and Maynwaring had spent the summer of 1704 in Windsor, presumably drinking in the atmosphere in preparation for *The Careless Husband,* which is set in Windsor, was given great significance.[21] In the process of legend building, the patience and determination that it took to establish her line in comedy were ignored.

There is no doubt that *The Careless Husband* was important for Anne's development. It mattered greatly that a role in a successful new play was so strongly identified with her. More than anything else, Lady Betty enabled Anne to emerge from the shadow of Verbruggen and Bracegirdle. Henceforth playwrights would think of her when they created new roles. The manners of silly, stylish Lady Betty would be reproduced in numerous, if not necessarily better, characters for the next twenty-five years.

5
Principal Comedienne

*W*hen the new theater in the Haymarket was completed in the spring of 1705, the Lincoln's Inn Fields company moved in, under Vanbrugh's management. A period of renewed rivalry began. Competing for audiences, the two companies resorted to such undercutting maneuvers as simultaneous premieres of new productions, with predictably bad results for both houses. Among the unsuccessful new productions at Drury Lane were Thomas Baker's *Hampstead Heath,* in which Anne played Arabella, a pretentious "City Wife" who has come to Hampstead to enjoy the fashionable pastimes of gambling and flirting with young beaux; Susanna Centlivre's *Basset Table,* in which Anne portrayed Lady Reveller, a giddy, aristocratic young widow given to gambling and flirting; and Cibber's Roman tragedy, *Perolla and Izadora,* in which Wilks and Oldfield played the title characters, a pair of star-crossed lovers. (After the happy ending, in which the lovers were united, Anne spoke a sprightly epilogue written by Maynwaring.) But on April 8, 1706, the company had an undoubted hit on its hands— *The Recruiting Officer,* a new comedy by George Farquhar.

The success of *The Recruiting Officer* was important for Farquhar, who was in desperate financial straits,[1] and for the Drury Lane company, but it was especially significant for Anne and the development of her famous stage partnership with Robert Wilks. By the spring of 1706, she had been paired with Wilks in five new plays (including one tragedy, *The Albion Queens*) and in four stock pieces,[2] some of which exploited their nascent sexual chemistry. In *The Chances,* a popular stock piece adapted from the John Fletcher original by George Villiers, duke of Buckingham, they played two wordly lovers, the second

43

Constantia and Don John, whose scenes are notable for lively, suggestive repartee, such as:

> *2 Con.*   I would fain—
> *John.*   Ay, so would I; come, let's go.
> *2 Con.*   I would fain know whether you can be kind to me.
> *John.*   That thou shalt presently: come away.
> *2 Con.*   And will you always?
> *John.*   Always? I can't say so; but I will as often as I can.
> *2 Con.*   Phoo, I mean love me.
> *John.*   Well, I mean that too.[3]

Not all of their early pairings conformed to this pattern. In *The Tender Husband,* the strong sexual attraction between Biddy Tipkin and Captain Clerimont is never more than an undercurrent—which could, of course, be played up in performance, mitigating Clerimont's merce-
nary motives. But in *The Recruiting Officer,* Farquhar left little to the imagination, providing ample opportunity for the sexual sparring and double entendre that became the keynote of the Oldfield-Wilks stage relationship.

The play pulsates with verbal sex, although the action is innocent enough. Captain Plume, an officer on a recruiting mission in Shrop-
shire, is already acquainted with Justice Balance's daughter Silvia, to whom he has laid siege without success. "'Tis true," he admits to his friend Mr. Worthy, "Silvia and I had once agreed to go to bed together, could we have adjusted preliminaries, but she would have the wedding before the consummation and I was for consummation before the wedding. We could not agree. She was a pert, obstinate fool and would lose her maidenhead her own way so she may keep it for Plume."[4] Silvia is attracted to Plume for the very quality that makes him less than an ideal husband—his roving, inconstant nature—and she chafes under the restrictions placed upon a young woman of her age and social class. In this respect, she is reminiscent of Hellena in *The Rover,* who is attracted to the rakish Willmore and pursues him energetically in several disguises. But the beautiful, intelligent, rich, forthright, virtuous, and resourceful Silvia is a more attractive, far better developed character than Hellena.

Her first encounter with Plume, though brief, establishes the nature of their attraction. He kneels before her, declaring that "the height of conquest is to die at your feet." Fully aware of the sexual connotation of "dying," she replies in kind: "Well, well, you shall die at my feet, or where you will . . ." (p.29). During much of the ensuing action, the sexual tension between the lovers is maintained by hint and indirection, for Silvia disguises herself as a young man and allows herself to be recruited by Plume as a soldier in Her Majesty's Army. Farquhar skillfully employed the conventions of the breeches role, in which an innocent action or remark can be charged with double meaning.[5] Wooing the disguised Silvia for military service, Plume competes for her with another officer, Captain Brazen, who offers to make the young man a corporal.

> *Plume.*   A corporal! I'll make you my companion; you shall eat with me.
> *Brazen.*   You shall drink with me.
> *Plume.*   You shall lie with me, you young rogue. (Kisses her.)[6]

In this situation, and on another occasion when Plume offers quite innocently to share his bed with his new young recruit, the audience can enjoy Silvia's discomfiture or, alternatively, share the joke with her. In the tradition of the broad style of playing that she had inherited from Susannah Verbruggen, Anne undoubtedly managed to telegraph Silvia's desire to share Plume's bed.

It can be argued that nothing overtly sexual actually transpires during the play; Plume's bastard child by a village woman had been begotten before the action of the play begins and, despite appearances, he claims not to have seduced the country girl, Rose. But the triangular relationship in which Silvia, Plume, and Rose are involved keeps the subject of sex very much in mind. In one scene, omitted for reasons of indecency after the opening night, Rose is plainly disappointed that she is "neither better nor worse" for having spent the night with the young recruit—Silvia in disguise—who, it is clear, cannot give her "as many fine things as the captain can" (p. 96). Other scenes between them, and between Plume and Rose, focus attention on the frustrated romance of Silvia and Plume.

We may have the impression of an emphatic, relentlessly suggestive style, but that was apparently not the case. Cibber observed that "Mrs. *Oldfield* and Mr. *Wilks,* by their frequently playing against one another in our best Comedies, very happily supported that Humour and Vivacity which is so peculiar to our *English* Stage."[7] Lightness, vivacity, and good humor nicely balanced the lack of subtlety. The sexual current was there, but the actors also conveyed the impression that it was not to be taken too seriously. *The Recruiting Officer* contributed materially to the distinctive comic interplay between Wilks and Oldfield; its success is a splendid instance of the collaboration of actors and playwright.

During the summer of 1706, Vanbrugh at last began to put together an amalgamated company at his new theater in the Haymarket, very much as he had planned in 1703, with players from the old Lincoln's Inn Fields company and many of the leading actors from Drury Lane.[8] The possibility that one company might not be big enough for so many stars, each with his or her own perks and personal stock of roles, apparently did not concern him. Satisfied with his deal and busy with his architectural work on Blenheim Palace, he turned over the management of the company to an able deputy, Owen Swiney.

In the new company at the Haymarket, Anne was still ranked below Elizabeth Barry and Anne Bracegirdle. She was also on unfamiliar ground—an interloper, along with the rest of her colleagues from Drury Lane—and she had been a principal comedienne for only three seasons. If a part that she and Anne Bracegirdle had played in the past were to be cast, it would very likely go to the senior actress. Still, with recent successes such as *The Careless Husband, The Tender Husband,* and *The Recruiting Officer,* Anne Oldfield was in a much stronger position than she would have been if Vanbrugh's plans had gone into effect three years earlier. The stage was set for a legendary rivalry.

For the first two months, at least, there were no overt signs of difficulty. Both actresses were cast in enough of their popular roles to keep them and their followers happy. In November, they appeared together for the first time. The play, *The Platonick Lady,* a new comedy by Susanna Centlivre, ran for only four nights, but it gave spectators their first chance to make a direct comparison between the two actresses. Although it was probably not the author's intention, the cards seemed stacked in Anne Oldfield's favor.

Centlivre knew both women well, having created roles for them in earlier plays. We may assume that she tailored the parts accordingly. For Anne Oldfield she created the spirited Isabella, who single-mindedly pursues her heart's object, Belvil. Anne Bracegirdle played the charming, rather diffident Lucinda, "platonick lady" of the title, beloved by Sir Charles Richley and also—in his fashion—by Belvil. While Lucinda attempts to reconcile her attraction to Belvil with her "platonicks," Isabella embarks upon a dizzying sequence of disguise and deception, the better to spy upon Belvil, alienate him from Lucinda, and break off her own match with Sir Charles. Occasionally she pauses to reflect upon honor and reputation, but having assured herself that she has satisfied the former, she firmly proclaims "A Fig for the Censure of the World!" The play ends happily for her when it is discovered that Lucinda and Belvil are brother and sister; Lucinda graciously consents to marry Sir Charles, leaving the way open for Belvil and Isabella to marry.

As a fable of female striving, *The Platonick Lady* in some sense foreshadowed the rivalry of the two actresses. But its immediate importance was that Isabella provided Anne Oldfield with a showcase for her energy and versatility, while Lucinda was only a pale imitation of the witty ladies of fashion that Anne Bracegirdle had made her specialty. In their first appearance together, the younger actress had the clear advantage.

Within a few months, the rivalry began to heat up. On February 4, the two women appeared together in *Marriage à la Mode; or, The Comical Lovers*. This "new" comedy was really nothing more than a mélange of the comic subplots of two Dryden plays, *Secret Love; or, The Maiden Queen* and *Marriage à la Mode,* fairly obviously cobbled together by Colley Cibber to capitalize on the appearance of the two popular comediennes. Anne Oldfield played Florimell (a role originated by Nell Gwynn) opposite Cibber himself as the genteel lover, Celadon. Once more she had an opportunity to revel in masks and disguises and, in a famous breeches scene, to don men's clothing and mimic the airs of a young gallant. This time, however, Anne Bracegirdle had an equally fine role: Melantha, the delightful "female fop" who torments her long-suffering lover. The actresses' second appearance together would have to be scored a draw.

Matters did not rest there, for thespian rivalries are good for attendance. On February 7, the run of *The Comical Lovers* was interrupted by a performance of a popular stock piece, *The Amorous Widow; or, The Wanton Wife*. It is tempting to suppose that this was actually the second of two consecutive performances—the legendary contest in which Anne Bracegirdle and Anne Oldfield played the role of Mrs. Brittle (the wanton wife) on successive nights.[9] According to the only full account of the incident, the role of Mrs. Brittle had been selected as a test piece to determine who was the more accomplished comedienne. Mrs. Bracegirdle, "as being the Senior," was invited to perform on the first night, whereupon she acquitted herself admirably, "as might be expected from a long unrivall'd Superiority."[10] Since she had played the role frequently for more than a decade, her success was not unexpected.[11]

Anne Oldfield was at a disadvantage, for the role was unfamiliar to her and she had to appear at short notice. Learning her part would present no great problem; she would not be expected to know the entire play—merely her lines, cues, entrances, exits, and stage business—and like most successful repertory actors, she undoubtedly had a prodigious memory. The greatest challenge was to follow Mrs. Bracegirdle's performance, which she had either to equal or to excel. Even her partisans are said to have dreaded the outcome.

Theater audiences throughout the eighteenth century were neither reverential nor impartial. While outright riots were rare, rowdy groups of spectators in the pit often succeeded in disrupting performances, making it next to impossible for the actors to be heard above the din. The catcall had been perfected as the chief vehicle for disapproval. In the course of her career, Anne was to face many restive, openly hostile spectators. Now she appeared before an audience divided between her own and Mrs. Bracegirdle's supporters. But she had spoken only ten lines when: "such was the gracefulness and beauty of her Person, so enchanting the harmony of her Voice and softness of her Delivery, and so inimitable her Action, that she charm'd the whole Audience to that Degree, they almost forgot they had ever seen Mrs. *Bracegirdle*, and universally adjudged her the Preheminence."[12]

Whether the contest took place in this manner—or took place at all—is not certain, for no independent evidence exists. But if the story in *Authentick Memoirs* is correct, Mrs. Bracegirdle must have felt doubly aggrieved. It was bad enough to have a role from her own repertoire used as the object of contention; far worse, to witness her rival's triumph. Basking in public approval, Anne Oldfield is said to have begun putting on airs, coming to the theater in a sedan chair while the veteran actresses made do on foot. Years later, Anne Bracegirdle would recall hearing the cry at the stage door after a performance: "Mrs Oldfield's chair! Mrs Barry's clogs! and Mrs Bracegirdle's pattens!"[13]

Mrs. Bracegirdle was at another disadvantage, which could hardly be blamed on her rival. Her greatest triumphs had been in plays that were five to ten years old. Anne Oldfield had the distinct advantage of appearing in a number of popular current plays. It is difficult to believe that Mrs. Bracegirdle's fans had begun to desert her, yet everything seemed to contribute to her young rival's growing popularity.

These disappointments might have been borne if not for the matter of Anne Oldfield's annual benefit.[14] Position in the benefit schedule was a jealously guarded prerogative and a sensitive indicator of an actor's place in the company hierarchy. Higher ranking actors took their benefits in late February or March, when houses were fuller. At Lincoln's Inn Fields and later at the Haymarket, Thomas Betterton, Elizabeth Barry, and Anne Bracegirdle had been accustomed to precedence in the annual schedule. The introduction of leading actors from Drury Lane created a potentially sticky situation at the Haymarket in 1706. In the contract he signed with Vanbrugh that summer, Robert Wilks, who was coming from Drury Lane as leading actor and director of rehearsals, made certain that his benefit would be held "sometime in February." John Mills, an actor of lesser standing, was content to negotiate a benefit "some time before the first of April." But Anne Oldfield, who undoubtedly expected that Barry and Bracegirdle would take precedence over her, merely stipulated that she was to have a benefit, paying the standard house charge.[15]

By the end of February 1707, something—perhaps her success in the contest—had happened to alter her situation. Robert Wilks's benefit, the first of the season, was duly held on February 18. Then, on February 25, before any other senior members of the company had their benefits, a performance of *The Tender Husband* was given for Anne Oldfield's benefit.[16] Bracegirdle's response was quiet but unambiguous. She walked out, forgoing her own benefit and the considerable sum it would have brought. A fit of pique might be assumed. She would surely return, if not before the end of the season then at least by the opening of the new season in September; but she did not. In her mid thirties,[17] hardly ripe for retirement, with no apparent plans for marriage, she turned her back on the career she had pursued since childhood, returning to the stage only for the occasion of Betterton's benefit in 1709.

This was certainly more than anyone had bargained for, but perhaps it was inevitable in the unsettled state of the London stage. The actresses would never have met head to head if conditions had favored the existence of two healthy, competing companies. With the viability of Drury Lane in some doubt and too many stars under one roof at the Haymarket, Bracegirdle chose to give up her career rather than find employment elsewhere.

Anne Bracegirdle did not exercise another option: to stay and fight. It would be said later that Anne Oldfield's influential friends—probably a reference to Vanbrugh and Maynwaring—had brought pressure upon Owen Swiney to give her a favored position in the benefit schedule.[18] But Bracegirdle was not without her own supporters. Thomas Betterton, her mentor and foster-father for nearly thirty years, was a respected ally. Vanbrugh's former partner, William Congreve, who may have sublimated his love for Anne Bracegirdle by creating for her the roles of Angelica (*Love for Love*), Almeria (*The Mourning Bride*), and Millamant (*The Way of the World*), still had some influence. The Earl of Scarsdale, a devoted admirer and rumored lover, would very likely have come to her defense. (Although neither he nor she publicly acknowledged any such relationship they were popularly regarded as lover and mistress; an entry in the so-called Minute Book of the Kit-Cat Club links them with Anne Oldfield and Arthur Maynwaring, who were acknowledged lovers.)[19] The likely explanation is that she had no desire to create a stir, preferring in this instance, as in the general conduct of her life, to maintain a discreet silence.

If their positions had been reversed, it is inconceivable that Anne Oldfield would have given up her position, let alone her career, without a murmur. She was no stranger to backstage power struggles. When she joined the Drury Lane company in 1699, Vanbrugh, then not a manager but a successful playwright and important figure in the theater world, watched over her briefly and helped her to her first starring role. After that she was largely on her own, surviving her first important challenge in 1703, when she emerged from the scramble for the late Susannah Verbruggen's repertoire with several important roles.

Anne Bracegirdle, raised from childhood under the parental protection of Thomas and Mary Betterton, had little experience with professional rivalry. She had stepped easily into featured roles in her late teens and had become a star in the 1690s. Even as a star she seemed content to be overshadowed by Elizabeth Barry, often taking the lesser roles of chaste and modest ingenues in tragedy opposite Barry's tempestuous heroines. The lifelong friendship of the two women was rare in the annals of professional relations. When they were still acting together at Drury Lane, Bracegirdle had been offered some of Barry's roles in a maneuver designed by Christopher Rich to undercut the established tragedienne. She declined to play that game, expressing her belief that "the Stage was wide enough for her Success, without entring [sic] into any such rash and invidious Competition with Mrs. *Barry*."[20] It was in keeping with her past history and reputation for discretion that she should remove herself quietly from an unseemly backstage contention in the spring of 1707.

Anne Oldfield seems to have emerged from the rivalry not only triumphant but unscathed. After Bracegirdle's departure, the season continued as if nothing had happened. If Elizabeth Barry was also stung by the preferential treatment of Anne Oldfield, she gave no outward sign, but quietly took her own benefit on March 6.[21] Thereafter the two women continued to perform together without obvious friction through the remainder of the season. Anne did not, however, recede tamely into the background. It was reported that she and the author, Edmund Smith, had a disagreement over some of her lines during the rehearsal of his new tragedy, *Phaedra and Hippolytus* (in which she played Ismena to Barry's Phaedra), while he and Mrs. Barry remained "in perfect harmony."[22]

The Drury Lane refugees prospered at the Haymarket—Anne perhaps more than anyone. The articles she signed with Vanbrugh in August 1706 gave her a salary of thirteen shillings four pence "for every day a Play shall be acted by the Company under his [Vanbrugh's] direction, or any person deputed by him,"[23] which worked out to four pounds per week, or about £120 a year, a considerable increase over her salary at Drury Lane. With the departure of Anne Bracegirdle, she had become the principal comedienne at the Haymarket, and she gained another brilliant comic role when *The Beaux' Stratagem* opened on March 8, 1707.

She and Wilks were paired again in Farquhar's new comedy, but not as marriageable lovers. In *The Recruiting Officer,* the audience knows from the outset that Silvia and Plume will be united at the end, for the only barriers between them are her father's consent and his own roving nature, familiar and easily overcome obstacles in comedies of the period. In *The Beaux' Stratagem,* Anne played Mrs. Sullen, a handsome and spirited woman trapped in a loveless marriage. In an age in which divorce was virtually impossible, there was no solution to her problem that was both honorable and romantically satisfying.

Vanbrugh's *Provok'd Wife,* written for Betterton's company in 1697, features a mismatched couple, Sir John Brute and Lady Brute, who had married because he could not have her any other way and because she hoped that she would grow to like him for himself as well as for his money and position. Inevitably, he has tired of her, and she is so disappointed in her part of the bargain that she very nearly cuckolds him with an attractive young beau. At the end of the play, their situation has not really changed; there is no reason to believe, despite their temporary reconciliation, that he will not continue to occupy himself with drinking and whoring and that she will not eventually succumb to a persistent lover.[24]

The situation in *The Beaux' Stratagem* is similar in many respects. Mrs. Sullen, a wonderful new character for Anne in quite a different vein from Silvia, is the conventional town-bred lady, plunked down in the country with a bumpkin of a husband who lives only for hunting and drinking with his cronies and has no interest in her company or any of the fashionable pastimes that delight her. She longs for London, where a woman can properly manage a husband, where "a fine woman may do anything. . . . o'my conscience, she may raise an army of forty thousand men."[25] Caught between her scruples and her desire to arouse *some* feeling in her lump of a husband, even if it is only jealousy, Mrs. Sullen enters into a flirtation with Archer (Wilks), hovering deliciously on the brink of adultery. Money also enters into the equation, for unless she regains her ten-thousand-pound dowry she cannot live independently.[26]

Mrs. Sullen's scenes with Archer, especially his verbal seduction in the "gallery" scene in act 4 and a more physical seduction attempt in her bedroom in act 5, were clearly written with the lightly erotic Wilks-Oldfield style in mind. Mrs. Sullen's frequent asides, in which she admits the truth of her feelings for Archer, invite us to watch her struggles with detached amusement. His overripe importunings have much the same effect. The audience would be titillated, yet fairly certain that adultery will be forestalled, as it is (at the eleventh hour) by the entrance of Sullen's manservant, Scrub.

Mrs. Sullen is conceived throughout in a self-dramatizing fashion that makes it difficult to take her plight too seriously, though in real life it would be pitiable indeed. At her first appearance, she inveighs melodramatically against her circumstances. "Country pleasures! Racks and torments!" she complains to her sister-in-law Dorinda, "dost think, child, that my limbs were made for leaping of ditches, and clambering over stiles?" (p. 26). (Anne, whose way with double entendre inspired Alexander Pope to coin the term "Ofieldismos,"[27] may have paused after the first syllable of "country," for good effect; she may also have had fun with "racks and torments," parodying the high tragic style.)

In keeping with the elements of self-mockery in the character of Mrs. Sullen, her unhappy situation is resolved in a mock ceremony in which she and Sullen at last manage to agree about something— namely, that they cannot live together. Running through a list of their aversions—she cannot stand hunting, he hates dancing; she hates cock fighting, he abhors card playing, and so on—they agree at last to part.

Sullen: Your hand.
Mrs. Sullen: Here.
Sullen: These hands joined us, these shall part us.—Away!
Mrs. Sullen: North.
Sullen: South.
Mrs. Sullen: East.
Sullen: West—far as the poles asunder.[28]

Critical opinion has been divided on the subject of this "divorce" and its consequences for the relationship of Mrs. Sullen and Archer.[29] When Archer "liberates" the papers that contain Mrs. Sullen's marriage settlement and returns them to her, she is free to live apart from her husband. But she is not equally free to live honorably—that is, in marriage—with Archer. It was reported that Anne complained that Farquhar had "dealt too freely with the character of Mrs. Sullen, in giving her to Archer without a proper Divorce, which was not a Security for her Honour."[30] If she did make such an objection, it must have been with a nice sense of what would pass muster on the stage, rather than what would be acceptable in life—her own, for example. Whether she made the objection, or intended it to be taken seriously, the story indicates an uneasiness about popular opinion.

In a recent study of Restoration and eighteenth-century drama, Judith Milhous and Robert Hume argue that a great deal depends upon how a play is interpreted in performance. *The Beaux' Stratagem* can be performed as a satire, in which the issues of unhappy marriage and fortune hunting are presented seriously and Mrs. Sullen is separated from Archer at the end; or it can be presented as a "romp," in which matters such as motives and legality are not taken seriously and no one worries about Mrs. Sullen's honor as she goes off with Archer.[31] But what seemed to matter most was not that the characters played by Oldfield and Wilks should live happily, and legally, ever after. At the end of the play, Archer and Mrs. Sullen lead a dance set to a song about "trifles," which rounds off their relationship in a pleasantly teasing fashion. Nothing could have been more appropriate for the most famous stage couple of the era.

The Beaux' Stratagem ran for ten performances and became one of the most popular pieces in the Drury Lane repertory. For Anne, the bored, mismated Mrs. Sullen was a significant addition to her stock of roles. She would eventually give up breeches parts such as Alinda, Hellena, and even Silvia to younger actresses. But she played Mrs. Sullen at least once every season throughout her career and began to acquire a whole new set of mature, sophisticated, comic heroines.[32] In Mrs. Sullen, Farquhar, who wrote *The Beaux' Stratagem* while he was mortally ill and died not long after the premiere, left her a magnificent legacy.

Out of the popularity of *The Recruiting Officer* and *The Beaux' Stratagem* grew the legend of Anne's romance with Farquhar. In the absence of hard evidence, there has been considerable speculation about her personal life during the early years of her career, when the beautiful young actress, by all accounts no prude, would have been exposed to many fleshly temptations. John Oldmixon's hint that Maynwaring was not Anne's first lover[33] is especially provocative, for as the author of *The Grove* he must have known Anne as early as the spring of 1700 and been privy to a great deal of gossip about what he did not know firsthand. But Oldmixon did not elaborate, and in the urge to fill in the gap, George Farquhar was put forward as a likely candidate for Anne's youthful affections.

Farquhar had left Ireland in 1697 or 1698 to try his luck as a playwright in London. His first effort, the comedy *Love and a Bottle,* opened at Drury Lane late in 1698 and ran for nine performances, an encouraging beginning. With the publication of a pamphlet, *The Adventures of Covent Garden,* Farquhar could consider himself launched as a writer. His discovery of Anne would have occurred at about this time. The romantic details of that story, in which the young playwright is stunned by the girl's blushing beauty, inevitably fueled the legend of their affair. Additional "evidence" has been taken from *Love and Business,* a collection of miscellaneous verse and prose published by Farquhar in 1702.

A sequence of letters in *Love and Business* has to do with the romantic quest of a young gentleman, following his encounter with a mysterious masked young lady. Eventually he learns that her name is Penelope— all we ever learn about her, except that she is young and unattached. Pursuing her with his pen, the young man expounds wittily upon the game of love as well as topical matters, such as the funeral of Dryden, on May 13, 1700. Before long he begins to compose poetry and contemplate suicide. The affair, such as it is, follows a predictable pattern. When he learns that she has taken up with "a very good and worthy Gentleman" he bows out, expressing the dignified hope that "the Person you admire [may] Love you as sincerely, and as passion-ately, as he whom you scorn."[34]

While many of the letters allude to real events of the spring and summer of 1700, they are essentially epistolary exercises.[35] Neverthe-less, Farquhar clearly drew upon his experiences and associations. One passage can be read as a playful tribute to Susannah Verbruggen, the original Lady Lurewell in *The Constant Couple.*

> Well! [so the twelfth letter begins] Mrs. V——— and my Charming *Penelope* are to lye together to Night; what I wou'd give now, to be a Mouse, (God bless us) behind the Hangings, to hear the Chat. . . . it shall go hard but I prove as kind to my Companion, as you are to yours; tho' I must confess, that I had rather be in Mrs. V———'s Place, with all the little Pillows about me, or in that of Monsieur Adonis upon the Chair.[36]

But even if the reader is supposed to "see" Mrs. Verbruggen in this scene, "with all the little Pillows" and a lapdog named "Monsieur Adonis," there is no reason to connect the mysterious Penelope with Anne. In the spring of 1700, Anne was leading a busy, public life, having enjoyed her first stage success in *The Pilgrim.* It is always possible that she and Farquhar had an affair, but the letters from *Love and Business,* and from another collection, *Letters of Wit, Politicks and Morality,* cannot be used as evidence.[37]

When speculation is set aside, Anne's relationship with Farquhar in the early years of their careers makes neither a very good story nor a very complete one. (It is unlikely that she was alluding to a youthful fling when she observed that she had spent many "agreeable hours" in his company.)[38] Seven years passed between their first meeting and her first role in one of his plays. By that time, she had become another man's mistress, and he another woman's husband. By that time, also, they had both matured as artists. The result was two plays whose enduring popularity would link playwright and actress in the popular imagination.

6
Mrs. Oldfield Complains

*I*t is difficult to like Christopher Rich, impossible to admire him, but one must sometimes accord him a grudging respect. Since first becoming a major shareholder at Drury Lane, he had alienated and finally driven away most of the leading actors, he had struggled to keep his remaining players going until they became successful rivals to the rebels at Lincoln's Inn Fields, and with the defection of most of his leading actors once more in 1706, he had still managed to keep his theater going as a competitive, if not altogether healthy, enterprise. It seemed that playwrights and actors might come and go, but Christopher Rich would go on forever.

He knew that in Drury Lane he had a valuable property: not just the building, certainly not—from his perspective—the actors, but the royal patents granted originally to Thomas Killigrew and Sir William Davenant by Charles II after the Restoration. Under the patent rights, he held certain privileges derived directly from the Crown and safe (or so he thought) from government interference.[1] As long as he could make enough to fend off his creditors and placate his fellow shareholders, he felt secure. Cibber once observed that he had often seen Rich "inclin'd to be cheerful in the Distresses of his Theatrical Affairs, and equally reserv'd and pensive when they went smoothly forward with a visible Profit." When most of his leading actors deserted him in 1706, he seemed unconcerned, taking Cibber backstage to show him all of the minor alterations he had made during the summer, apparently oblivious to Cibber's repeated query, "*But, Master, where are your Actors?*"[2] But even a man who relished confrontation could not hold out against the combined forces of rebellious actors and the Lord

57

Chamberlain. In the struggle that came to a head in 1709, Anne Oldfield was to play a crucial role.

When the new season opened in the fall of 1707, two more Drury Lane players, Jane Rogers and Letitia Cross, defected to the Haymarket, leaving Rich only a few leading actors with whom he could expect to draw audiences—the comedians Will Pinkethman and Richard Estcourt, and George Powell in tragic and straight comic roles. There were also disquieting hints that a movement was afoot to break Rich's monopoly on musical theater, which he had been granted as part of the deal that led to the creation of Vanbrugh's amalgamated company in 1706. The rumors proved true when, on December 31, the Lord Chamberlain issued an order declaring that after January 10 there would be a united company of actors at Drury Lane, having the exclusive rights to perform spoken drama, and a company of singers and musicians at the Haymarket, with a monopoly on opera and musical entertainments. Stripped of his musicians and singers, Rich now faced the prospect of taking back the actors who had defected to Vanbrugh.[3]

The transition was accomplished in less than one week. On Saturday, January 10, Betterton appeared as Macbeth at the Haymarket. After a hiatus of only three working days, "Her Majesty's United Company of Comedians" made its debut at Drury Lane with *Hamlet*. Once again there was the potential for backstage strife over such matters as the assignment of roles and the arrangement of the benefit schedule. For the junior players, chances of survival, let alone progress, were now greatly diminished. In the preceding October, Mary Porter at the Haymarket had complained to the Lord Chamberlain that parts had been given to "those below her," and that another actress—probably Jane Rogers—had been taken into the company "over her head."[4] With an even larger number of actresses under one roof at Drury Lane, prospects were not likely to improve.

When the time came, wily Christopher Rich was able to capitalize on such discontents, but for the moment his strategy was to remain discreetly in the background. A new figure appeared upon the scene, Colonel Henry Brett, a longtime personal friend of Cibber.[5] In the summer of 1707, Brett obtained an interest in the patent from a major Drury Lane shareholder, Sir Thomas Skipwith, and began to involve himself in theatrical affairs. Because he lacked managerial experience, one of his first moves was to appoint Wilks, Cibber, and Estcourt as his deputies, with responsibilities for rehearsals and the daily business of management. Throughout the rest of the season of 1707–8 the affairs of the new united company went smoothly.

Anne returned to Drury Lane with a considerable repertoire. Between October 13, 1707, when the season opened at the Haymarket with *The Recruiting Officer,* and June 11, 1708, when it closed at Drury Lane with *Hamlet,* she played twenty-eight different roles in seventy-five appearances.[6] Among her new roles was the gentle Ethelinda in Nicholas Rowe's tragedy, *The Royal Convert.* The play was unsuccessful and the part was wrong for Anne, since Ethelinda was essentially a "Bracegirdle" part, second in importance to Barry's passionate Saxon princess, Rodogune. Anne was also miscast as the villainous Countess of Nottingham in a revival of John Banks's historical tragedy of Elizabeth and Essex, *The Unhappy Favourite.*[7]

She did, however, appear to advantage as Semandra in Nathaniel Lee's *Mithridates.* It may be this production of which Chetwood wrote: "When *Mithridates* was revived, it was with much Difficulty she was prevail'd upon to take the Part; but she perform'd it to the utmost of Perfection, and, after that, she seem'd much better reconcil'd to Tragedy."[8] The central female figure in the play, Semandra is pitiable but not pathetic—a distinction that can be made in most of the tragic characters for which Anne became famous. Beloved of Ziphares (played by Wilks in this and later productions), she is forced to marry his father the king, who rapes her on their wedding night. Madness and death are the inevitable consequence. Wandering about the palace in her deranged state, Semandra is accidentally stabbed by Ziphares who, Romeo-like, swallows a death potion and dies nobly with her. Strong stuff for Anne, who generally left the business of madness and passion to others. But evidently she liked the role enough to play it from time to time and to choose it for her benefit in 1723.

In addition to the popular roles she had originated—Alinda, Lady Betty, Biddy Tipkin, Silvia, and Mrs. Sullen—and the stock roles that she had acquired in 1703, her comic repertoire now included Lady Heartwell, a young widow "handsome and of a high reserv'd Behaviour," in a new adaptation of the Fletcher comedy, *Wit Without Money,* and the Silent Woman (Mistress Epicoene) in Ben Jonson's *Epiceone; or, The Silent Woman.*

This last play, in which Anne played an unmanageable woman married to one of the world's greatest misogynists, was immensely popular on the Restoration stage and throughout the early eighteenth century, but it created a problem for its interpreters. The surprise ending, in which Mistress Epicoene (the no longer silent woman) is revealed as a boy in woman's clothing, depended upon a sexual disguise so impenetrable that the audience would be completely taken in. This was not a problem when the play was performed in Jonson's lifetime, for in the original production all the roles were played by young men, and Jacobean audiences were accustomed to the convention of male actors playing female roles. But after 1660, when women began to play women's roles and female impersonation was no longer the norm, it was evidently felt that a female impersonator could not be completely convincing as Mistress Epicoene. The role began to be played by a woman. Now, however, there was a new problem. How on earth did an actress manage to pass herself off, at the end, as a boy disguised as a woman? The original text calls for Mistress Epicoene's wig to be pulled off, revealing the boy's cropped hair underneath. A late eighteenth-century adaptation of the play indicates that this key piece of business was changed to make the denouement both possible and reasonably plausible: at the climactic moment, according to a stage direction, "Epicoene throws off female apparel, and appears in boy's cloaths."[9] That is probably the way the scene was played in Anne's time—giving the actress a brief opportunity to strut about in breeches. The "maleness" of Mistress Epicoene could not, of course, be taken seriously, but by the end of the play that was perhaps not so important. The chief element of the comedy, in which Anne undoubtedly reveled, was the transformation of the meek and humble "Silent Woman" into an outrageous shrew.

For her benefit on January 8, 1708, Anne chose the leading female role in *Rule a Wife and Have a Wife,* the perennially popular comedy by Beaumont and Fletcher. Estifania is a clever servant who passes herself off as a wealthy, marriageable aristocrat to ensnare a young officer, Perez. Upon discovering that his pretensions to wealth are as false as hers, she dubs him the "Copper Captain," by which name the character was popularly known. At the end, Estifania and Perez are content to have married for love rather than for wealth or position, but the way to reconciliation proves rocky. What Anne made of one small incident was, fortunately, recorded by Tom Davies:

When Oldfield drew the pistol from her pocket, pretending to shoot Perez, Wilks drew back as if greatly terrified, and, in a tremulous voice, uttered, *What! thy own husband!* Oldfield replied, with an archness of countenance and half-shut eye, *Let mine own husband, then, be in his own wits,* in a tone of voice so exactly in imitation of his, that the theatre was in a tumult of applause.[10]

Another admiring spectatator noted that Anne "turn'd herself into a roguish wheedling artful Miss."[11] Estifania, formerly played by Anne Bracegirdle and Susannah Verbruggen's daughter, Susannah Mountfort, became one of her most frequently performed roles.

Before leaving the Haymarket, Anne appeared in two new comedies by Cibber. Lady Dainty, in *The Double Gallant; or, The Sick Lady's Cure,* became another of her most popular roles. Here was Cibber in one of his characteristic modes: resourceful hack, pasting together pieces of at least three plays[12] to create a vehicle for the company's leading players. For himself he reserved the showy role of Atall, a tireless and inventive rake who manages to woo three ladies at once. For Wilks and Oldfield he created, or rather constructed, the characters of Careless and Lady Dainty, conflating the plots of two comedies by William Burnaby.

When Lady Dainty is not enjoying her "fragile" health to the hilt, she fawns mindlessly upon everything that is foreign and exotic. Careless successfully courts her in the guise of a Russian prince who has come to London with Peter the Great.[13] Since Lady Dainty is really attracted to Careless, she accepts the revelation of his true identity good-naturedly, pausing to declare, "and were but my Health recoverable, I should think myself completely happy."[14] The audience is left in little doubt that Careless has the cure for what ails her.

In *The Lady's Last Stake; or, The Wife's Resentment,* Anne played Mrs. Conquest, who disguises herself as a young man to save her friend Lady Gentle from the clutches of Lord George Brilliant and, in the process, to marry Lord George herself. Cibber blamed the failure of the play upon the poor acoustics at the Haymarket, whose high, arched ceiling produced echoes that often reduced spoken dialogue to an indistinct gabble.[15] But unlike *The Double Gallant, The Lady's Last Stake* was written in Cibber's heavy, moralizing vein. It was revived infrequently in the years to come, with another actress playing Mrs. Conquest, no doubt because Anne had acquired a considerable body of roles more to her own liking.

On February 7, 1708, the united company at Drury Lane staged

Congreve's *Love for Love*. The play had been written originally for
Betterton (then sixty years old) as the romantic lover, Valentine; Anne
Bracegirdle as the wealthy young lady of fashion, Angelica; Thomas
Doggett as Valentine's seagoing brother, Ben; and Elizabeth Barry as
Mrs. Frail. It was so strongly identified with these players that it
remained exclusively in the Lincoln's Inn Fields repertory. But over
the years, *Love for Love* had declined in popularity to the point that it
was sometimes performed as a curiosity with an all-female cast. The
Drury Lane production of 1708 marked a revival of interest and a new
lease on life for a fine play.

In his study of the history of Congreve's plays in the eighteenth
century, Emmett Avery attributes the success of the revival largely to
Anne, observing that when she began to play Angelica, *Love for Love*
was performed more frequently.[16] Anne had wonderful material to
work with, as Angelica calmly picks her way through a company of
fools, wears down her foolish old uncle, and twists Sir Sampson
Legend around her finger. She and Wilks, as a young, attractive Valentine, certainly struck more sexual sparks than their famous predecessors. *Love for Love* became a popular vehicle for them, as well as for
Estcourt (as Sir Sampson) and Drury Lane's other superb comedians.

The opening of the season of 1708–9 was disrupted by the death of
Queen Anne's consort, Prince George, on October 28, 1708, which
closed the theaters for a seven-week period of national mourning. It
was therefore probably not until after the first of the year, when the
benefit schedule was being worked out, that Rich dropped a bombshell.
A crucial section of the agreement that Brett had concluded with Wilks,
Cibber, and Estcourt dealt with actors' benefits. According to its
provisions, which were not to go into effect until the following year,
in arranging for a benefit an actor would have to deposit forty pounds
with the company treasurer—a safeguard that assured the managers
that they would be able to cover house expenses. This provision was
surely daunting, for few actors would be able to lay their hands on
that much money *before* their benefits; they were accustomed to having
the charge deducted from the night's receipts. Even worse was the
new provision whereby, in addition to the house charge, all actors
whose salaries did not amount to four pounds per week—and that
would be the majority—would have to hand over *one-fourth* of their
share of the profits; those who did not earn more than fifty shillings
per week—again, that would be quite a few—would have to hand over

a *one-third* of their share of the profits; and those at the bottom of the heap, who did not earn more than two pounds per week, would have to part with *half* of their profits.[17] This amounted to a tax upon benefits, which struck hardest at those who could least afford it. The actor-managers would not be affected, since their salaries were higher than four pounds per week, but few of their colleagues would fail to feel the bite.

Rich, who had not been a party to the agreement, nor indeed to any agreements with the members of the united company, had remained pleasantly vague throughout the period following the merger, allowing the actors to believe that their most recent contractual arrangements were still in force. Now he saw an opportunity to benefit himself. Suppose one were to waive the forty-pound deposit and, far from discouraging requests for benefits, actively encourage them? The underpaid players would, after all, do their best to fill the house on "their" nights. The management would then tax the profits "for the use of the patent."

Actors' contracts with Rich had always been verbal, but Cibber states that Rich now stipulated that they could have their benefits only if they signed a statement agreeing to the tax. When several principal actors at first refused to sign this so-called indulto, Rich offered it to the next lowest in rank, with the expected result that "some of the fearful [got] the Preference to their Seniors; who at last, seeing the time was too short for a present Remedy, and that they must either come into the Boat, or lose their Tide, were forc'd to comply, with what, they, as yet, silently, resented as the severest Injury."[18]

Anne, whose contract with Vanbrugh was still in effect, was not affected—or so she thought—by the terms of the agreement. Her benefit, *The Beaux' Stratagem,* went forward as scheduled on March 3, 1709, with receipts totaling £134.3. But, to her consternation she learned that the Drury Lane treasurer kept out not only the forty pounds house charge but an additional third of the remainder, "for the use of the patent," leaving her with a total profit of only £67.7.9.[19] The levy had been made as if she had been making only fifty shillings per week. The very next day she took her grievance to the Lord Chamberlain. In the conventional language of such appeals, the document began, "Mrs. Oldfield Complains," and went on to summarize her past and present situation, stating that at the Haymarket her contract had called for a salary of four pounds per week and an annual benefit, from which only forty pounds was to be deducted. She asserted that she had been assured by the Lord Chamberlain that these terms would be honored at Drury Lane, after the merger. "But Mr Rich, having consented to have a Play acted for her Benefit the 3d of this inst March, refuses to pay her the profits exceeding ffourty pounds of such Play, He absolutely demanding seventy one pounds for the use of the Patent, & insists upon her having only the remainder." The complaint concluded with the wish that the Lord Chamberlain would use his authority to "oblige Mr Rich to keep the Agreemt she had at the Hay=market."[20]

In a lengthy response, "The Answer of Mr Rich the Patentees & Adventurers, to a Paper intitled Mrs Oldfields Complaint," Rich attempted to kick a great deal of sand over the traces. He asserted first of all that her five-year contract, which was of course verbal, was still in force, and that it provided for a salary of fifty shillings (£2.10) a week "and no Agreement for a Benefit Play."[21] He declared himself to be a "stranger" to any articles she had concluded with Vanbrugh as to salary or benefits but added, in words damaging to his case, that since her return to Drury Lane in January of 1708 she had been paid four pounds every week, although "no woman 'till of late years had above 50 s." He further asserted that, when arrangements were made for her benefit on March 3, she had agreed not only to the deduction of the house charge but to the deduction of one-third of the remainder. Only thirty-one pounds, not seventy-one pounds as she claimed, was "for the use of the patent," for the remaining forty pounds was the standard house charge, which, he added, was not really enough. *His* expenses were really far greater than Vanbrugh's, "by reason of both Companies coming together." In fact, he was really being generous to actors who, in any case, no longer needed benefits, since they were now paid their full salaries quite punctually.

Anne in turn could argue that, in paying her four pounds per week since her return, Rich had in effect been honoring her contract with Vanbrugh, and that when she signed the hated "indulto" she had no idea that it affected her. While other actors based their complaints on different grounds, arguing custom or asserting that they had been coerced into signing the tax provision, she pleaded the terms of her contract with Vanbrugh. Her legal case might have been strong, but the Lord Chamberlain did not take action for more than a month, and by that time matters had taken quite a different turn.

By the end of April, more than twenty actors had taken their benefits. Betterton's, on April 7, was an especially grand occasion for which both Barry (who had left the company in the summer of 1708) and Bracegirdle came out of retirement—performing their original roles in *Love for Love,* with an epilogue written especially by Nicholas Rowe. No more complaints were made, according to Cibber, the actors deciding to wait until their benefits were over before taking some kind of mass action. There is no record of any such protest, but on April 30 the Lord Chamberlain at last acted, issuing an order restraining Rich from deducting any more than the customary house charge of forty pounds.[22]

In the meantime, a number of the company's leading actors had taken their own steps to undermine Rich. On March 10, only six days after Anne's complaint to the Lord Chamberlain, Wilks, Cibber, and Thomas Doggett signed an agreement with Owen Swiney for the joint management of an acting company at the Haymarket Theatre—poor acoustics or no. The agreement, made of course in secret, was a violation of the Lord Chamberlain's order of December 1707, giving Rich a monopoly on spoken drama, but from subsequent events it is clear that the Lord Chamberlain tacitly approved these negotiations. By the end of March, a number of Drury Lane actors began to sign articles with Swiney—all under the eye of the Lord Chamberlain.[23] On April 21, Anne joined them.

Anne's contract with Swiney made her not only the highest-paid, most privileged actress in the history of the English stage but the highest-paid member of the company, after the actor-managers. The agreement, good for thirteen years, promised her a salary of two hundred pounds per season, in nine equal monthly payments. In the event that the theater had to close for any reason during the season, "a reasonable abatement" of her salary would be made, "in proportion to the time of Such Cessation, or Non-performance." She was to have a play acted for her benefit each February, "the whole and intire receipts whereof, wthout [sic] any Deduction whatsoever" to be paid her; and she would not be obliged to perform before September 10 or after June 10.[24] The contract was witnessed by Margaret Saunders, an actress who had joined the company during the previous season and was to become Anne's devoted friend, and by Maynwaring, who was a personal friend of Swiney's and presumably acted as Anne's advisor during the negotiations.

The very advantageous terms—the high salary, the "clear" benefit (from which no house charge would be deducted)—would seem more impressive if they had not been intended as recompense for her exclusion from the management. From Cibber we know that she had been under consideration as a manager, along with Wilks, Doggett, and himself. As such, she would have earned far more than two hundred pounds per year. According to the terms of the actor-managers' contract with Swiney, each was to have a salary of two hundred pounds and a clear benefit. (Wilks was to have an extra fifty pounds, as he had for some years, for directing rehearsals.) In addition to their salaries and benefits, the three actor-managers would share equally in half of the company profits, the other half going to Swiney. This was the first formulation of an arrangement that made the actor-managers very rich indeed over the next two decades.

Anne's exclusion from management was not a personal reflection upon her. Except for the brief period of cooperative management at Lincoln's Inn Fields, when three women—Elizabeth Barry, Anne Bracegirdle, and Elinor Leigh—had been equal partners and shareholders with Betterton and four other actors, women had not participated in the management of theatrical companies in England. This situation was probably a reflection of the unequal status of women when they were first admitted to the acting profession in the early 1660s.[25] For reasons that had nothing to do with the inclusion of the three women as joint sharers at Lincoln's Inn Fields, the experiment in cooperative management had not been successful; Barry and Bracegirdle, in particular, had come in for criticism.[26] When Anne was suggested as a manager of the new company in 1709, Doggett, who had been unhappy under the regime of Betterton, Barry, and Bracegirdle, vetoed the proposal, noting that although he had no doubts about Anne's merit as an actress and professional colleague, "our Affairs could never be upon a secure Foundation, if there was more than one Sex admitted to the Management of them."[27] As compensation, Anne was to be offered carte blanche in the terms of her articles; the contract that she signed on April 21 was the result. Barred, as a woman, from participation in profits and managerial decisions, she would have to exercise her power in less formal ways. (Social scientists make a useful distinction between power and authority.) Accounts of her threatened walkouts and tantrums are more understandable in this context.

Rich apparently had no inkling of the plans to form a new company at the Haymarket. Throughout the spring of 1709, the schedule of performances at Drury Lane continued as usual. All of the principal actors continued to appear regularly—except Anne. After mid-March, she performed only twice: for Mills's benefit on March 31, and for John Bickerstaffe's benefit on April 16. During this period, other actresses played her roles: Lucretia Bradshaw took over Hellena in *The Rover* as well as Carolina in *Epsom Wells* (a popular revival this season), Frances Knight played Lady Lurewell in *The Constant Couple,* and Henrietta Moore played Teresia in *The Squire of Alsatia* and Silvia in *The Recruiting Officer.* One of Anne's biographers has inferred that Rich was punishing her for her role in his troubles by giving her parts to others. (As far as we know, she was the only member of the company to make a public complaint to the Lord Chamberlain, although Cibber speaks of others "who had distinguish'd themselves in the Application for Redress.")[28] In a pamphlet, *Concerning the Poor ACTORS, who under Pretence of hard Usage from the PATENTEES, are about to desert their Service,* the aptly named treasurer of Drury Lane, Zachary Baggs, claims that Anne had simply walked out, refusing to "assist others in their Benefits."[29] But her absence throughout most of March and April and all of May was probably unrelated to professional matters. At the end of March she was six months pregnant.

Rich's protest, through Baggs, was an attempt to stir up support, but it had no effect on his legal situation. On June 6, the Lord Chamberlain exerted his authority once more, issuing a silencing order that closed Drury Lane altogether. (Since the season was nearly over, the order lost some of its force.) According to Cibber, the word reached the theater while a rehearsal was in progress. There followed a melodramatic scene in which a tardy actor (probably Cibber himself), chided by Rich, had the satisfaction of watching the messenger deliver the order, at which, "throwing his Head over his shoulder, towards the Patentee, in the manner of Shakespear's Harry the Eighth to Cardinal Wolsey [he] cry'd *Read o'er that! and now—to Breakfast, with what Appetite you may.*"[30] For many of the Drury Lane actors it would be a moment to savor; not quite the end of Christopher Rich, but the end of their bondage to him.

Anne's motives in the affair are not entirely clear. She was a logical candidate to confront Rich because she had a strong case and because her lover had social and political connections with the Lord Chamberlain. A degree of calculation undoubtedly governed her actions. At the very least, Rich might have been enjoined to honor the terms of her contract with Vanbrugh. But with Cibber, Wilks, Swiney, and the rest of the defectors, she gambled that the contentious patentee would play for higher stakes, and lose.

Throughout the season of 1708–9, Anne had also been occupied with domestic affairs. On June 1, 1708, she signed a lease for a parcel of land just off Covent Garden, on which she was to build her first house, number 23 Southampton Street. The lessor was Wriothesley Russell, duke of Bedford. In 1705, the young duke had decided to pull down the great mansion in the Strand that had housed the Russell family since the sixteenth century and to lease the property for residential development. A new street, named after his maternal Southampton relatives, was put through from the Strand to Henrietta Street, on the south side of Covent Garden, and lots suitable for townhouses were laid out. The new development, which attracted "respectable" rather than "fashionable" residents, proved especially convenient for affluent theater people—who did not fit into either category—since it was within easy walking distance of Drury Lane.[31]

Many of the leases were quickly snapped up by carpenters and bricklayers, who, like contractors building on speculation today, put up houses for sale or rent. Robert Wilks lived briefy at number 24, built on a plot leased by the carpenter Thomas Barlow. But Anne leased her lot directly from the Duke of Bedford, which suggests that it was still vacant at the time and that she made her own arrangements for the construction of the house. According to the terms of the sixty-year ground lease, Anne Oldfield, "a Spinster of the Parish of St. Paul Covent Garden," was to pay the Duke of Bedford a ground rent of eight pounds a year. Exception was made for the first two years, for which, in compensation for the building costs incurred, she would be required to pay only the token annual rent of one peppercorn.[32] As lessee she was expected to be scrupulous in the upkeep of the property, was to allow the landlord to inspect it at any time, and would, of course, pay the annual poor tax "charged upon the Houses of the Inhabitants of the said Parish of St. Paul Covent Garden."

No trace whatever remains of the house today. In 1876, it was demolished, and the land was subsumed into a large corner lot now occupied by a branch of Lloyds Bank.[33] Of all the houses built in the early 1700s, only two escaped demolition or major reconstruction in the nineteenth and twentieth centuries. One is number 27, for many years the home of the actor David Garrick. To look at now, the narrow, four-storied, rather plain building seems far too modest to have been the home of the most famous actor of the eighteenth century. (He moved into grander quarters eventually.) Anne's house, with a frontage of only sixteen feet, was even smaller. Yet in 1709, the move to number 23 Southampton Street must have represented hitherto unknown comfort, security, and status.

In 1749, Garrick thought he had gotten a "very good Bargain" when he paid five hundred guineas for number 27.[34] Anne presumably paid far less for her smaller house. Even so, at the time she signed the lease, she had been earning the relatively high salary of four pounds per week for only two years, hardly enough time, one would think, in which to accumulate the purchase price. She undoubtedly depended upon Maynwaring for a portion of the payment, but despite his comfortable income he was not possessed of a "saving" disposition. Indeed, in April 1708, he had written to his patroness, the Duchess of Marlborough, asking for a loan "to make my next payment into the Bank, or loose what is there allready [*sic*]." As an excuse for his financial problems he explained that money was still owing to him for "Business done above two years ago," and concluded—perhaps in deference to Sarah Churchill's views on the management of money—"it is certain that I am not made of a borrowing temper."[35]

It should be remembered that the season of 1708–9 was a difficult period for Anne, as for actors generally. Salaries had been reduced when the theaters were closed for seven weeks in November and December after the death of Prince George. Then in March came the confrontation with Rich over the matter of the benefit tax, followed by her temporary retirement from the stage in mid-April, and in late April the expense of entering into a one-thousand-pound bond to seal her articles with Swiney. According to Zachary Baggs's pamphlet, Anne's salary for the season came to only £56.13.4. It is not surprising that she fought to keep the full amount of her benefit proceeds.

Baggs noted that, in addition to her salary and two-thirds benefit, she had been given £10.15 "to wear on the Stage in some Plays, during the whole Season, a Mantua and Petticoat," and that she did not return any of that money although she had stopped acting three months early. He also estimated that she obtained £120 "by Guineas"—that is, by selling tickets to wealthy patrons at a premium price—in addition to two-thirds of the profits for her benefit.[36] But this was not a great deal, considering her small salary that year and the expenses of building her house.

There were pressing reasons for Anne to be securely in possession of her own home and a lucrative, long-term contract with Swiney. Sometime in the summer of 1709, probably at the end of June, her son, young Arthur Maynwaring, was born. In *Faithful Memoirs,* Edmund Curll states that Anne's first son was seven years old at the time of his father's death,[37] which would place his birth sometime in 1705. But Curll set the record straight in his later *History of the English Stage* by reprinting a letter from Margaret Saunders in which, among other things, it was noted: "There is an Error about the Child. He was no more than three Years old when his Father died."[38] There is no reason to doubt Mrs. Saunders, who may already have been living with Anne at the time of the child's birth. Other evidence also serves to pinpoint his birth during the summer of 1709.

To begin with, there are Anne's infrequent stage appearances after mid-March, and her absence altogether after April 16. Clothing styles made it possible to conceal pregnancy until it was fairly far advanced. Certainly there are no surviving comments about her condition, as there would be about her pregnancy in 1713. Out of respect for Maynwaring, and because he was able to look after her, she would not have continued working past the point of concealment. The date and circumstances of young Arthur Maynwaring's marriage, thirty years later, also suggest that he was born in the summer of 1709. On June 23, 1739, he married Katherine Pyne in the church of St. Bene't, Paul's Wharf.[39] According to the terms of Anne's will, he did not come into full possession of his inheritance of five thousand pounds until his thirtieth birthday. It seems likely, therefore, that he was born in mid or late June 1709, and that he did not marry until he was old enough to claim his legacy.

His military career provides additional evidence of his birth in 1709 rather than in 1705. He did not follow his father's example in education or choice of careers but was influenced, and also helped, by Anne's second lover, Colonel Charles Churchill, a career military officer and courtier. Young Arthur received his first commission on December 4, 1724, as an ensign in Colonel Stanhope Cotton's regiment of the Somerset Light Infantry.[40] A few months later, in April 1725, he transferred to a more elite regiment, the Tenth Hussars, in which he was commissioned cornet to Lieutenant Colonel Powlett. (This was

Charles Churchill's own regiment, and Churchill was probably responsible for the change.) If Arthur was born in June 1709, he would have been not quite sixteen when he joined the Tenth Hussars, very young by modern standards, but not according to the pattern of military life in the eighteenth century. Ensign and cornet were the lowest ranking commissioned officers in the infantry and cavalry, and it was not uncommon for boys far younger than Anne's son to hold such rank. Colonel Churchill, himself the son of a career officer, had been commissioned as an ensign at about the age of ten and was a captain before he was twenty. Arthur's half-brother, young Charles Churchill, was already a lieutenant in the Sixth Dragoons at the age of sixteen. Young Arthur Maynwaring, therefore, probably began his military career as soon as he had completed his youthful education.

The story that Anne had a daughter, born in about 1700, was related by a woman well known to readers of eighteenth-century literature—the august Mrs. Delany, Fanny Burney's elderly friend. In her memoirs, Mrs. Delany recalled that in 1706 she attended school with Anne Oldfield's daughter, a "Miss Dye Bertie," who in later life was "the *pink of fashion* in the beau monde and married a nobleman."[41] The young lady unquestionably existed, but Mrs. Delany's memory was at fault in connecting her with Anne. That she was the daughter of Peregrine Bertie, Vice-Chamberlain from 1694 to 1706, is clear from Bertie's will, dated June 27, 1711, which contains a handsome bequest to "Elizabeth Allen commonly call'd Mrs Poltney," and an additional provision of two hundred pounds a year "in trust and for the use and benefitt of Diana and Harriett my two daughters by the said Mrs Allen. . . ."[42] One cannot but be grateful to "the old Vice," as Maynwaring called him, for being so explicit. Too often, wills of the period are cagey about mistresses and illegitimate children.

Apart from the month and day of young Arthur's birth, it would be interesting to know whether Anne welcomed the prospect of motherhood and what kind of a mother she was. The chief evidence of maternal devotion seems to be her concern for her son's financial security, specifically the large legacy she left him and the care she took to protect it.[43] One thing is certain, however: no matter how much she may have welcomed motherhood and fulfilled her responsibilities, she did not let it interfere with her career. When she resumed a heavy schedule of acting at the Haymarket on September 22, 1709, the child would have to be cared for, and nursed, by others, if he had not already been put out to nurse.

It is difficult to imagine Arthur Maynwaring as a father, according to the modern, child-centered ideal of family life. That would have been out of keeping both with the practices of his social class and his own inclinations. During the years of Anne's residence on Southampton Street, his letters to Sarah Churchill are full of references to dining out with political friends, and his manifold activities took him to Windsor Lodge, St. Albans, and Woodstock, where Blenheim Palace was slowly gestating. But the birth of his son, described by Oldmixon as "very like him in Person and Vivacity," seems to have caused some alteration of his former ways. He worried about what would become of the boy after his death, since he had so little to leave him.[44] If he was not able to change his spendthrift habits he did the next best thing: he helped make sure that Anne would be secure in her career and able to support the child. The house on Southampton Street would, of course, be a haven for both Anne and their son.

A distinctly plump Anne Oldfield. Portrait attributed to Sir Godfrey
Kneller. Courtesy of the Garrick Club.

Robert Wilks. Engraving from a portrait by John Ellys dated 1732 (the year of Wilks's death), showing him to be every inch the fine gentleman. Reproduced by permission of The Huntington Library, San Marino, California.

Colley Cibber in the character of Lord Foppington. Engraving from a portrait by Grisoni. Reproduced by permission of The Huntington Library, San Marino, California.

The Kit-Cat portrait of Arthur Maynwaring by Sir Godfrey Kneller, possibly painted in 1709. Reproduced by permission of the National Portrait Gallery, London.

Anne Oldfield. Engraving from a portrait by Jonathan Richardson. The pose is conventional, but the overall effect is suggestive of the liveliness and charm for which she was famous in comedy. The Latin inscription reads: "Ornament and Delight of the Stage." The Harvard Theatre Collection.

Mrs Oldfield Complains. 101

That when She acted at the Queens
Theatre in the Haymarket: She had an Agreem.t
four four pounds of Week Sallery, and a Benefit=Play
every year paying, only, out of the Receipt Fourty=
=pounds, wch Agreem.t was Enterd in the Lord Cham=
=berlain's Office: That upon my Lords assureance
of his Protection, and her being continu'd at the Same
Sallery, and terme of a Benefit=Play at the Theatre
=Royall, She return'd to act there: But Mr. Rich
having consented to have a Play acted for her Benefit
the 3.d of this ins.t March, refuses to pay her the
profits exceeding fourty pounds of such Play, He
absolutely demanding Seventy one pounds for the use of
the Patent, & insists upon her having only the remainder

Mrs Oldfield Therefore, Humbly hopes, the Lord
Chamberlain will Use his Authority to Oblige
Mr. Rich to keep the Agreem.t She had at the
Hay=market.

Ann Oldfield

March ye 4th 1708/9

Anne Oldfield's petition to the Lord Chamberlain, March 4, 1709, complaining about the reduction of her benefit proceeds. Copyright reserved. Reproduced by permission of Her Majesty's Stationery Office (Public Record Office).

Barton Booth. Engraving from a drawing by G. Clint. The Harvard Theatre Collection.

Anne Oldfield. Engraving from a portrait by Jonathan Richardson. The pose and the surrounding details suggest the "majestical dignity" of her tragic roles. The Harvard Theatre Collection.

The "Richard Savage" letter. Comparison with the signature on Mrs. Oldfield's petition to the Lord Chamberlain indicates that the letter is not in her handwriting. Loyola University of Chicago Archives: Edward Carrigan, S.J. Theatre Collection.

Drawing depicting Ellen Terry and Gordon Craig in a scene from the Mildred Aldrich comedy, *Nance Oldfield*, 1894. Drama Library, Yale University.

7
The Distrest Mother

Still only in her mid twenties, Anne was established as the leading actress at the Queen's Theatre in the Haymarket.[1] The next few years would be a time of great creative growth and development. Although she continued to perform her popular breeches roles—Alinda, Hellena, Silvia—she began to expand her repertoire to include a more worldly, often amoral set of characters. In the popular Restoration comedy, *The Man of Mode,* she took the role of Mrs. Loveit, a cast-off mistress who schemes against her former lover and raves enthusiastically, breaking her fan in one notable fit of pique. (A regular entry in the property bills was "a new Fann" for Mrs. Oldfield in *The Man of Mode.*)[2] A small but showy part that gave Anne a chance to flounce about the stage in great style, Mrs. Loveit became a staple of her repertoire. As Mrs. Brittle in *The Amorous Widow; or, The Wanton Wife* (the role she is supposed to have played in competition with Anne Bracegirdle in 1706), and as Laetitia in *The Old Batchelor,* she played a lively young "city" wife who cheerfully cuckolds her ineffectual husband. In both instances, Wilks played the dashing, aristocratic seducer. Their erotic byplay in *The Old Batchelor* must have been noteworthy, for an avid theatergoer claimed that the memory of it caused him to lose his concentration—and a trick—in a game of whist.[3]

Another important addition, in a different vein, was the title character in Fletcher's *Scornful Lady.* Here she was involved in a more conventionally romantic situation—as a headstrong young woman who torments her faithful suitor and is finally tricked into admitting her love for him. (With Wilks as the suitor, Loveless, there was little doubt as to the outcome.)

Laetitia and the Scornful Lady, as well as an earlier acquisition, the

Silent Woman, had belonged to Frances Knight at Drury Lane, and when she and Anne were performing in the same company they seem to have shared the roles for a while before Anne took them over altogether. That Anne was able to expand her repertoire in this fashion suggests that stock roles were not "property" in quite the same way as original parts and that Frances Knight was never very popular, despite the importance of many of her roles.[4]

With the silencing of Rich at Drury Lane, the Haymarket company expected to enjoy a monopoly on theatrical entertainment. But the season of 1709–10 was not long underway when William Collier, a lawyer and minor shareholder in the Drury Lane patent, approached the investors in the theater building (as opposed to the sharers in the patent) for permission to operate his own company on the premises. Since they received no rent while the building stood unused, they were happy to back Collier's application to the Lord Chamberlain for a license to establish his own company. According to the terms of the license, Collier had to agree to give up his own interest in the Drury Lane patent, to exclude Rich and the other patentees from any share in his company, and to place himself directly under the control of the Lord Chamberlain. Rich's patent rights were thus neatly circumvented.[5]

Meanwhile at the Haymarket, affairs were not prospering. In addition to dramatic offerings, the management was responsible for expensive, twice-weekly operatic productions, which were not drawing the audiences that opera had formerly attracted. Now, faced with the threat of renewed competition, Swiney explored the possibility of reorganizing his partnership with Wilks, Cibber, and Doggett on more favorable financial terms. Once more Anne's name was mentioned as a partner, but nothing came of the proposal for reorganization.[6] Competition was not a great threat initially, in part because Rich had managed to strip Drury Lane of the costume stock and all but a few pieces of old scenery before Collier took physical possession on November 22.[7] But as the Drury Lane company gradually recovered, its offerings began to attract spectators from the Haymarket, especially with the great success of Charles Shadwell's *Fair Quaker of Deal; or, The Humours of the Navy,* starring the charming dancer-actress Hester Santlow.

If renewed rivalry were not problem enough, events in the political world also provided unexpected competition. On November 5, 1709, the anniversary of William III's landing on the southern English coast, which had triggered the Glorious Revolution of 1688, a cleric named Henry Sacheverell had preached a fiery sermon in St. Paul's cathedral, appealing to growing distaste for the Whig ministry and the increasingly unpopular war that the Whigs were promoting. When the sermon was published a week later, it became an instant best-seller and the "Sacheverell Affair" was underway. In short order, the cleric was impeached for sedition by the House of Commons and tried before the House of Lords, which, dominated by Whigs, seemed certain to vote for conviction. The trial had to be held in Westminster Hall to accommodate the huge crowds, which, according to Cibber, included many of the "better Rank of People" who were temporarily lured away from the theater.[8] Sacheverell was duly convicted, but the relatively close vote and light sentence—barring him from preaching for three years and ordering his sermon burned—gave disturbing evidence of defections within the Whig ranks.

Maynwaring became deeply involved in the crisis, as a journalist and propagandist. He was also concerned about the worsening position of his patrons, especially the Duchess of Marlborough, in Queen Anne's court. In 1704, after the Battle of Blenheim, the duke and duchess had been showered with additional honors, including the magnificent palace at Woodstock. Within just a few years, however, the queen and the duchess had become estranged. Part of Maynwaring's task as "secretary" to the duchess had been to encourage her to mend the breach, for in her absence new favorites, opposed to the Whigs and the war effort, had gained the queen's confidence. But the volatile duchess only managed to make matters worse. During a private interview on April 6, 1710, she was guilty of an intemperate outburst in which she taxed the queen for her "inhumanity."[9] The two women, close friends since childhood, never saw each other privately again.

Anti-Marlborough sentiment was growing amid rumors that the Captain General had swelled his private coffers at public expense. In the summer of 1710, the controversy spilled over into the theatrical world. A German visitor to London, Zacharias Conrad von Uffenbach, witnessed an impromptu political demonstration during Estcourt's benefit performance of The Recruiting Officer on July 13. As part of a "prodigiously satirical" entertainment between the acts, singers, dressed as English troops, sang a song that praised the generosity of Prince Eugene of Savoy and criticized Marlborough for his avarice.

"When the song was at an end," von Uffenbach reported, "there was such a clapping and yelling that the actors were unable to proceed for nearly a quarter of an hour."[10]

That Estcourt was having a benefit on July 13 was itself a bad sign. The regular season at the Haymarket had ended on June 10 with a loss of £206 and considerable ill feeling on the part of Cibber, Wilks, and Doggett, who had become uneasy about Swiney's financial and managerial methods. At a time when the company's leading actors would normally have begun their summer vacations, the theater was reopened for a second series of benefits in the hope that the actors might compensate for their reduced salaries and the slim pickings at their earlier benefits.

Anne was fortunate that her first benefit had been held early in February, before the Sacheverell trial began to compete for audiences. For much of the month of May, she was absent from the stage, probably due to illness; her roles in *The Beaux' Stratagem, The Chances,* and *The Pilgrim* were played by Mary Porter, Margaret Bicknell, and Mary Willis.[11] She returned by mid-June in time to assist her colleagues by appearing in all six of the second series of benefits. Her own, *The Chances,* was helped along by an item in the June 29 issue of the *Tatler* that cited the roles of Constantia and Don John as "acted to the utmost perfection." Despite such stratagems, the extended season was not entirely successful. When the benefits were over, Cibber, Wilks, and Doggett reimbursed themselves from the treasury to the amount of £350—without the knowledge of Swiney, who was away in Ireland.[12]

Political matters continued to preempt public attention during the summer and fall of 1710, with rumors of the impending demise of the Whig ministry and the dissolution of Parliament. On August 7, Sidney Godolphin, the able and loyal Lord Treasurer, was dismissed; in September, after dismissing more Whig ministers, the queen at last dissolved Parliament. Elections were scheduled for early October. There seemed little doubt that the political campaign would be hard-fought, but the Whigs were still hopeful of preserving their majority in the House of Commons.

In early October, with the help of John Oldmixon, Maynwaring undertook the publication of a two-page political weekly, the *Medley,* in opposition to the Tory *Examiner*.[13] He was not optimistic about the outcome of the election, and in fact lost his own seat at Preston, in what turned out to be a crushing, nationwide defeat for the Whigs.

Shortly afterward he fell ill. In a letter to the duchess in early November, he tried to make light of not having stirred from the house for the last four days and having "taken more Remedies than in twenty years."[14] This was the beginning of a series of fevers, which, increasing in intensity, badly undermined his health.

During the election campaigns in the fall of 1710, another theatrical revolution occurred, which brought Anne and her colleagues back to Drury Lane once more—this time to stay. New licenses were issued by the Lord Chamberlain, authorizing Collier to take charge of an opera company at the Haymarket, while Swiney, Cibber, Wilks, and Doggett returned to Drury Lane as the managers of a united company of actors. (The separation of opera and spoken drama into two monopolies was exactly the plan proposed by Vanbrugh and briefly implemented in 1708–9, but he was no longer involved in theatrical management.)[15] Once again, there was only one company of actors in London. In addition to the tension that was normal for a situation such as this, ill feeling seems to have existed between the actors who had gone over to the Haymarket company and those who had stayed at Drury Lane. It was particularly galling for Barton Booth, who had declined the tempting offer of a higher salary at the Haymarket, to be under the direction of the three actor-managers.[16]

As it happened, Anne was absent during much of the fall of 1710. Either she herself was ill or she was preoccupied with Maynwaring, whose health deteriorated gravely during this period. In November, he wrote to his friend Thomas, Earl of Coningsby: "I have been very ill since I had the honour of your Lordship's letter, & heard nothing worth troubling you with." He had developed a "lurking feavour and cold," which was only temporarily remitted by taking "Peruvian bark."[17] This illness, and an even worse fever in late May, caused temporary partial deafness and an alarming weight loss; "fallen away to a Skeleton," he would describe himself. For one whose happiness depended upon the social round of coffeehouses and dinners with friends, the isolation of deafness and invalidism were especially hard to bear.

During Anne's absence, from early November 1710 until early January 1711, her roles were taken by a variety of substitutes. Lucretia Bradshaw played Elvira in *The Spanish Fryar*, Angelica in *Love for Love*, Carolina in *Epsom Wells*, and Hellena in *The Rover*. Jane Rogers played Louisa in *Love Makes a Man*, Mary Porter was Leonora in *Sir*

Courtly Nice, Mary Willis was Alinda in *The Pilgrim,* and Margaret
Bicknell played Silvia in *The Recruiting Officer.*[18] Several plays—*The
Careless Husband, The Tender Husband,* and *The Beaux' Stratagem*—
with which Anne was particularly associated were not performed at
all. Of the actresses who took her place, both Bicknell and Bradshaw
were promising younger performers who undoubtedly welcomed the
chance to play Anne's roles, but they gave them up again, as would
be expected, when she returned on January 8.

When Anne reclaimed her parts there was, inevitably, a domino
effect, with the lower-ranking actresses trying desperately to hold onto
their positions. But the only problem that became public involved an
established performer, Letitia Cross. When Mrs. Cross did not appear
at all during the season of 1710–11 a group of seventy-three devoted
followers threatened to create a disturbance at Doggett's benefit, a
performance of *She Wou'd If She Cou'd,* if Cross were not allowed
to play "her" part of Gatty. They also threatened to prevent any
performances in which other actresses played her roles.[19] The managers
replied that she was at fault for refusing to act. She would later claim
that, to the contrary, in November 1710, the actor-managers had
turned her away, "saying that now they had Actors enough." The
threat evaporated when Doggett's benefit was held on March 19 without incident—and also without Mrs. Cross.[20] The affair was disquieting, however, indicating that the public could be aroused on behalf of
a beleaguered actress.

In this uneasy atmosphere, Anne contemplated a new direction in
her career. She would be famous for a lighthearted complaint about
tragic acting: "I hate to have a Page dragging my Tail about. Why do
they not give Porter these Parts? She can put on a better Tragedy Face
than I can."[21] Nevertheless, in the season of 1711–12, she took up
tragedy with apparent enthusiasm. This circumstance has led some
biographers to see a connection between her career and the tragic
events in her private life. It is true that before the end of 1712, Anne
found herself, in effect, a widow with a young son to support. But it
is clear that she became a tragic actress because there were compelling
professional reasons to do so.

The death of Thomas Betterton on April 28, 1710, and the retirement
of Elizabeth Barry soon afterward, had left a gap in the ranks of tragic
actors. Even though they had been relatively inactive in the last few
seasons, their mere presence in the company affected the way audi-

ences—and playwrights—thought about tragic heroes and heroines. Finding successors would involve more than providing exact copies of the originals. Who among the younger players might capture the popular imagination, as Betterton had done in the early years of the Restoration, or Barry in the 1680s? Which actors and actresses would play well together in tragedy as Wilks and Oldfield did in comedy? And—perhaps the most delicate issue—which players would *expect* to inherit the positions of Betterton and Barry?

Betterton's logical successor was George Powell, who had remained with the Drury Lane company in 1709, playing such important roles in tragedy as Hamlet, Lear, Timon of Athens, and the noble Torrismond in *The Spanish Fryar*. In the last fifteen years, he had also taken over many of the more fiery roles of Betterton's youth. But Powell himself was no longer young; he seemed to have lost his own fire. In the new united company at Drury Lane, he had to compete with Wilks, who claimed Hamlet for himself, and stolid John Mills, to whom Wilks gave a number of plums, including Macbeth. It was symptomatic of a general uncertainty that Betterton's tragic repertoire was distributed among five different actors: Powell, Wilks, Mills, Theophilus Keen, and Barton Booth. In a remarkably short time, however, Booth would emerge as the company's leading tragedian.

In 1711, Booth was about thirty.[22] At least chronologically, his career had paralleled Anne's. In 1700, after serving a promising apprenticeship at the Smock Alley theater in Dublin, he had been admitted to the Lincoln's Inn Fields company. While he was fortunate to work under Betterton and to observe at close hand the noble and dignified manner for which the great tragic actor was especially noted in his later years, he did not have Anne's opportunity for early advancement. Both Jack Verbruggen and George Powell had outranked him for many years; one of his few major new roles was the romantic lover Axalla in Nicholas Rowe's *Tamerlane,* a character he later gave up to play Tamerlane himself. His decision to remain with the Drury Lane company in 1709 had proved wise, for with less competition from established actors he was able to add a number of important roles, including Othello, to his repertoire.

It was probably at this time that he began to attract a personal following and to evolve a style that owed something, no doubt, to the gravity of the elder Betterton, but also to his own personality. A heavy drinker in his youth, Booth did not abandon his love of food and good company, but nothing seemed to taint his august stage presence. Admirers never failed to comment upon his striking attitudes (inspired by his familiarity with classical sculpture and fine painting), smooth manner, and mellifluous voice. Above all, there was his supreme self-restraint. In a strongly emotional role, such as Othello, he managed his voice so expertly "that in the highest Expression of fury and Distraction it never became untuneful."[23] His heartbreaking anguish as the noble moor "would have drawn Tears from the most obdurate;—yet all his Grief, though most feelingly expressed, was never beneath the Hero."[24] Merely to see Booth walk across the stage was a memorable experience, so strong was the impression of calm dignity and majesty. His unfailing decorum, so different from present-day notions of great acting, represented the ultimate in "politeness," the other side of Wilks's graceful urbanity in comedy. Othello, Mark Antony, and Brutus were all touched by the same loftiness.

Just as there was no immediate successor to Thomas Betterton, it was also not clear who would become the company's leading tragedienne after Elizabeth Barry's retirement in 1710. The managers seemed to be waiting to see who would catch the public fancy. Not counting Anne, who evidently did not see herself, at first, as a contender, there seemed to be several possibilities. Jane Rogers and Mary Porter had become competitors for a number of leading roles in their line of pathetic, emotional heroines and stood a chance of inheriting some of Barry's roles. Lucretia Bradshaw, known as a faithful student of Barry, was a third candidate. When Barry's roles were distributed, Bradshaw received two plums: Lavinia in *The History and Fall of Caius Marius* and Monimia in *The Orphan*. Two popular pathetic heroines, Belvidera in *Venice Preserv'd* and Isabella in *The Fatal Marriage,* fell to Rogers. A significant number of important roles were taken by Frances Knight, in some cases because she had been playing them at Drury Lane in Barry's absence: Leonora in *The Spanish Fryar,* Queen Elizabeth in *The Unhappy Favourite,* Evadne in *The Maid's Tragedy,* Gertrude and Lady Macbeth, and Almeria in *The Indian Emperor.* Mary Porter, who would eventually eclipse all three actresses, did not receive any of Barry's tragic roles during the initial distribution.

In the fall of 1711, Anne had reached a point in her career at which some new development might be expected. She had begun to give up some of her youthful roles: Alinda (*The Pilgrim*), Florimell (*The Comical Lovers*), Florella (*Greenwich Park*), and Maria (*The Fortune Hunters*), but with so many potential competitors, she could not afford to give up too much ground in the new united company.

It may merely be coincidental that there was a dearth of good new comedy at this time. Farquhar was dead, Vanbrugh had retired from theatrical activity, Steele was immersed in the *Tatler* and the *Spectator*, and Cibber's time was taken up with managerial duties, not the least of which involved continual peacemaking between his fellow managers: the hot-tempered Wilks with his favorites—"the Achilles of our Confederacy"—and grumpy, miserly Doggett. Only Susanna Centlivre was turning out good comedies on a fairly regular basis. A new piece by Charles Johnson, *The Wife's Relief; or, The Husband's Cure,* in which Oldfield and Wilks played two sentimentalized sophisticated lovers, was unexpectedly successful in November 1711, gaining its author three hundred pounds, so hungry was "the Town" for new plays.[25] The lack of good new comic roles, though perhaps not the most important, was certainly a factor in Anne's decision to make her first serious attempt at tragedy. She was also protecting herself. For if she did not take whatever good new roles were available—in tragedy if need be—a gifted younger actress might rise to challenge her.

Accordingly, at the beginning of the season of 1711–12, she showed a more than passing interest in tragedy, appearing in *The Albion Queens, Mithridates,* and three performances of another historical tragedy by John Banks: *Vertue Betray'd; or, Anna Bullen,* in which she played the title character. That she had not attempted to get her share of Barry's famous roles when they were first distributed suggests that she did not find them congenial. Instead, she began to assemble a tragic repertoire that would be distinctively hers, playing to her strengths: a statuesque figure, a commanding stage presence, and a melodious voice. By all accounts, her emotional range was not especially great. Barry was far more passionate, entering into her parts so wholeheartedly that, as she once told Betterton, she could never speak the lines "Ah! poor Castalio!" in *The Orphan,* without weeping.[26] Anne's tragic characters were chiefly noted for "Majestic dignity." If strong passion did not suit her, she made the most of the qualities that made her a successful comedienne. The conscious artifice that gave her comic portrayals a delightful hint of self-mockery was translated into a studied grace that matched Booth's. A successful new stage partnership was in the making.

As Maynwaring had been her coach and advocate in the past, he continued to interest himself in her career. His health seems to have improved in the fall of 1711, or at any rate he was free from the debilitating fevers that had plagued him earlier that year. A delightful epilogue that he created for her to recite at the end of *The Wife's Relief* proposes a "Parliament of Women," which would banish jealous husbands and make sure that

> . . . those Dull, Uncomfortable Wights,
> Who sleep all Morning, and who sot at Nights,
> Shou'd find, when they reel home, with Surfeits cloy'd
> Their tender Wives with better Friends employ'd.[27]

It was the sort of sprightly, faintly indecent performance that she always managed to bring off with great success.

Still deeply involved in the propaganda campaign for military victory in the war with France, Maynwaring slipped into the epilogue a tribute to the "Glorious Character of Soldiers" and a pious hope: "The War, 'tis said, is drawing near an End." But the war was not ending as Maynwaring and his fellow Whigs hoped. Peace negotiations unfavorable to England's allies had been underway since early in 1711, and in the fall, Tory propagandists made one last move to undermine the Duke of Marlborough. In a pamphlet published in late November, *The Conduct of the Allies,* Jonathan Swift charged the Captain General with prolonging the war for his own economic advantage. Maynwaring and the Whig propagandists rushed to Marlborough's defense in pamphlets of their own, but the damage had been done. Even if the specifics of Swift's charges could not be made to stick, Marlborough was seen as an obstacle to the achievement of peace. On December 31, the queen finally asked for, and received, his resignation.

Supporters of the war effort hoped that the appearance of the popular Prince Eugene of Savoy in London, in January 1712, might rekindle public support for the allied cause. Susanna Centlivre, a fervent Whig, hastily added several lines in praise of both Prince Eugene and the Duke of Marlborough to the epilogue that Anne was to speak at the premiere of *The Perplex'd Lovers* on January 19. But, as Centlivre later explained, "the Managers of the Theatre did not think it safe to speak it, without I cou'd get it licens'd, which I cou'd not do that Night, with all the Interest I cou'd make: So that at last the Play was forc'd to conclude without an Epilogue."[28] Although she obtained a license

from the Vice-Chamberlain the next day, "by this Time there was a
Rumour spread about Town that it was a notorious whiggish Epilogue;
and the Person who design'd me the Favour of speaking it, had Letters
sent her to forbear, for that there were Parties forming against it, and
they advis'd her not to stand the Shock." Whether or not Anne felt
threatened, she did not recite the epilogue. Instead, on the second night
of the run, Henry Norris, dressed in mourning, delivered a hastily
written substitute alluding to the author's difficulties; there the controversy ended. The episode, trivial in itself, serves to illustrate how
strongly feelings were running against the war.

At about this time Drury Lane undertook to produce a new tragedy
by Ambrose Philips, *The Distrest Mother,* and Anne became the center
of a new controversy, the noisiest professional dispute of her career.
At the heart of it was the development of her line in tragedy. According
to *Faithful Memoirs,* Philips had created the title role for Jane Rogers.
"But the Author, as well as his Friends, were soon convinced that
Mrs. OLDFIELD was infinitely the more accomplished Person for so
Capital a Part. Upon its being given to Her, Mrs. *Rogers* raised a Posse
of Profligates, fond of Tumult and Riot, who made such a Commotion
in the House, that the Court hearing of it sent some four of the Royal
Messengers, and a strong Guard, to suppress all Disorders."[29]

The play itself would hardly have aroused controversy. Based upon
Jean Racine's *Andromaque, The Distrest Mother* is a tragedy of unrequited
love set in the aftermath of the Trojan War. Most of *The Distrest
Mother,* like *Andromaque,* is concerned with the frustrated passions of
the central characters—Orestes loves Hermione, who loves Pyrrhus,
who loves the Trojan princess Andromache, his prize of war. But
Philips shifted the emphasis slightly toward Andromache and her
dilemma: to protect her son, she must marry Pyrrhus, but she has
sworn to remain faithful to the memory of her dead husband, Hector.
In both plays, the dilemma is resolved happily for Andromache; although she intends to commit suicide after marrying Pyrrhus, her new
husband is killed by Orestes immediately after the marriage ceremony.
As the widow of Pyrrhus, Andromache is at last able to protect both
her son and her honor. Philips added a scene at the end in which
Andromache embraces her son and exults in their salvation.

The role of the noble, beautiful, captive princess was perfectly suited
to Anne's small but growing stock of tragic heroines, but Jane Rogers
did not relinquish it gracefully. In a broadsheet titled "The Memorial

of Jane Rogers Humbly Submitted to the Town," she gave a highly colored account of her struggle for professional survival.[30]

> A new Tragedy being lately brought to the House, Mr. *Wilks* sent for me to the first publick Reading of it, and the Author seeing me home from the House, was pleas'd to compliment me, with telling me, he design'd the Part of *Andromache* for me. About Three Days after, Mr. *Wilks* with a great deal of seeming Civility came to me into the green Room, and told me, that he and the Author were both asham'd to see me, for having sent for me to the Reading of the Play; for they design'd me the Part of *Andromache,* which they thought would become me, and was more in my way than any Part I had played a long time. But that as Mrs. *Oldfield* had declared, she would not play unless she had that Part, they must oblige her with it.[31]

The matter soon came to an open dispute between the two women, at which point, according to Rogers, Anne threatened to have her turned out of the theater. In this power play, we are told, Anne was strongly backed by Wilks, who informed Mrs. Rogers "that had I ten times the Merit I fancy'd I had, I should never set foot on that Stage again for affronting Mrs. *Oldfield.*" It would be far better, Wilks hinted, for her to leave quietly, as Mrs. Bracegirdle had done five years earlier at the Haymarket. If she did not, he would go to the Lord Chamberlain and obtain permission for her immediate dismissal. The injured actress's response was to bring the whole mess out into the open:

> I thought my self obliged not so tamely to recede from the Stage, to which I had been bred since my Childhood, but to address myself to the Town with laying the Truth of my Sufferings before the publick Audience; and accordingly in all Duty bound, I return'd them my hearty Thanks for the many great Favours I had received from them, letting them know that I was to be forced to quit my Business, for daring to contend with Mrs. *Oldfield* for a Part in Tragedy.

Her "address to the town" probably took place at the end of the first week of February, when she appeared in *Love's Last Shift,* for that was her last appearance on the Drury Lane stage for some time. But she was not without her partisans. A letter dated March 1, 1711/12 describes a disturbance at Drury Lane on the previous Thursday night, February 28, which caused the managers

> to let down ye Curtain, to return ye Money, occasion'd by some rudeness shown to my Ld Salisbury some time ago and a dispute happening between Mrs Rogers & Mrs Oldfield about ye cheif [sic] part in ye New play, upon wch she was suspended, wherein ye Town have thought fit to Interest themselves, as well as to condemn ye management of ye Directors of ye House in their discouragement of some other of ye Actors. All these things have for ye present put a stop to our Diversions of this kind.[32]

The occasion was Anne's benefit, the revival of Fletcher's *Humourous Lieutenant*.

The demonstrators had been incited, in part, by a scurrilous broadside, "A Justification of the Letter to Sir John Stanley, relative to his Management of the Play-house in Drury Lane."[33] Among the charges alleged by the anonymous author are that Swiney owed Letitia Cross three hundred pounds in back pay, that Jane Rogers had been turned out of the company "without any reason," that Lucretia Bradshaw had been "used with . . . insolence, only to gratify the pride of Mrs Oldfield, who cannot bear any one should shine above her," and that the salaries of Estcourt, Powell, Booth, George Pack, and Benjamin Johnson, "in short almost all" of the actors' salaries, had been abated (pp. 420–21). The latter half of the document is devoted to a personal attack upon Anne, so vicious that one begins to suspect that it was motivated by considerations other than the search for justice at Drury Lane.

The references to Anne begin mildly enough with a query about her high salary, especially in view of the greatly reduced salaries of the other actors. But allusions to her personal as well as her professional conduct are soon forthcoming. Can she really be worth so much, "She who, if 'tis possible is more infamous than her Character?" The tone of the attack turns particularly nasty in a series of allusions to venereal disease. Adopting an air of mock-solicitude, the author regrets the death of a Dr. Wall—a notorious "pock doctor"—who might have "purified the whole mass of her blood, which had been corrupted by a series of complicated distempers, [so] that she need not have been obliged to the very last extremity of trepanning her skull to effect the Cure" (p. 421). (Trepanning was no longer standard medical practice but was sometimes used, along with other painful and outlandish procedures, in the treatment of syphilis.) In his closing remarks, the author kindly offers the suggestion that Mrs. Oldfield might fill the house at her upcoming benefit, even if it were "a deal larger than it is," by the simple expedient of requiring every man she had lain with to purchase a ticket.

We may wonder what Anne could have done to inspire such vituperation. Except for the incident of *The Distrest Mother,* Jane Rogers's real threat seems to have come from Mary Porter, whose lines in comedy and tragedy were almost identical to those of Rogers and quite different from Anne's. In 1707, Porter had complained that another actress, probably Jane Rogers, had been taken into the Haymarket company over her head, but in more recent seasons her fortunes had begun to prosper. It is possible that Anne was using her influence to promote Porter at the expense of other actresses because she did not regard her as a serious rival. (Wilks is said to have advanced the career of John Mills for the same reason.) If the charges about abatement of salaries are true, a number of actors at Drury Lane had legitimate grievances against the management, but that hardly explains the slanderous attack upon Anne. The allegations of promiscuity had no obvious connection with backstage politics.

The attack on her morals makes more sense if Maynwaring, not she, was the chief target. Striking at her, the author struck at her lover— for if she was a whore, what did that make him? Maynwaring was a tempting target on several counts. His labors as a Whig propagandist in 1711 and 1712 had earned him many political enemies. He himself had not scrupled to employ sexual slander and could expect little mercy in return.[34]

It is not easy to judge Anne's involvement in the Andromache wars. No one has ever denied that the character was first promised to Jane Rogers. *Faithful Memoirs* treats the matter lightly, hinting that Rogers, then only in her middle or late thirties, was past her prime and not a serious candidate for the role.[35] It is a little surprising that Andromache had been offered to her, for by 1712, although hardly over the hill, she was not secure in her position in the company. Indeed, that was part of the problem.

Whatever the truth of her charges, Jane Rogers would hardly have created such a storm if she had not felt injured and desperate. In a pathetic postscript, she pointed out that unlike Anne Bracegirdle she could not afford to give up her career. Her salary had never been high enough to provide the financial security that enabled Mrs. Bracegirdle to live comfortably in retirement, and she had a young daughter to support. The theater was her only livelihood. London at this time had only one acting company. At best she could look forward to returning meekly to Drury Lane, as if nothing had ever happened. And indeed, she did return to the stage before the end of the season, appearing as Belvidera in *Venice Preserv'd* on May 9 and Alibech in *The Indian Emperor* on June 19, and perhaps in other stock pieces for which no casts were advertised.[36]

Though we might wish Anne *had* told her side of the story, she remained silent through all of this, and afterward. Others were willing to speak for her, and success has a way of justifying itself. She emerged from this episode, as from the contest with Anne Bracegirdle, with her popularity intact. Cibber would characterize her as "tractable and less presuming in her Station than several that had not half her Pretensions to be troublesome," adding that she "had every thing she ask'd, which she always took care should be reasonable, because she hated as much to be *grudg'd* as *deny'd* a Civility."[37] If Cibber's Anne Oldfield sounds far too good to be true, let alone to have survived in a highly competitive profession, it seems clear that she got along quite well with her male colleagues at Drury Lane and probably with the women who were neither real nor potential rivals. Over the years, she had obliged her associates, shouldering her share of responsibilities and gracefully accepting her status as a salaried player—on very favorable terms. She expected to be obliged in return. Beneath the calm reasonableness in Cibber's portrait there is an undeniable toughness. Her biographers tend to gloss over that toughness as if it were unbecoming or inconsistent with the legends of her charm and lightheartedness. But it is a quality that Lady Betty, Andromache, and Anne Oldfield possessed in common.

The premiere of *The Distrest Mother* came off without incident on March 17, 1712, and was as successful as actors and author could wish. This was partly due to skillful promotion by Addison and Steele in the *Spectator,* both before and after the premiere. The February 1 issue reported on a touching scene during a rehearsal, in which an actor became so deeply affected that he "frequently threw down the Book, till he had given Vent to the Humanity which rose in him at some irresistible Touches of imagined Sorrow," an open display of emotion in which he was joined by the rest of the cast, "who had long made it their Profession to dissemble Affliction." In a leavening mood, the March 25 issue was devoted to the humorous "natural criticism" of Addison's country squire, Sir Roger de Coverly, who seemed to sum up the whole business with a comment from his own experience: "You can't imagine, Sir, what 'tis to have to do with a Widow."

As added insurance, Addison and his cousin, Eustace Budgell, provided Anne with a comic epilogue—one of the most famous of her mini-performances. Still wearing her Andromache gown and ostrich-plumed headdress, she stepped forward to address the audience rather in the manner of Lady Betty than Hector's noble relict:

I hope you'll own, that with becoming Art,
I've play'd my game, and topp'd the Widow's Part.
My Spouse, poor man, could not live out the Play,
But dy'd commodiously on his Wedding-day;
While I, his Relict, made at one bold Fling,
Myself a Princess, and young Sty a King. . . .
'Twas a strange Scape! Had Pyrrhus liv'd till now,
I had been finely hampered in my Vow.
To die by one's own Hand, and fly the Charms
Of Love and Life in a young Monarch's Arms!
'Twere a hard Fate—ere I had undergone it,
I might have took one Night—to think upon it.[38]

The piece proved so popular that Anne had to repeat it twice each night during the first part of the run, and audiences continued to call for it long after it would ordinarily have been dropped.[39]

The Distrest Mother was clearly a personal triumph for its stars. It would be said of Booth that Pyrrhus "plac'd him in the seat of Tragedy, and Cato fix'd him there."[40] When the fame of *The Distrest Mother* reached Oxford, a fellow of Balliol College, Francis Reynardson, was inspired not only to travel to London to see it but to compose a poetic essay on the "art, rise, and progress of the English stage." He was full of praise for the actors, especially the "Godlike Air, Quick Eye, and Accent smooth," and "the Manly Graces," of Barton Booth as Pyrrhus. But even such a Pyrrhus could hardly be expected to prevail over the noble Andromache, when her virtue was united with the "complicated Charms" and "Form divine" of Anne Oldfield. "All, all would love her like Achilles' Son, / All would like him be ta'en, all like him undone."[41] Anne was given a second benefit on April 3, presumably to compensate for the one that had to be called off in February. This time there were no disturbances.

In a letter to the Duchess of Marlborough in the summer of 1712, Maynwaring complained of a "continued headake" which made writing difficult.[42] This was the precursor of a devastating illness that is unusually well documented. Absent from the scene, Sarah Churchill nevertheless directed operations. A flood of correspondence passed between London and the Marlborough estate at St. Albans, with the duchess receiving letters from one of the attending physicians, Sir Samuel Garth, from Owen Swiney, from Sidney Godolphin, and most often from Maynwaring's sister, Grissel. No symptom or treatment was too trivial to escape comment; even the tardy arrival of one of the physicians was reported to the duchess. In response, she sent cordials and advice by return post.

By the fourth or fifth of August, Grissel Maynwaring arrived on the scene. In the first of her letters to the duchess, dated August 6, she writes: "My poor Brother had a dismal night raved without ceasing till 7 a clock when he began to slumber & be a little more quiet." The physicians, Garth and Sir Richard Blackmore, had prescribed a course of purgatives and blisters, which Grissel describes in detail.[43] On August 7, Owen Swiney reported the hopeful news that after he had sat with Maynwaring through the previous night, he "continues to rave but not so frequently nor wth the tenth part of the Violence which I look upon to be a sign that they have chequ'd his Distemper."[44] Maynwaring had better and worse days, "as in ague," and was delirious much of the time. August 7 through 9 was a particularly bad period, but by the time Sidney Godolphin looked in on Sunday, August 10, he was able to converse briefly with Maynwaring, who seemed lucid enough, but very weak.

In all of this voluminous correspondence, there is one notable omission: any mention whatsoever of Anne. Perhaps this was out of deference to the duchess; Maynwaring himself never referred, even indirectly, to Anne in any of his correspondence with Sarah Churchill. Was Anne present but tactfully ignored in the letters? Or was she barred from the bedside by the redoubtable Grissel, who, Oldmixon often hints, was hostile to her? A letter dated August 9, which appears to be in the hand of Margaret Saunders, indicates that the scene of the illness was not Anne's house on Southampton Street and that Maynwaring's sister was complicating matters by keeping his trusted servants away from his bedside.[45] From Grissel's own letters it is clear that she was always at her brother's side, sometimes sitting up all night with him. It is impossible to believe that she moved into Anne's house and took charge, yet take charge—somewhere—she did. We are left with the impression of a determined sister standing guard, and the Marlborough circle drawing tightly around Maynwaring.

According to Oldmixon, Maynwaring, having fallen ill in September, lingered for two months and then died. But by mid-August he was writing to Sarah Churchill again, and by the end of the month he was well enough to travel to Woodstock to inspect Vanbrugh's work on the Blenheim Palace project and enjoy a hearty meal of fish, mutton, and quantities of fresh fruit. Writing about this occasion to the duchess, Sidney Godolphin was happy to report that, contrary to what she had heard, Maynwaring's health continued to improve.[46]

Meanwhile, Maynwaring was to undertake one last service for his patrons. The Duke of Marlborough had in effect exiled himself to the countryside during the summer of 1712, where, on the anniversary of Blenheim, he held court at St. Albans for his band of loyalists. But he decided at last to leave England for the more agreeable political climate of the Allied states in Europe. First, however, it was necessary to obtain a passport, and to make it clear that his departure was both voluntary and in accordance with the wishes of the queen. And so, beginning in early September, a number of letters passed between Maynwaring and the queen's trusted adviser, Robert Harley, in which the subject of the passport was broached with diplomatic indirection. On October 30, the queen finally signed the passport and Maynwaring arranged to meet Harley the next day to pick it up. The meeting never took place. Instead, on November 3, Marlborough wrote to the Lord Treasurer directly. "My giving you the trouble of this letter is occasion'd by the illnesse of poor Mr Manwayring [*sic*] and the desire I have of waiting upon your Lordship this evening, or to morrow night, which may be most convenient to your Self; if you please to send two lines to Mr Manwayring, I shall be sure to have itt."[47] Except for a terse letter from Grissel to the duchess later that month, enclosed with some of her brother's papers, this is the last reference to Maynwaring in the Marlborough correspondence. In a letter to the duchess on September 29, he had expressed the "hope to be still some years your Secretary," but on November 13 he was dead.

His last illness was not protracted; there would be no discussions of symptoms and treatment. Oldmixon reported that in his last sickness he was visited by many great people, "of both Sexes," of whom only two were admitted to his bedside. "And it is to his Glory, that the greatest Lady in *England,* wept often by the side of his Death Bed, which he water'd, as often with his Tears, being sensible how much he ow'd to such an Illustrious Mourner."[48] By the "greatest Lady" he referred, of course, to the Duchess of Marlborough, but the touching scene probably owes more to the biographer's desire to flatter the duchess than to his knowledge of the events. It is likely that Maynwaring lay ill, this time, on Southampton Street, cared for by Anne and his own servants. For it is surely significant that Anne was absent from the stage between November 6 and November 25, a time when she would ordinarily be performing two or three times a week.

Her presence at his bedside was a matter of no small consequence. As his mistress, she had no legal standing. If Maynwaring had died in August, she might have been barred from his funeral and any claim upon his estate. He had not yet made a will that properly provided for her and their son. That oversight was corrected on September 27.

His only heir, besides Anne and young Arthur, was his sister. To Grissel he left the lump sum of one thousand pounds, later estimated to be about one-third of his estate. Maynwaring then named Anne his executrix and bequeathed "all the Rest, Residue and Remainder of my Estate, both Real and Personal . . . unto Mrs. *Anne Oldfield,* now living in new *Southampton-street* . . . and to her Son commonly called *Arthur Maynwaring,* otherwise called *Arthur Oldfield,* to be equally divided between them the said *Anne* and *Arthur.*"[49] These are dry, lawyerly terms, but they constitute a daring and unprecedented expression of Maynwaring's regard for Anne and a deliberate rebuke to Grissel. It was common for a wife to be named executrix; for a mistress, it was virtually unheard of, especially if the testator had living relatives or responsible male friends, as in Maynwaring's case. The bequests to Anne and young Arthur were generous and certainly welcome, but they alone would have aroused little comment. (A few months earlier the Earl Rivers had died, leaving bequests to an impressive number of mistresses—one of whom, Arabella Field, has been mistaken for Anne

Oldfield.) In naming Anne his executrix, Maynwaring not only saw to it that the bequests to Anne and Arthur would be protected, since Anne would administer his estate, but that the responsibility for his funeral arrangements would be in Anne's hands, surely a rebuff to his sister. The nomination also suggests that Anne had little in common with the giddy ladies she played but could be trusted to carry out her testamentary duties.

During part of the time after Maynwaring's death, Anne would have been occupied with rehearsals for Cibber's new play, *Ximena; or, The Heroick Daughter,* which opened on November 28. Rehearsals presumably would not have prevented her from discharging her responsibilities as executrix, including the arrangements for Maynwaring's interment with his father and grandfather in the parish church of Chertsey, in Surrey. At some time they must have discussed the place and manner of his burial, for in his will he specified no details, leaving the matter entirely to "the Discretion of my Executrix." An autopsy was conducted partly to dispel rumors that he had died of a venereal disease. The cause of death was given as consumption.[50]

Oldmixon summarized Maynwaring's life and character in this fashion: "His Learning was without Pedantry, his Wit without Affectation, his Judgment without Malice, his Friendship without Interest, his Zeal without Violence, in a Word, he was the best Subject, the best Friend, the best Relation, the best Master, the best Critick, and the best Writer in Britain."[51] Allowances, of course, must be made for the conventions of the eulogy.

It is less easy to speak about the nature of his love for Anne, and hers for him, since he merely hinted at it in the confidence he bestowed upon her in his will, and she left no record of her feelings. They were together for about ten years. During that time, they actively pursued their respective careers, had one living child, and established a settled, if unorthodox life together. He took an interest in her work and was doubtless responsible, in part, for her early success as an actress and for the financial rewards that she later reaped. She was apparently sympathetic with his political endeavors, for her future alliances remained staunchly Whig. Partly on his behalf, she endured slanderous accusations. In remaining loyal to her, he courted the disapproval of powerful friends. The moralists of a later age, who sentimentalized their relationship, only succeeded in cheapening it.

8

Tragedienne

In Authentick Memoirs, the story is told that soon after Maynwaring's death Anne brought young Arthur onstage when she recited the epilogue to *The Distrest Mother,* pointing to him when she spoke the name of Andromache's son, "young Sty." The audience was charmed at the "similitude" between her own recent bereavement and that of Andromache.[1] But the similarity was, after all, not so great. Andromache had lost a husband she never wanted and gained a kingdom for her son. Anne had lost a lover and protector, the father of her child and of her child to be. At the time of Maynwaring's death she was nearly three months pregnant. By the following spring every theatergoer in London knew she was pregnant, and it would be rumored that the biggest hit of the season, Addison's *Cato,* had to be terminated abruptly because of Mrs. Oldfield's imminent accouchement.

If anything attests to the sudden alteration in her circumstances, it is this episode. While Maynwaring was alive, there had been no thought of exposing him to scandal or ridicule by continuing to perform so late in her pregnancy—parading his bastard *in utero,* as it were. For herself, apparently, there was no such concern. The yards of petticoat that enhanced an actress's "figure" onstage, would in any case conceal her condition for some months. As late as the end of March, she had no qualms about accepting the role of Cato's virginal daughter in Addison's new tragedy, hardly anticipating that she would still be playing it in May.

During the early stages of her pregnancy, she was evidently healthy and able to withstand the rigors of a season in which she appeared in no fewer than four new plays. The first, which opened not long after Maynwaring's funeral, was *Ximena; or, The Heroick Daughter* (better known by its subtitle), Colley Cibber's determined attempt to cash in on the success of *The Distrest Mother* by "improving" yet another French neoclassical drama. For his source he chose Pierre Corneille's famous tragedy, *The Cid,* which he rather plundered than adapted. His Ximena is allowed to suffer nobly the conflict between love and filial duty—the centerpiece of Corneille's play—without any of the real consequences. Her father is only wounded in the duel with her lover Don Carlos, and when this fact is discovered she can with an easy conscience withdraw her demand for Don Carlos's death. According to Cibber's hollow notion of poetic justice, willingness to suffer was sufficient proof of virtue.

Once more Steele worked mightily to promote a work that was surely designed to improve the English stage. The November 26 issue of the *Spectator* reports on a rehearsal in which the actors outdid themselves, especially Mrs. Oldfield, who, in the title character, "had so just a Conception of her Part, that her Action made what she spoke appear decent, just, and noble." Anne was sufficiently pleased with her part (which permitted her to be alternately tender and noble) to choose it for her benefit in March. But advance publicity and good acting, which had contributed so much to *The Distrest Mother,* were no guarantees of success. His authorship at that time unknown, Cibber watched the production from one of the side-boxes with his hat pulled low over his eyes, the better to conceal his mortification as the "merry-making Criticks, that call themselves the *Town*" burlesqued his efforts.[2]

Following the run of *Ximena,* Anne appeared in an impressive array of her popular stock characters—Mrs. Brittle, Leonora in *Sir Courtly Nice,* Laetitia, Lady Heartwell in *Wit Without Money,* Andromache, Lady Dainty, Estifania, Angelica, Lady Lurewell, Mrs. Sullen, and Mrs. Loveit—until the premiere of Charles Shadwell's *Humours of the Army* at the end of January. If Shadwell hoped to borrow some glory from his enormously successful earlier play, *The Fair Quaker of Deal; or, The Humours of the Navy,* he must have been disappointed with the lukewarm reception of his new comedy about army life. *The Humours of the Army* featured scenes of lowlife among the enlisted men and a love intrigue between Victoria, a general's daughter (played by Anne), and a dashing young officer (played by Wilks). One memorable line, the young officer's declaration that he does not give a rap if his beloved is disinherited—"I'll take her stark Naked, and settle all I have upon her!"—was obviously written with Wilks and Oldfield in mind. Shadwell's treatment of the military situation is worthy of note, perhaps reflecting the mood of a war-weary nation as peace negotiations were nearing completion at Utrecht. Stationed in Portugal in the waning days of the war, the officers are restive and quarrelsome, but the anticipated battle never takes place. In the final scene, a general truce is announced; the epilogue expresses the hope that soldiers will still be valued in time of peace.

Although the real war was all but over, the paper war between Whig and Tory journalists flared up again, and during the run of *The Humours of the Army,* Anne's private life was aired in the press. When the terms of Maynwaring's will were made known, his enemies seized the opportunity to attack. A passage in the February 6–9 issue of the *Examiner* pulled no punches.

> Suppose I were able to tell the World, that the most active Enemy against this Paper, was *One,* who got to be Poor in the *Jacobite* Cause, and then ran over into Two desperate Extreams, and was resolved at once to grow Rich and Honest in the Cause of the *Whigs;* that he out-liv'd his Works a little too long, till, having parted with Religion and Morality, he threw away his Honour in a careless manner after it, together with his Humanity and Natural Affection to a *kind Sister,* his Estate, Fortune, and even the *Vouchers* belonging to his Office; all which were bestow'd, as the Monumental Legacies of *Whig-Honesty,* on a *Celebrated Actress,* who is too much admired upon the Stage, to have any Enquiry made into her Conduct behind the Curtain.

Warranted or not, such attacks were bound to happen. An actress who deliberately cultivated a glamorous public image would not automatically command respect and sympathy as a poor widow. (The anecdote about bringing her son onstage at the end of *The Distrest Mother* should be read in this light.) Men who had respected her position as Maynwaring's mistress would now feel free to make their addresses, and she, for a variety of reasons, may not have discouraged such attention. Although she enjoyed a rare degree of independence, she had not lived independent of male companionship and protection.

Not long after the attack in the *Examiner,* a defense of sorts appeared in the Whig *Flying-Post,* acquitting Maynwaring of the imputation of Jacobitism and praising him for his integrity and disinterested loyalty to the Whig cause. But Maynwaring's passion for Anne, as it offended "all who esteem'd him," was characterized as lamentable. Her conduct behind the curtain, it was agreed, might not bear looking into. However, "if the *Whiggs* do lose her, they will bear it with the same Patience that they have already the Defection of others of like Virtue, tho' greater Quality, and higher Obligations to be constant to us."[3] The writer spoke, he admitted, "only from general Rumour." He personally did not doubt Mrs. Oldfield's loyalty to the Whigs, indeed he had been "credibly inform'd" that she "insists upon her Lover's voting on our Side."[4]

While her name and reputation were thus dragged through the muck of the political press, she appeared in another new tragedy, *Cinna's Conspiracy*, based upon another play by Corneille. Once more she portrayed a daughter who seeks revenge for the death of her father and is willing to sacrifice her personal happiness in the process. With her lover Cinna (played by Booth), Emilia becomes a conspirator in the assassination plot against Augustus Caesar, who had destroyed her father but now "loads her with Honours" as if she were his own daughter. When the plot is betrayed, Caesar—the model of an enlightened autocrat—demonstrates his magnanimity by pardoning the conspirators. His example inspires Emilia to master her unruly passions and be reconciled. The formula should have found favor with Augustan audiences, but *Cinna's Conspiracy* did not even fare as well as *Ximena,* lasting only three nights.

Undaunted by the poor response to the two Corneille adaptations, the Drury Lane managers proceeded with the production of a third new tragedy in the "correct" neoclassical manner. This time they were fortunate beyond their imaginings. Addison's *Cato* filled the theater for an unprecendented first run of twenty nights, at a time of the year when only actors' benefits were expected to draw crowds. The "unexpected After-crop" yielded the managers a profit of £1,350 apiece for the season, nearly twice what they might have earned in an especially good year.[5]

No one could have been more gratified or surprised by this phenomenal success than Addison, who had written most of *Cato* during his travels on the continent more than ten years earlier but received little encouragement to complete it. At Steele's behest, he had shown the manuscript, then consisting of the first four acts, to Cibber, who (as he remembered many years later) read it with great enthusiasm. But the diffident Addison was swayed by the objections of one whose opinion he especially respected: Arthur Maynwaring, "the best Critick of our Time."[6]

In Maynwaring's judgment, the very plan of the work was deficient, and by this he referred to the "fable," which Addison had taken chiefly from Plutarch's account of the death of Cato in the civil wars that followed the fall of the first triumvirate. Striving for the regularity of French tragedy, Addison focused upon the last twenty-four hours of Cato's life, when, besieged by Caesar's superior forces in Utica, the exiled senator calmly oversaw the safe departure of his followers before committing suicide. It did not require great critical acumen to perceive the theatrical deficiencies in this situation. Romantic subplots and an abortive uprising afforded some interest, but the fact remained that Cato, a professed Stoic and staunch republican, unwavering in his determination and unruffled in temperament, was above conflict; his death held no dramatic interest.

Maynwaring's negative response is said to have been chiefly responsible for Addison's decision to put aside the uncompleted play for many years, but in the winter of 1712–13 he was finally persuaded to complete it.[7] In the early months of 1713, the manuscript passed through a number of hands and Addison incorporated many minor suggestions into the finished product, which was accepted for production immediately after the Passion Week recess.[8]

"Good God! what a Part would Betterton make of Cato!" was Steele's judgment when he and Cibber first discussed the play in 1703.[9] In 1713, young Lady Mary Wortley Montagu, invited to comment upon the manuscript, predicted that its "blemishes" would escape the attention of "the croud of Hearers and Readers."[10] Although she felt that the tribulations of the lovers in the subplot have nothing to do with the story of Cato's death, she confessed that she could not read "without tears" the scene in act 4 in which Marcia admits her love for Juba, on her knees before his supposed corpse. There was good material for actors to work with, and if Addison did not supply Anne with one of the greatest roles of her career, the character of Marcia was very much in her line of self-sacrificing heroines.

Juba, the young Numidian prince who inspires Marcia's love and is inspired by Cato's selflessness, was perfect for Wilks, who preferred to play romantic lovers in tragedy even though they were often supporting rather than leading roles. Cato's son Portius, rival of his brother for the affections of Lucia, was George Powell's last part in a new play. Portius dies honorably in putting down the mutiny of Sempronius and Syphax. In what is probably the best-known scene, his body is brought before Cato, who, instead of mourning his personal loss, regrets that "we can die but once to serve our Country." *His* tears are reserved for the fate of his country, now fallen to the tyrant Caesar. It is easy to imagine the effect of these and other fine patrotic sentiments when spoken in Booth's beautifully modulated tones.

Addison had shown the script to half of literary London, even soliciting approval from the Tory leaders, Robert Harley and Henry St. John, Viscount Bolingbroke. As a result, there was considerable interest in the production before its premiere. On March 27, George Berkeley, the future Bishop of Cloyne, wrote to his friend Sir John Percival that "the town is full of expectation of it, the boxes being already bespoke." Addison, he added, intended to give his benefit money to the actors, "in proportion to their performing," a very fine gesture, indeed.[11]

It had long been the custom to invite influential outsiders to attend rehearsals, in the hope that they would report enthusiastically to their friends, but Jonathan Swift, attending a rehearsal on April 6, reported with disdain the sorry spectacle of Addison directing the actors, who were evidently not fully prepared. He was especially amused by the sight of his late enemy's pregnant mistress—"the drab that Acts Catos daughter"—forgetting her lines "in the midst of a passionate Part, & then calling out, What's next?"[12]

During the reading of the play, Anne is said to have objected to a passage in act 3. A past mistress of the double entendre, she saw the possibility for unintended lewd humor in Portius's passionate address to Lucia:

Fixt in astonishment, I gaze upon thee;
Like one just blasted by a stroak from Heaven,
Who pants for breath, and stiffens as he stands.

The brilliant young poet Alexander Pope, who was present, suggested that the troublesome phrase be changed to "stiffens, yet alive," a correction that hardly seemed to improve the situation but was accepted by the nervous playwright, along with many other suggestions.[13]

For the opening night, Steele had taken care to pack the house with discerning and sympathetic auditors (a stratagem that had worked well for *The Distrest Mother*).[14] Feelings ran high from the moment that Wilks, as Juba, began to speak Pope's prologue. Rumors that *Cato* was a "party play," favoring the Whigs, disposed the more fervent spectators to hiss or clap at the slightest provocation. Berkeley was pleased to report that "Whiggish" lines evoked more claps than hisses, but Pope professed great indignation at being "clapped into a stanch Whig sore against [my] will, at almost every two lines."[15] Whigs saw themselves as champions of liberty—for which read constitutional monarchy and the Protestant succession—and vigorously applauded not only every mention of liberty itself, but every reference to republican Rome. A group of Tories, not to be outdone, summoned Booth to a box between acts and presented him with a gift of fifty guineas—in acknowledgement, said Bolingbroke, for "defending the cause of liberty so well against a *perpetuall dictator*."[16] In so doing, they hoped to call attention to their success in frustrating the Duke of Marlborough's ambition to become Captain General for life.

By a happy coincidence, the play could be read either as favoring Marlborough (as the exiled champion of liberty) or as opposing him (in the guise of Caesar, the dictator). No one looked too closely at the ambiguous ending, in which Cato's followers prepare to treat with the victorious Caesar. It was more satisfying to see oneself as the heir of Cato—"A brave Man struggling in the storms of Fate, / And greatly falling with a falling State!"—than to consider the implications of survival and political compromise.

Stimulated by political passions, helped along by the brilliant performances of Booth and his colleagues, *Cato* captured the popular imagination as no other tragedy of the period. Mondays excepted (for the actors would not be cheated of their benefits), Addison's tragedy played for twenty consecutive performances. The unprecedented length of its first run was due in part to the gradual increase in the size of the theatergoing population. Once it would have been possible for every Londoner who wanted to see a new play to do so in the first three days; by the time of *Cato,* a successful new play usually ran its course in six days, and it would soon be common practice to extend a first run to nine days, giving the author a third benefit night. But the success of *Cato* amounted to a craze; many spectators must have seen it more than once.

By April 30, the text of *Cato,* published on April 27, had gone into a third edition, and Pope reported that orange sellers in the park were hawking copies to passersby in their coaches. By way of demonstrating the general lunacy, Pope created an Oxford undergraduate, one "Damon," whose whole world revolved around *Cato,* even to the point of dating everything from its first, second, or third night, going up to Oxford only when *Cato* was not playing, and falling in love with Mrs. Oldfield "for no other reason than because she acted Cato's daughter." Indeed, Pope insisted, this eccentric behavior had given rise to a scurrilous epigram that had been making the rounds of the coffeehouses:

> You ask why Damon does the College seek?
> 'Tis because *Cato's* not rehears'd this week.
> How long at Oxford then will Damon stay?
> Damon returns not till they *Cato* play:
> Oldfield wants Damon—when will he be at her?
> Oh, not till Oldfield shall be Cato's daughter:
> Why then, if I can guess what may ensue,
> When Cato's clapped, Damon will be so too.[17]

Anne's pregnancy, which by the end of April must have been obvious, did not shield her from the abuses of coffeehouse wits. For some of the sterner moralists, it must have seemed a blatant reminder of the difference between herself and the character she was playing. But we know of only one direct comment upon the situation, hardly more than an aside, in a letter from Berkeley to Percival on May 7: "Mr Addison's play has taken wonderfully, they have acted it now almost a month, and would I believe act it a month longer were it not that Mrs Oldfield cannot hold out any longer, having had for several nights past, as I am informed, a midwife behind the scenes, which is surely very unbecoming the character of Cato's daughter."[18] Whether or not the play could have run for another month, Berkeley was evidently right about Anne's condition. The play closed after two more nights, and she did not appear in any other productions during the remainder of the season.

Nothing was ever said about the child, which suggests that it was stillborn or died in early infancy. In an age of high infant mortality, parents were more accustomed, although not necessarily hardened, to such losses. Evidently Anne felt well enough in body and spirit to rejoin her colleagues in late June, when they were honored by an invitation to perform at Oxford as part of the annual festivities—the "Act"—that marked the end of the university term.

Cato figured prominently in the Oxford repertory, which also included *Julius Caesar, Othello, Sir Courtly Nice,* and a popular farce, *Hob; or, The Country Wake.* No cast information exists for these performances, but Anne probably appeared in *Cato* and *Sir Courtly Nice.* The financial incentive for the journey was considerable. In previous visits to Oxford, it had been the custom to perform twice a day, once before the midday meal, and once in the early evening; the actors received double pay for their dual labors. This year, in an expansive mood at the end of such a successful season, the managers retained the custom of double salaries while eliminating the extra daily performance, hoping that the difference would be offset by the improved seating capacity of the theater. It was a happy decision all around. *Cato* proved to be as great a drawing card in Oxford as in London, filling the house for three days running. Something of the dignity of the play seems to have rubbed off on the players, for when they completed their engagement, they were commended by the vice-chancellor for their conduct, an honor, Cibber noted, that had not always been paid. In financial terms, which mattered most of all, the tour was also successful. After paying the actors their promised double salaries and donating the customary one night's proceeds (in this case, fifty pounds) to the repair of the university church, each manager netted £150. Cibber had cause to reflect upon the rewards of virtue.[19]

The fall of 1713 saw another change in the management of Drury Lane. While Booth rode the crest of the *Cato* craze, Cibber, Wilks, and Doggett became uneasy, for they could see that his prestige had been greatly enhanced, and they were aware that he had been complaining about his hireling status to his friends at court. At first, Doggett proposed that they offer him fifty guineas, matching the gift that had been tendered so ostentatiously by the Tory leaders; Wilks seconded him. In vain did Cibber insist that Booth would not be bought off so cheaply, when the real plum—admission to the ranks of the actor-managers—was within his grasp. Booth received the fifty guineas with every appearance of gratitude, but he continued to campaign for a share in the management. Doggett remained strongly opposed, but his obstinacy, which had kept Anne out of the management in 1709, did not prevail against the influence of Booth's friends and the insistence of the Lord Chamberlain. In November 1713, Booth's name was included in a new license issued by the Lord Chamberlain. Seeing no recourse, Doggett thereupon walked out on his partners, returning to Drury Lane only for special appearances in some of his popular comic roles a few years later.[20]

The managerial triumvirate of Cibber, Wilks, and Booth reigned for the remainder of Anne's lifetime. The new partners followed much the same procedure as before, with Wilks as director of rehearsals, and Cibber chiefly responsible for reading new manuscripts. Each partner signed bills for the ordinary running expenses. A number of the bills for wardrobe and property items, preserved in the theater collection of the Folger Shakespeare Library, attest to the minutiae that concerned them, from the outlay of sixpence for a rose "for Mad[am] Oyelfel" (one of the more creative spellings of Anne's surname) for *The Distrest Mother,* to rather considerable expenses for George Powell's funeral in December 1714.[21] Booth was far more complaisant than Doggett had been, and although the managers did not always agree about expenses, there were no longer so many wearying clashes among the partners. An era of prosperity and internal peace had been inaugurated.

The season of 1713–14 was nearly as successful as the last, with profits totaling thirty-six hundred pounds.[22] This was due in large part to the monopoly that Drury Lane enjoyed during a period when theater attendance was on the increase, but Cibber and his colleagues prided themselves on attracting discerning audiences in larger numbers than ever with fine serious offerings, such as *Cato* and *The Distrest Mother,* unadulterated by farcical afterpieces and other entertainments of a less refined nature. The enormous success of *The Tragedy of Jane Shore* in February seemed to bear that out, but most new plays, however wretched, now ran for at least six performances. The quality of new drama was, unfortunately, not equal to the demand.

In January, Anne had her first new role of the season in *The Victim,* a new tragedy by Charles Johnson. It was little more than a close adaptation of Racine's *Iphigenie,* which in turn had been based upon *Iphigenia at Aulis,* by Euripides. Racine had added the character of Eriphile, who is sacrificed at the last moment in place of Iphigenia. Anne was certainly miscast as the passionate and jealous Eriphile, but she spoke a delightful comical epilogue by Cibber in which she apologized for not appearing in a manner more suitable for a dead heroine. She could hardly be expected to spoil her face, and possibly her gown, by daubing herself with white powder, and how was she to rise in a ghostly fashion through the narrow trapdoor while wearing "nine wide Whale bone Yards of Petticoat?"[23] The mockery was richly deserved.

Not long after the run of *The Victim* ended, there were rumors that a new tragedy by Nicholas Rowe was ready for production. Interest was piqued when the title of his new play—*The Tragedy of Jane Shore*—became known, for there were those who questioned the propriety of making Edward IV's mistress, the wife of a goldsmith, the heroine of a tragedy. Before the play opened, several opportunistic booksellers capitalized on the preproduction publicity by publishing brief lives of Jane Shore, for the greater edification of theatergoers.[24]

The first run, beginning on February 2, 1714, nearly duplicated the record set by *Cato*—seventeen consecutive nights, followed by two more performances in March and April. The brilliant cast included Anne as the penitent and vulnerable, yet morally stalwart heroine, whose beauty is fatally attractive; Booth as the noble libertine, Lord Hastings, whose solicitude for Jane Shore is tainted by lust; Mary Porter as Alicia, Hastings's cast-off mistress; Wilks as Will Shore, who, disguised as the exile, Dumont, returns to witness his wife's suffering and pronounce her redemption; and Cibber as the villainous, hunch-backed Duke of Gloucester, a role for which he was already famous in his adaptation of *Richard III*. As a mark of her satisfaction and success, Anne chose the play for her benefit on March 1.

Despite its great success, *Jane Shore* did not escape adverse comment. Some of Rowe's critics were content to mock his pretentions in claiming to write "in imitation of Shakespeare's style."[25] Others, notably the poet and critic Charles Gildon, attacked him on firm, if ludicrously rigid, neoclassical grounds. In a satirical playlet titled *The New Rehearsal; or, Bays the Younger,* one of Gildon's characters argues that "A Shop-keeper's Wife of the City can never rise above the Soc, and her having lain with the King and two or three Lords, will never be thought ennobling enough to fit her for the Buskin, since that very Crime renders her entirely incapable of it."[26] Indeed, he insists that the play be regarded as a comedy, since "Of the 8 characters, the 2 women are whores, and three of the men villains, one a Cuckold and another a debocher of young ladies." But few of Rowe's detractors or admirers understood the truly revolutionary nature of *Jane Shore*.

He had once before explored the theme of female sexual frailty and penitence—a central preoccupation of popular literature in the eighteenth century. But in that earlier play, *The Fair Penitent* (1703), he had not been altogether successful. The fallen heroine's eventual repentance seemed to have been grafted onto a different kind of tragedy, one that exalted and glamorized its sinful lovers. After the death of Calista's seducer in act 4, the dramatic energy seemed to seep away, and despite the excellence of the casting, and many fine moments in the early acts, the play was not a success.[27] Rowe turned his attention to more a conventional type of tragedy, but the plays that followed *The Fair Penitent* were also unsuccessful.

Jane Shore marked a return, with a difference, to Rowe's earlier interests. In Jane herself he chose a heroine from the material of popular ballads, underscoring her simplicity in his prologue: "Justly they drew the fair, and spoke her plain, / And sung her by her Christian name— 'twas Jane." As a redeemed sinner and martyr, she did not conform to conventions of tragic character. There had long been a tendency to polarize female characters, equating sinfulness with self-aggrandizement and often with undeniable glamor—like the bitch-goddesses of modern popular literature and television—while virtue was equated with youth, innocence, and pathos. In Jane Shore, and in the character of Hastings's mistress, Alicia, Rowe blurred these distinctions. Woman, he saw, was weak, the inevitable prey both of man and her own emotional (read "sexual") nature. Jane Shore was the perfect embodiment of a divided, fundamentally tragic, femininity—"sense and nature's easy fool." History portrayed her as an essentially good woman who used her influence with Edward IV to reward the meritorious and relieve the poor. Thomas More, the first to tell her story, partly excused her transgression on the grounds of her too-youthful, loveless marriage. Unprotected after Edward's death, stripped of her possessions, and turned out into the streets to starve, she became both a monitory and a pathetic figure.

Rowe made the most of the didactic and melodramatic elements in her story. Jane's path to redemption is strewn with obstacles. When Hastings (in most historical accounts, her lover and protector after the king's death) expects her to reward his kindness with sexual favors, he interpets her refusal as calculated coyness and tries to force himself upon her. In the subsequent duel between Hastings and Dumont, Jane's dependence upon the "right" kind of masculine protection is tellingly demonstrated, and Dumont's victory becomes the triumph of a new, more bourgeois morality over decadent libertinism.

Jane wishes only to live out her days in humble surroundings, far from the scene of her former vanity, but the jealousy of Hastings's cast-off mistress and the ambitions of the Duke of Gloucester provide further impediments. Falsely accused of "seducing" Hastings to the cause of the boy king, Edward V, she attains moral grandeur in defying Gloucester. In an impassioned outburst she prescribes the very punishment that Gloucester ultimately decrees:

> Let me be branded for the public scorn,
> Turned forth and driven to wander like a vagabond;
> Be friendless and forsaken, seek my bread
> Upon the barren, wild, and desolate waste,
> Feed on my sighs, and drink my falling tears,
> Ere I consent to teach my lips injustice
> Or wrong the orphan who has none to save him. [28]

What might in a less resolute woman appear maudlin, even masochistic, becomes heroic.

The final, harrowing scene of her suffering achieves additional moral and dramatic power when Dumont at last decides to reveal himself as her husband, Will Shore. It is doubtful whether Jane, in her weakened condition, will be able to withstand the shock of seeing him; he, for his part, may not be able to forgive her. Shore risks death merely by coming to Jane's aid, since Gloucester has decreed that anyone doing so will be punished for treason. The climactic moment of their reconciliation is followed by their agonized parting, torn from each other's arms by Gloucester's henchmen. Jane dies content in the knowledge of her husband's forgiveness; Shore goes bravely to his death, having fulfilled his last duty in pardoning her. [29]

Even an extensive summary of *Jane Shore* cannot convey its revolutionary nature as tragedy in the early eighteenth century. The positive light in which marriage, and especially the dignity and authority of the husband, are viewed was quite new. That a "shopkeeper from the City," and a cuckold to boot (if the two were not synonymous), should attain heroic status was sufficiently daring to provoke adverse comment from critics such as Gildon; that his love for his wife rendered him strong and noble, rather than whining and effeminate, was an equally radical innovation.[30]

The revolutionary ideology of the play was, however, served up in conventional dress. The historical setting, with its clear echoes of *Richard III*, removed the story from the realm of domestic tragedy, and Rowe insisted upon historical dress of some kind for Jane Shore and Gloucester,[31] perhaps with the notion of dignifying Jane. He need not have worried. It is quite unlikely that Anne played Jane as a shopkeeper's wife.

Anne would later observe that the best school she had known was hearing Rowe read her part in his tragedies.[32] Nevertheless, she had her own notion of how things should be done. She is supposed to have opposed the playwright's wish that Wilks play the role of Hastings, insisting that Wilks be cast as Will Shore, "otherwise she would take that of Alicia."[33] (The threat sounds a bit hollow, since Alicia was hardly in her line.) Anne may have sensed that if Wilks played Hastings, the attempted rape in act 2 would remind audiences of similar scenes she played with Wilks in comedies, in which the woman was not altogether averse to being carried off to the boudoir. Or she may have reckoned that only an actor as popular as Wilks could make make the once-despised character of the husband as attractive as Rowe wished. In any event, if the story is true her wishes were respected. Until Booth's retirement in 1728, Wilks played Dumont/Shore and Booth played Hastings. The great success of the play undoubtedly owed much to its excellent cast.

With the roles of Hermione in *The Distrest Mother,* Lucia in *Cato,* and Alicia in *Jane Shore,* Mary Porter established herself as a leading actress at Drury Lane. More than any other member of the company, she would be regarded as Elizabeth Barry's heir, eventually taking over many of Barry's most famous tragic roles: Monimia in *The Orphan,* Belvidera in *Venice Preserv'd,* Isabella in *The Fatal Marriage,* and Zara in *The Mourning Bride,* as well as Lady Macbeth, the queen in *Hamlet,* Roxana in *The Rival Queens,* and Queen Elizabeth in *The Unhappy Favourite.* In appearance, we are told, she was "tall and well-shaped; of a fair complection, but not handsome."[34] Commentators frequently refer to her regal quality and her excellence in portraying strong emotion. But in some important respects she was quite different from Barry. Benjamin Victor speaks of her "naturally tender Voice," which "was enlarged by Labour and Patience into sufficient Force to fill the Theatre," by means of which she developed a tremor "which was a Singularity that nothing but Custom could reconcile."[35] Barry's grandeur did not come naturally to Mary Porter. In the characters that were created for her there is often a fragile quality. Alicia is "a dainty-fingered girl"; Lucia is formed by nature "of her softest mould," and "enfeebled . . . with tender passions."

Like Anne, but in quite a different way, she left her mark upon a body of roles, taming the powerful, sensual tragedy queen and injecting a greater degree of pathos into strongly emotional characters. Appearing with Anne in numerous comedies and tragedies, she was more Bracegirdle than Barry, no matter how much emotion she generated. In this way, the balance seemed to shift between the two traditional female types, with Anne's virtuous heroines gaining strength and importance. Perhaps this change reflected an evolution in popular taste, for by the middle of the century aggressive, amoral female characters virtually disappeared from new drama, and there would be a greater emphasis than ever upon hapless mothers, wives, and daughters.[36]

In their personal, as well as professional, relationship Mary Porter seemed content to remain in Anne's shadow. Although the two women were about the same age, Porter's natural gravity made her seem older, and Anne teasingly called her "mother."[37] She lived quietly, untouched by scandal or notoriety—one of the good women of the theater about whom virtually nothing is known.

In tragedy, Anne was fortunate in such partners as Porter, whose delicacy was a perfect complement, Booth, whose dignified deportment matched hers, and Wilks, whose romantic lovers were always attractive and sympathetic. With Cibber principally playing the heavy villains, and John Mills as the noble villain or dignified soldier, a pattern was established that would prevail through most of Anne's career. There is no evidence to suggest that audiences tired of the formula. In any case, with their busy schedules, actors could not afford the challenges of experimentation.

Anne's repertoire at this time consisted of about eighteen comic roles and six tragic roles, not all of which she performed every season.[38] An important new role was Caelia in Fletcher's *Humourous Lieutenant*. The popular comedy—worthy of modern revival—is reminiscent of Shakespeare's later plays. In the potentially tragic main plot, a lustful king and his noble son are both in love with a beautiful captive; the underplot involves the comical adventures of a whimsical soldier—the "humourous" lieutenant of the title.

Caelia appears at first to have more in common with Anne's growing collection of tragic heroines than with her sprightly comic heroines. Tricked into coming to the corrupt court of Antigonus, Caelia must summon up every ounce of moral fortitude and wit to defend her virtue. She triumphs over her would-be corrupters but nearly loses her lover, Demetrius, who cannot believe that she was able to live in his father's court unscathed. In the last act, a playful note is introduced when Caelia decides to torment Demetrius for his unreasonable jealousy: "If I must play the knave with him, to die for't; / 'Tis in my nature."[39] But her game nearly gets out of hand when her playfulness fires his jealousy almost beyond remedy. Anne and Wilks could be called upon, of course, to play these scenes in such a way as to set the stage for the lovers' eventual reconciliation.

The Humourous Lieutenant was a logical addition to her repertoire at this time. The serious earlier scenes were a showcase for her majestic, tragic manner. The last act demonstrated her versatility. More than most of her predecessors in the role,[40] Anne could play Caelia's shining virtue as convincingly as her playful wit.

9
Soldier and Courtier

Sometime in 1714, Anne moved from Southampton Street to a fine new house on the east side of the Haymarket, near Piccadilly. The street was described by John Strype in his *Survey of the Cities of London and Westminster* (1720) as large and spacious, "with well built Houses, especially the East Side."[1] The move from Southampton Street was a move upward in the social scale, the first of several choices that, over the years, tended to detach Anne socially from her theatrical colleagues. The building itself no longer stands, and nothing is known about its size, external decoration, or architectural features. That she was proud of her house and its furnishings is suggested by a passage in a satirical play *The Confederates,* published in 1717, in which "Mrs. Oldfield" threatens to leave Drury Lane and her acting career:

> On Market fam'd for *Hay,* a House full high,
> With Sashes bright, and Wainscot Rooms have I;
> Rich Beds, and Damask Chairs (I thank my Stars!)
> And Cabinets are there with China Jars.
> What hinders then, but I enjoy my Store,
> As famous BRACEGIRDLE has done before?
> (Mock'd by Spectators, and by Poets crost)
> And quit the Scenes where all my Glory's lost?[2]

The situation is imaginary, but the description of the house was probably accurate, for it would have been well known to local residents. Its furnishings no doubt aroused comment as the property of an actress who had come up in the world and was proud of it.

Along with the move to the Haymarket, there was another significant change in her life. The interval between Maynwaring's death and the acquisition of a new protector was certainly "decent," yet some of her biographers, especially those who see Maynwaring as the great love of her life, wish that she had waited longer.[3] Passion aside, there was good reason for her to reestablish herself publicly in a quasi-marriage. Since Maynwaring's death, she had been the object of gossip and perhaps unwanted attentions. Neither promiscuity nor celibacy had any attraction for her. What she needed was another lover who could offer both affection and protection and would not feel degraded by her occupation. Colonel Charles Churchill answered her needs admirably. They were to live together until her death.

In view of the objections by the Duke and Duchess of Marlborough to her affair with Maynwaring, it is interesting that she ended up with a Churchill of her own, but it is not entirely surprising. Charles Churchill's political affiliations would have drawn him into Maynwaring's orbit. Both men were famous for their devotion to the Whigs and to Anne. On the surface, they had little else in common, but the judgment on Churchill may be in need of revision. The historian J. H. Plumb has described him as the bastard nephew of Marlborough and the "hard drinking, hard hunting, half-literate friend of Walpole."[4] That he was the bastard son of Marlborough's younger brother, General Charles Churchill, has never been disputed. That he was the devoted friend and political ally of Sir Robert Walpole is attested to in numerous anecdotes. His reputation for semiliteracy is another matter, for it seems to rest entirely on the often-quoted assertion that Churchill "professed never having read a whole book through his life, and his letters were so ill wrote and so ill spelled that Sir Robert Walpole used to keep them unread till he saw him, and then he often could not read them himself."[5]

Churchill's educational deficiencies were no greater than those of most Englishmen of his class and occupation. He was a soldier, not a man of letters. Soldiering was the Churchill family trade. Of the first Sir Winston Churchill's four surviving sons, three entered the military and served with distinction. The eldest, John (the future Duke of Marlborough), rose from the ranks as a junior officer in the Duke of York's foot regiment to become one of the most brilliant military commanders in modern history.

The Churchills were also courtiers and diplomats. The elder Charles Churchill was appointed page of honor in the Danish court when he was only thirteen and became a gentleman of the bedchamber to Prince George of Denmark four years later. When Prince George married Princess Anne of England in 1683, this association, along with Sarah Churchill's friendship with the princess, cemented Churchill family ties with the future queen. Toward the end of the second Dutch War, in 1674, Charles returned to England to begin his military career as an ensign in Captain John Churchill's company of foot in the Duke of York's regiment. Afterward, he advanced rapidly, becoming a lieutenant in 1675 and a captain in 1678.[6] At about this time he sired a natural son, his only child, Charles Churchill.

The biographer A. L. Rowse is probably correct in surmising that the child's mother is the Elizabeth Dodd to whom General Churchill left an annuity in his will,[7] for this terse document contains only three bequests. The bulk of his estate was left to Mary Gould Churchill, the heiress he married in 1702. To his "natural son, Charles Churchill," he left the sum of two thousand pounds, not a great fortune, but an adequate nest egg, which, if invested conservatively, would yield an income of one hundred pounds per year. (Charles had income from his army commissions, as well as a small legacy from his grandmother Churchill.) Finally, there was a bequest of fifty pounds to be paid in equal installments, on the twenty-fifth of March and September each year, to Elizabeth Dodd "during her naturall life."[8] The relatively large bequest suggests that she was more than a family servant. Churchill gave the child his name and raised him as if he were a legitimate heir, demonstrating an affection and concern for the boy that transcended mere decency. It was a pattern that young Charles would follow not only with his own son by Anne but with another natural child.

If the boy had much formal education, it was not at one of the well-known schools in England. In 1688, when he would have been about ten years old, he was commissioned as an ensign in the third regiment of foot. (He was too young, of course, to have had any part in the Glorious Revolution, in which the Churchills figured prominently among those who threw in their lot with William of Orange and the Protestant cause.)[9]

Nothing of importance is known about young Charles until 1697, when he was stationed in Flanders as a captain in his father's regiment. He rose through the ranks, almost always in infantry regiments and usually under his father's command. At Blenheim, where Lieutenant General Churchill's troops played a decisive role, his son served as his aide-de-camp. Though nepotism might be suspected, there is every reason to believe that he was a competent and dedicated officer and that he owed his position in the army and the world at large as much to his own ability as to his family connections. When Anne first knew him, he was in his early or mid thirties and a man of the world, certainly far more polished than the stereotypical bluff soldier he is sometimes said to have been, who could not speak a complete sentence without uttering an oath. (The speculation that he was the model for Colonel Ranter in the tenth issue of the *Tatler* seems entirely without foundation.) His tours of duty abroad, on his father's staff, must have given him at least a working knowledge of French, Dutch, and German. Robert Walpole would later make use of his services on missions to the Continent, reporting on the activities of exiled Jacobites. In his old age, lame from gout and missing several front teeth, he was a figure of fun to the wits, but one of them—Sir Charles Hanbury Williams—paid tribute to the graces of the youthful colonel:

> Frank and good-natur'd, of an honest heart,
> Loving to act the steady friendly part:
> None led through youth a gayer life than he,
> Cheerful in converse, smart in repartee.
> Sweet was his night, and joyful was his day,
> He din'd with Walpole, and with Oldfield lay.[10]

In 1708, General Churchill suffered a disabling stroke and retired to the family estate in Dorset, where he died in 1714. Since the signing of the Peace of Utrecht in 1713, Charles had been living in London, at least part of the time in a house on Sherard Street, in Soho.[11] It is likely that when he came into his modest inheritance and was free of family commitments, he made his addresses to Anne. He was not a particularly wealthy man at the time. Indeed, unless he had resources in addition to the income from his inheritance and his military pay (which was reduced by half when he was not on active duty), his annual income would have been less than Arthur Maynwaring's. But Anne herself was a woman of property who earned perhaps four hundred pounds a year. She did not have to live off her lover, nor, apparently, did she wish to. A deciding factor may have been Churchill's evident pride in her, and his determination to make it "his sole Business and Delight to place her in the same rank of Reputation . . . with Persons of the best Condition."[12] Maynwaring had contributed to her development as an actress but seldom included her in his social life. Churchill, then, may be seen as completing an important element of Anne's public character. Through him she at last entered the world of Lady Betty Modish.

At first he needed a position of his own, and after the death of Queen Anne in the summer of 1714 and the return of the Duke and Duchess of Marlborough from self-imposed exile, his prospects appeared good. In September 1714, Marlborough attempted to obtain an appointment in the royal household for his nephew, but he was not successful, for he no longer enjoyed his former great influence, and George I objected to the young man's illegitimacy.[13]

In the meantime, there were still friends in the Walpole circle— Whigs who declared their loyalty to the brilliant Parliamentarian and party leader, Robert Walpole—to whom Charles could introduce his charming mistress. Among Anne's first aristocratic friends were the Earl and Countess of Bristol. As John and Elizabeth Hervey, landed gentry from Suffolk, they had been protégés of the Duchess of Marlborough, who was instrumental in obtaining a barony for John Hervey in 1703. His dedication to the Hanoverian succession earned him an earldom soon after the accession of George I. Perhaps because their elevation to the nobility was so recent or because they were not at all stuffy, Lord and Lady Bristol welcomed Charles Churchill's actress-mistress to their home. The countess loved card playing and gossip, those staples of London social life.[14] Anne had been portraying her type for many years.

Their eldest son John, Lord Hervey, was a passionate lover and hater, a learned and vivid correspondent, a charming conversationalist with a touch of malicious wit, and in later life, a political pamphleteer. Among his many writings, his memoirs of the reign of George II are especially valued by modern readers. Like his parents, he was a devoted Whig and Walpole loyalist. He, more than his parents, seemed to be Churchill's and Anne's particular friend.

In the summer of 1716, having completed his education at Cambridge, young Hervey was in Paris on the first leg of the obligatory grand tour. There he appears to have encountered Anne, on what may have been her first holiday abroad. How long she was there, and how she amused herself, we do not know, but by the second week of September she was back in London, paying a social call on Lord and

Lady Bristol. She was "wellcome to us both," Lord Bristol wrote to his son on September 13, "because she brought me a letter from you, which entertaind us better than she with all her witt & ridicule on France could do; your simile of the Invalides was worth her whole conversation."[15] Although the reference to Anne may seem slighting, Lord Bristol probably meant to pay his son a high compliment in comparing him favorably to a woman famous for her "witt & ridicule."

The accession of George I in 1714 had significant consequences for the theater. Like the earlier Stuart monarchs, but unlike William III and Queen Anne, the Hanoverians loved the theater. From 1714 onward, command performances and the appearance of members of the royal family at the theater—duly noted in the press—were frequent occurrences. Renewed royal interest in the theater was probably crucial for Anne's acceptance into the social world of courtiers and the court. For Drury Lane there were two important new developments.

Ever since the silencing of Christopher Rich in 1709, the Drury Lane company had operated under a series of licenses, issued first to William Collier, then to Owen Swiney and the actor-managers, and once again to Collier and the actor-managers. But Collier was a Tory, with no standing in the Hanoverian court. Since the accession of a new monarch meant that their license would have to be reissued, Cibber, Wilks, and Booth looked about for a more suitable partner, hitting at last upon Richard Steele, whose work as playwright and unofficial publicist had contributed so much to their past success, and whose journalistic efforts in the cause of the Protestant succession would soon earn him a knighthood. A license for Steele, Cibber, Wilks, and Booth was duly issued on October 18, 1714.[16] The new partnership proved even more successful when Steele was able to obtain a patent on January 19, 1715, the first new theatrical patent to be granted since 1663. Unlike the perpetual patents of Thomas Killigrew and Sir William Davenant, which had descended to Christopher Rich, Steele's patent was valid only for the period of his life plus three years. Still, it conferred greater independence than a mere license—or so Steele and his partners believed—and was potentially worth a great deal. One of Steele's first actions was to assign shares in the patent to the actor-managers.

While the actor-managers were, as they thought, solidifying their position, Christopher Rich decided that it was time to improve his. He had never given up hope of regaining the use of his patent, which had lain dormant ever since his silencing in 1709. Accordingly, he acquired the lease to Thomas Betterton's old theater in Lincoln's Inn Fields and bided his time until conditions seemed favorable for renovating the building and creating a new company. The increase in patronage in the last years of Queen Anne's reign seemed promising for his new venture, and after her death, he appealed to the new monarch to rescind the ban against his patent. The king was happy to do so, recalling that throughout most of the reign of his Stuart cousin, Charles II, there had been two patent companies in London. As it turned out, Rich did not live to see the opening of the new theater in December 1714. Ownership of the patent passed to his sons, one of whom, John (in many ways as remarkable a character as his father), enjoyed a long and successful career as an actor-manager at Lincoln's Inn Fields and Covent Garden.

The effect of the establishment of a new company was felt immediately at Drury Lane, for a number of actors were eager to join forces with John Rich. They included the veteran comedians William Bullock, Francis Leigh, and George Pack, dignified Theophilus Keen and young Christopher Bullock, and Frances Knight and Jane Rogers. With Mrs. Rogers went her daughter, young Jane, who—first as "Mrs. Rogers, Junior" and then as the wife of Christopher Bullock—became a popular and highly esteemed performer. The Drury Lane ranks were further reduced by the retirement of Lucretia Bradshaw, who left the stage to make a respectable marriage.[17] Opportunity to advance in the hierarchy was undoubtedly a major factor in the mass defection. In the new company, Frances Knight and Jane Rogers were able to claim top billing, and they were joined by several other veteran actresses who had dropped from sight after the union of the two companies in 1709.[18]

With the departure of Knight and Rogers, Anne added two more important stock roles to her repertoire: Berinthia in *The Relapse* and Imoinda in *Oroonoko*.[19] The two characters could not have been more different. Berinthia, a lively young widow, became part of Anne's stock of worldly, amoral ladies of fashion. The seduction scene, with Wilks as the errant husband, Loveless, was especially delightful. (As Loveless carries Berinthia off to her bedchamber she cries—"very softly," according to the stage direction—"Help, help, I'm ravished, ruined, undone! O Lord, I shall never be able to bear it.")[20] In marked contrast was the nobility and pathos of Imoinda, the beautiful wife of the slave prince, Oroonoko—an appropriate addition to Anne's roster of tragic heroines. After Jane Rogers left Drury Lane, Anne played

Imoinda for five seasons, opposite Booth as Oroonoko, before relin-
quishing the role to a young newcomer to the company, Sarah
Thurmond.

Throughout the spring and summer of 1715, when George I had
been on the throne for less than a year, there was much uneasiness
about Jacobite risings in England and about possible invasion by
supporters of James II's son, who was recognized in France as his
father's legitimate successor, James III. By July, it was clear that the
military, greatly reduced since the peace of Utrecht, would have to be
reactivated.

The anticipated invasion was foiled in the fall of 1715 and the ring-
leaders arrested or put to flight, but risings in the north posed a serious
threat. Colonel Charles Churchill raised a troop of dragoons and served
in a series of frustrating engagements along the Tweed, in the north-
east, and with greater success at the siege of Preston, in Lancashire,
where the numerically superior Jacobite forces surrendered on November 13.[21] At about the same time, the threat in Scotland was turned
back by the Duke of Argyle at Sheriffmuir. In the midst of one of the
bitterest winters in recent memory, the Stuart pretender finally landed
in Scotland, but by then his cause was clearly lost.

Meanwhile, in London, the theater dealt with the Jacobite threat in
its own fashion. Just after Passion Week in the spring of 1715, Drury
Lane produced Nicholas Rowe's violently anti-Catholic historical
drama, *The Tragedy of Lady Jane Gray,* with Anne as a very different
kind of Jane from her popular character of the previous season—a
patriot who dies not as a repentant sinner but as a Protestant martyr.
Rowe had taken up the subject in the summer of 1714, when, in the
waning months of Queen Anne's reign, the Protestant succession
appeared imperiled.[22] By the time the play was ready for production,
the tragic story of the "nine-day Queen," established briefly on the
throne after the death of young Edward VI as an obstacle to the lawful
sucession of Catholic Mary Tudor, addressed a slightly different threat:
the specter of a successful invasion by French-financed Jacobites.

Perhaps because political considerations were uppermost, the result
was not Rowe at his best. The character of Lady Jane, described in the
prologue as a heroine, martyr, queen, and "beauteous saint," is drearily
virtuous rather than stirring. Marrying Guilford Dudley for reasons
of filial duty as well as love, she insists that they spend their wedding
night in mourning for the young Protestant king and for England's

uncertain fate at the hands of his Catholic successor, Mary Tudor. When she reluctantly agrees to accept the crown, it is in the same spirit of mournful resignation.

> Invest me with this Royal Wretchedness;
> Let me not know one happy Minute more.
> Let all my sleepless Nights be spent in Care,
> My Days be vex'd with Tumults and Alarms . . .[23]

Only in the final scenes, when the attempt to place her on the throne has failed and she is faced with the choice of death or conversion to Catholicism, does she begin to show some spirit. Here Rowe pulled all the theatrical stops at his disposal. After Guilford Dudley is led to the place of execution, the back scene opens and reveals the scaffold, hung in black, awaiting Lady Jane herself. She parts with her waiting women in a scene that is understated and moving.

Despite its topical appeal and the excellence of the cast, which included Booth as Guilford Dudley and Cibber as the scheming Bishop of Winchester, the play was only moderately successful. The run of ten nights, interspersed with actors' benefits, was sufficient to earn Rowe two author's benefits, but it hardly equaled the impressive showing of *Cato* or *Jane Shore*. Except for one performance in the following season, it was never revived during Anne's lifetime. The reason may have been, in part, political. Few Englishmen, in 1554, had been willing to lay down their lives for the Protestant Lady Jane Gray; the hereditary rights of Mary Tudor were ultimately upheld. In the spring of 1715, and for some time afterward, the Hanoverian monarchs may have preferred to forget that historic episode.

In December, the Jacobite leaders who had surrendered at Preston were taken to London, amid jeering mobs; in February 1716, they were tried for treason in a great show trial reminiscent of Henry Sacheverell's and publicly executed. In the partisan climate there were incidents—some spontaneous, some carefully orchestrated—in the theaters. An old reliable stock piece could suddenly take on topical significance. A spectator attending a performance of *The Spanish Fryar* at Drury Lane on February 13, noted that derogatory references to priests drew enthusiastic claps from the Whigs and hisses from the Tories.[24]

At the end of her benefit performance on March 5, Anne appealed directly to popular sentiment in an epilogue "Recommending the

Cause of Liberty to the Beauties of Great Britain." Skillfully employing her lighthearted epilogue manner in a political cause, she exhorted the ladies in the audience to consider how they might best use their vaunted power:

> The Thing's so plain—for those, that would destroy all,
> Reserve your Frowns, your Favours for the Loyal. . . .
> With Scorn relentless treat those wretched Elves,
> That durst be Slaves to any, but your selves.
> For where's the Glory to make him your Slave,
> That would not die, his Liberty to save? . . .
>   Since then such Joys in *Britain* only flow,
> How much to guard them, Ladies, lies on you?
> And as the World can no such Monarch boast,
> Let Royal GEORGE be ev'ry Beauty's Toast.[25]

Published the next day, the epilogue enjoyed its own successful run, being repeated several more times. Hearing it on March 13, theatergoer Dudley Ryder found the beginning to be dull but was "very well pleased to hear it clapped by a full house, and a general approbation of the sentiments."[26]

Political considerations were also responsible for the revival of Rowe's *Tamerlane* at Drury Lane on November 5, 1716, with a new prologue by the author "in honour of King William and in memory of what he did for us."[27] The success of the revival of 1716 assured that it would be performed every season on November 4, the birthday of William III, and November 5, the anniversary of his landing at Torbay, as long as the Whigs were in power. Anne played the role of the tragic Grecian noblewoman, Arpasia (originally written for Elizabeth Barry), in love with a fellow Christian, Moneses (played by Wilks), but forced to marry the cruel heathen chieftain Bajazet, who, in Rowe's propagandistic version of the Tamerlane story, stood for Louis XIV and the evils of the French monarchy. Undoubtedly she felt that she was doing her part in the anti-Jacobite cause, but Arpasia was evidently not one of her favorite or more successful roles; after 1721 she dropped it.

Anne did not automatically gain entrée to the highest levels of society through Churchill's connections. The story that "she was to be seen on the terrace at Windsor, walking with the consorts of dukes, and with countesses, and wives of English barons, and the whole gay group might be heard calling one another by their Christian names,"[28] seems greatly exaggerated. But through friends such as the Earl and Countess of Bristol, especially the countess, who became a lady of the bedchamber to the Princess of Wales in 1718, Anne was probably introduced to the Leicester House set (who supported Walpole during a split within the Whig ranks) and the Prince and Princess of Wales. The clever, strong-willed princess, Caroline of Anspach, was just Anne's age, spoke English well, and liked to be surrounded by lively, attractive, witty people. She herself was something of an actress, able to use her "regal tone" when it suited her,[29] and like all members of the royal family she loved the theater.

On one occasion, according to Tom Davies, Princess Caroline, encountering Anne at a social gathering, remarked that she had heard rumors that Anne and Churchill were married. Anne responded enigmatically, "So it is said, may it please your highness, but we have not owned it yet."[30] The story is generally told as an example of Anne's quick wit and tact, but it also suggests a certain unease, on the part of the princess, over Churchill's domestic situation. Anne's reply may have been intended to satisfy appearances.

During the season of 1716–17 Anne added no important new roles to her repertoire, with the exception of Arpasia. Three new plays in which she appeared—Susanna Centlivre's *Cruel Gift,* Charles Johnson's *Sultaness* (based on Racine's *Bajazet*), and Delariviere Manley's *Lucius, The First Christian King of Britain*[31]—failed quietly. A fourth new play, also a failure, involved Anne in a notorious theatrical incident that reflected, at least indirectly, upon her new social connections. The young playwright John Gay and his collaborators, Alexander Pope and Dr. John Arbuthnot, submitted the manuscript for a farce titled *Three Hours After Marriage* for production at Drury Lane. Wilks and Booth evidently wanted to have nothing to do with it, nor did Anne at first, but three of Princess Caroline's maids of honor, who patronized the project, persuaded Anne to take part in it, and the production went forward, opening on January 16.

The premiere was jammed with spectators, many of whom were lured by rumors that the nominal author, Gay, had been abetted by Pope and Arbuthnot. Pope's deadly wit was particularly anticipated and feared. Although he may have been guilty of malicious mischief, it is difficult to understand—from a mere reading of the text—why such a fuss ensued. The plot of *Three Hours After Marriage* deals with the efforts of the new young bride, Mrs. Townley, to cuckold her husband Dr. Fossile, assisted by her would-be lovers, the actors Plotwell and Underplot. Contemporary spectators would have recognized several prominent satirical targets: the poet-critic John Dennis, in the character of Sir Tremendous; and the physician and scientific experimenter, John Woodward, in the character of Dr. Fossile. Several well-known women writers could have served as models for Phoebe Clinkett, a pretentious, unsuccessful playwright.[32]

If Pope's reputation aroused partisan feeling before the event, it is difficult to account for the clamor that all but drowned out the dialogue during the first two performances. *Ad hominem* satire was nothing new on the Augustan stage. In this case, however, the actors may have added to an already-tense situation by engaging in some malicious mimicry.[33] A satirical play, *The Confederates,* which was published in March 1717, offers evidence of such an occurrence and of Anne's involvement in it. The events of *The Confederates* purport to take place in a nearby tavern and backstage at Drury Lane immediately after the first performance of *Three Hours.* In one scene "Mrs. Oldfield" threatens to quit the stage, where she has been so grievously insulted, and retire to her house in the Haymarket; she then falls to lamenting that she ever took part in the proceedings in the first place.

> Ill-judging Beauties (tho' of high Degree)
> Why did you force this wretched Part on me?
> And Thou, fat *Baroness,* with cheeks so Red,
> Whence came this Maggot in thy ancient Head?
> Oh! That I had (with BOOTH and WILKS combin'd)
> Obdurate as at first, not chang'd my Mind!
> Or, since I could not from the Task be freed,
> Had mimick'd Lady M——N, not Mrs. M—D.[34]

While the meaning of this passage is obscure to modern readers, it was clear enough to that limited group of Londoners who constituted "the Town" in 1717. From various clues, knowledgeable readers would conclude that Princess Caroline's charming maids of honor had not only persuaded Anne, against her better judgment, to take the role of Mrs. Townley but had also persuaded her to mimic the wife of the noted Dr. Mead, Pope's friend and personal physician.[35] If this was true it was doubly mischievous, for how were the spectators to know that the idea of mimicking Mrs. Mead had not originated with Pope, but with the actress and her friends? Anne may have come in for her share of criticism.

By the end of the second performance, tempers seem to have cooled, for it was reported that "while the inimitable Oldfield was speaking the epilogue . . . the storm subsided—And to speak poetically, my friend—The billows seem'd to slumber on the shore."[36]

By the third night the uproar had completely subsided, and the remainder of the run passed with only one incident—a hilarious bit of unintended slapstick that occurred during a scene in which Plotwell and Underplot gain entry to Dr. Fossile's house by disguising themselves as a mummy and a crocodile. Will Pinkethman's crocodile costume was a cumbersome affair that projected far above his own head (his eyes peeped out of the beast's belly) and was anchored with an enormous tail. On the fourth night of the run, the unwieldy tail struck the actress who was playing Mrs. Townley's maid, Sarsnet, and knocked her flat on her back, displaying her undergarments and quantities of bare flesh. If this were not enough, Pinkethman, in attempting to help her to her feet, not only stepped out of character but lost his balance and fell into the open mummy case, becoming so tightly wedged that stage carpenters had to be summoned to cut him loose. Far from objecting to an interruption of some thirty minutes, the audience enjoyed the spectacle so hugely that a repetition of the impromptu scene was called for—but not presented—on the next night.[37]

The Confederates is an amusing if unreliable account of Anne's involvement in the affair of *Three Hours*. Whether she was culpable or not, or threw such a tantrum, in good satirical fashion the author presented "Mrs. Oldfield" at her imperious best and titillated his readers with bits of gossip about her private life. The story is interesting for what it reveals about her public image at the time. That her fine house and social connections were objects of satire suggests, at the very least, that they were well known to the theatergoing public. Clearly, Charles Churchill had already begun to make good his project of placing her in the company of "Persons of the best Condition."

10

The Patent Company

Mindful of competition from Lincoln's Inn Fields, and perhaps too conscious of their position as the established "Old House," the Drury Lane managers pursued a conservative policy, emphasizing their big stars and treating plays as vehicles for them. The results could sometimes be brilliant, but successes became fewer. The company of young players that had successfully challenged Betterton, Bracegirdle, and Barry was sinking into complacent middle age. In the season of 1717–18, Anne appeared in only one new play, *The Non-Juror*, Colley Cibber's anti-Jacobite adaptation of Molière's *Tartuffe*. Molière's characters were transferred to an English setting, with Anne playing the daughter, Maria, a coquette in the Lady Betty tradition. Owing to its topical interest, the play ran for sixteen consecutive performances, finishing the season with a total of twenty-three. The theater was crowded as it had not been for years and Cibber was rumored to have made nearly one thousand pounds,[1] but except for one performance by a summer company at Richmond Hill and one more performance at Drury Lane in October 1718, the play was not performed again during Anne's lifetime.

In September and October 1718, the Drury Lane company was invited to perform in the new theater that George I had constructed in the Great Hall of Hampton Court.[2] The bill of seven plays included *The Beaux' Stratagem*, *The Constant Couple*, and *Rule a Wife and Have a Wife*, in which Anne undoubtedly appeared. The German-speaking monarch, who seems to have preferred comedy to tragedy, demonstrated his appreciation in tangible fashion by paying the company's expenses and proffering a gift of two hundred pounds.

Basking in the favor of the royal family and the public, the actor-managers felt secure enough to spend nearly six hundred pounds—an unprecedented amount—on costumes and scenery for a revival of Dryden's *All for Love* on December 3. The expenditure was well repaid, for the revival ran for six consecutive performances and a total of ten for the season, a more successful showing than for many new plays—and there were no author's benefits to deduct from the profits. Dryden's decorous dramatization of the love and death of Antony and Cleopatra had premiered at Drury Lane in 1677 and later passed into the repertory of Betterton's company at Lincoln's Inn Fields, where Betterton played Antony opposite Barry as Cleopatra and Bracegirdle as Octavia. But over the years it had been performed infrequently; the revival of 1718 was advertised, if slightly inaccurately, as "Not perform'd these Twelve Years." No doubt some of its success can be attributed to the lavishness of the production, with new costumes and scenery "proper to the play." But the cast was new, too, and excitement was certainly generated by the prospect of seeing, for the first time, Booth as Antony, Oldfield as Cleopatra, and Porter as Octavia.[3]

On the surface, at least, the adulterous Egyptian queen was a departure for Anne in tragedy. But one should never underestimate the power of a stage persona. As Anne played her, Cleopatra was cut from much the same cloth as Andromache, Mary, Queen of Scots, and Cato's daughter. "Majestical Dignity" was the keynote. A great favorite with audiences was Cleopatra's first encounter with Antony in act 2, just after his stalwart general, Ventidius, has persuaded him to abandon her, become a Roman and a man again, and join battle with Octavius Caesar. In this scene, in which Cleopatra must use both her considerable wiles and her wit to find favor with Antony again, we are told that Anne's dignified bearing and manner, like Booth's, "commanded the applause and approbation of the most judicious critics."[4] That was apparently what Augustan audiences wanted to see, for *All for Love* became a popular addition to the repertory.

In embarking upon a series of handsomely costumed and decorated revivals, the actor-managers performed an important service, rekindling interest in important but neglected works. *The Way of the World* is Congreve's best known, most highly regarded comedy, but its early stage history gave no sign of its eventual success. John Downes, the prompter at Lincoln's Inn Fields when the play was first presented in 1700, observed that it had been brilliantly acted, but, being "too Keen a Satyr," did not find the receptive audiences that Betterton's company had anticipated.[5] Thereafter, the play was seldom performed. During the period of reorganization and eventual union of the rival companies it did not migrate into the Drury Lane repertory along with other Congreve comedies such as *Love for Love* and *The Old Batchelor*. The revival of *The Way of the World,* in January 1718, was therefore advertised as new at Drury Lane, with "All the Characters being new drest."[6] Why did the actor-managers at long last perceive its many fine qualities? Very likely they were on the lookout for any comedy that might be a vehicle for Wilks and Oldfield and saw it chiefly in those terms. (It should be remembered that Cibber cherished the memory of Anne Bracegirdle's portrayal of Millamant.) Whatever their motives, the success of the revival was decisive in establishing the popularity of the play. In Millamant, Anne had a sparkling new comic heroine, all too rare a commodity in this period.

If audiences flocked to see Booth and Oldfield in *All for Love* and Wilks and Oldfield in *The Way of the World,* the destructive side of a managerial policy geared for a few stars could be seen in the occasionally insensitive treatment of a good piece that did not quite fit the formula. In 1719, a new playwright, John Hughes, offered his tragedy, *The Siege of Damascus,* for production at Drury Lane. There is some evidence that the actor-managers had to be compelled by the Lord Chamberlain to accept it at all[7] and considerably more evidence that they treated the play in cavalier fashion, insisting upon a major change in the text and disregarding the playwright's wishes in the casting of the three leading roles. Hughes had written the role of the ambitious young warrior, Phocyas, for Wilks, who, he felt, could "more truly touch all the tenderness of the heart and variety of passions in the character" than any other member of the company. He had designed Caled for Booth, who could give the Saracen chief "very great strength and lustre," and the devout Christian heroine Eudocia for Anne, whose "grace and beauty" had added to the attractions of so many virtuous heroines.[8] By the time the play went into rehearsal, Hughes was mortally ill and unable to take any part in the proceedings. The premiere on February 17, 1720, featured Mary Porter instead of Anne as Eudocia, Booth instead of Wilks as Phocyas, and Mills as Caled. With the exception of Mills, clearly a second-rank actor, the players could not be objected to on grounds of popularity or general excellence. The point, however, was that Hughes had conceived the characters with the qualities of specific actors in mind, and that such casting would have provided a "reading" of the play that was quite different from the production that reached the stage.

In looking at the generally sorry record of new drama during the reign of George I, it is hard to know where to lay the blame. Between 1715 and 1730, Anne appeared in no fewer than twenty-three new plays, of which only two were successful enough to become stock pieces. Some of these were works by established playwrights: Rowe (*The Tragedy of Lady Lady Jane Gray*), Addison (*The Drummer*, which closed after only three performances at Drury Lane in 1716 but was revived with great success at Lincoln's Inn Fields in 1722), Cibber (*The Non-Juror; The Refusal; Caesar in Egypt*), Centlivre (*The Cruel Gift; The Artifice*), and Thomas Southerne (*The Spartan Dame*). Some were the early efforts of writers who would become famous later: Edward Young (*Busiris*), John Gay (*Three Hours After Marriage; The Captives*) and Henry Fielding (*Love in Several Masques*). Charles Johnson, the author of several moderately successful comedies, failed with *The Sultaness*, a tragedy adapted from Racine's *Bajazet*, and a comedy, *The Masquerade*. Ambrose Philips was unable to repeat the success of his Racine adaptation, *The Distrest Mother*, with his Shakespeare adaptation, *Humfrey, Duke of Gloster*.

Anne's appearance in two Shakespeare adaptations in the 1720s raises the issue of the curious position of Shakespeare's plays on the early eighteenth-century stage.[9] On the one hand, most of his major tragedies—*Hamlet, Othello, Julius Caesar, Macbeth,* and *King Lear*—had been performed regularly since the reopening of the theaters in 1660, *Macbeth* and *King Lear* in Restoration adaptations. Shakespeare's reputation as a tragic poet was such that Rowe invoked his spirit to bless the enterprise of *Jane Shore*. But after the early years of the Restoration, Shakespeare's comedies fared poorly, especially in comparison with works by other Elizabethan playwrights: Jonson, Beaumont, and Fletcher. Performed rarely, and then often in adaptations that were effectively new plays, such as *The Jew of Venice* and *The Taming of the Shrew; or, Sawny the Scot*, the comedies that so greatly pleased later generations of playgoers apparently did not suit early eighteenth-century audiences. Thus it was that Anne, who seemed born to play Beatrice opposite Wilks as Benedick, and who, in her youthful days of breeches roles, would have been a delightful Rosalind or Portia, never appeared in a Shakespeare comedy. Her only association with Shakespeare was tenuous and deservedly unsuccessful.

In *Humfrey, Duke of Gloster,* she played the uncharacteristic role of the evil and manipulative Queen Margaret. The author admitted taking "one or two hints," and a few lines here and there, from the second part of Shakespeare's *Henry VI.* Beyond that he greatly enlarged, but did not improve, the central female roles. Aaron Hill's *King Henry V,* in which Anne played the French princess, Catharine, was likewise unsuccessful. Claiming to have built *"a new fabric"* on Shakespeare's foundation, Hill added a melodramatic subplot involving a conspiracy to kill the king and the character of Henry's cast-off mistress, Harriet (a fine fifteenth-century name!). Catherine, torn between love and patriotism, behaves with unfailing nobility. Since Hill found no place for the charming scenes in Shakespeare's *Henry V* in which the French princess practices her English and the king woos her in broken French, Anne was to be denied even a snippet of Shakespearean comedy.

In the winter of 1719, the fortunes of the new patent company changed when it ran headlong into opposition from the Lord Chamberlain, the Duke of Newscastle.[10] The reasons were partly political, for Steele had become one of Newcastle's most vocal opponents in Parliament, where the Whigs had become deeply divided. But there were echoes of Christopher Rich's troubles in 1709. This time it was the actor-managers who needed to be shown their place. Newcastle ordered that a part belonging to Booth be given to another actor. In doing so, he may have been legally within his rights, but he was trampling on actors' cherished prerogatives. In arrogant language that seemed calculated to inflame the Lord Chamberlain, Cibber refused to obey the order,[11] heaping more fuel on the fire with his fulsome praise of Steele in the preface to *Ximena,* published that fall. The inference seemed clear: the actor-managers were firmly supporting their partner, however unpopular he had become with a powerful faction of the Whigs.

Then, on November 11, John Dennis's version of *Coriolanus—The Invader of His Country; or, The Fatal Resentment*—was produced at Drury Lane under circumstances that reflected badly on the management. The subtitle was very nearly prophetic. The version of the play that reached the stage had been altered against Dennis's wishes, and he was outraged by the epilogue Cibber had written for Anne (who had no part in the play itself), calling it "a wretched Medley of Impudence and Nonsense."[12] Feeling that Cibber had betrayed him and that his play had, in general, been treated with contempt by the actor-managers, in his dedication to the published text Dennis urged the Lord Chamberlain to exert his power to chastise and control the offenders.

In contrast to a different Lord Chamberlain, who held off for several months before silencing Rich in 1709, Newcastle acted quickly. On December 19, he directed Wilks, Booth, and Steele to prohibit Cibber from acting and from engaging in his managerial duties. Exercising his powers as master of the royal household, Newcastle then proceeded to close Drury Lane until the managers would agree to the issuing of a new license with Steele's name omitted. Cibber's biographer, Richard Barker, believes that the Lord Chamberlain "compelled the managers to accept a license in which Steele's name was not included."[13] In any event, on January 27, 1720, after Drury Lane had been shut down for three days, the license originally issued to Steele, Wilks, Cibber, and Booth was revoked and a new one was issued to the three actor-managers. The legal nicety was that Steele remained in possession of the patent, but without a license he could not participate in—or profit from—the company management.

On January 28, 1720, Drury Lane reopened with a performance of *The Careless Husband.* The Lord Chamberlain demonstrated his intention to keep a close rein on Drury Lane, administering a special oath of obedience to the members of the company, ordering the afore-mentioned production of *The Siege of Damascus,* and issuing an order that prices could not be raised without his permission, a move that struck at the practice of charging higher prices not only for new but for "new-drest" productions, such as the revival of *All for Love.* On February 2, 1720, he required that the "Managers of the Sd Company Acting under his Majts Licence . . . take care that no benefit might be Allowed for the future to any Actor before Mrs Oldfield and Mrs Porters benefitt Night."[14] The reasons for this order are not clear. The two actresses were already at the top of the benefit schedule, with Anne's coming first and Porter's third, after Mills. For a brief time, Mary Porter did move into second place, but when the earlier pattern was reasserted, the order was not invoked. Perhaps the point was that one could never be sure when and for what purpose the Lord Chamberlain would intervene.

A more serious personal problem was shortly to occupy Anne. At the age of thirty-seven, she was pregnant again. Apparently healthy and vigorous during the first three months, she performed as usual in the spring of 1720, appearing in the last production of the regular season, *The Old Batchelor,* on June 2. In the fall, she was conspicuously absent. Plays in which she routinely appeared could not just be dropped from the repertory; audiences expected to see them, and other actors had important roles in them. The result was that some of her parts were taken by rising younger members of the company, Sarah Thurmond and Christiana Horton.[15] Some plays with which she was particularly associated—*The Careless Husband, The Tender Husband, The Distrest Mother, Jane Shore, All for Love,* and *The Way of the World*—were simply not performed.

Her son, named Charles after his father, was probably born in the late fall of 1720, for his age was given as nine when he entered Westminster School in 1730. By the new year, Anne had returned to her daunting routine of evening performances and daytime rehearsals. An advertisement in the *Original Weekly Journal* for January 7, 1721, only hinted at the reasons for her long absence: "Last Monday Night the Celebrated Mrs. Oldfield performed at the Theatre in Drury Lane, for the first Time since her Indisposition." It is difficult to believe that the nature of her "indisposition" was not common knowledge in the small world of London theatergoers.

There had been rumors of a grave illness. On December 3, 1720, the *Weekly Journal, or Saturday's Post* had gone so far as to report that "On Tuesday last in the Evening died Mrs. Oldfield, the famous Actress at the Drury-Lane Play-house." The *Weekly Journal, or British Gazetteer* hastened to assure its readers on December 31 that "The Celebrated Mrs. Oldfield, who had long been indispos'd, and reported to be dead, is so well recover'd that she will act her Part next Monday Night, in the Comedy of Sir Foppling Flutter [*The Man of Mode*], when 'tis expected there will be an Extraordinary crowded House." If the first report was, in Mark Twain's memorable phrase, greatly exaggerated, the second sounds suspiciously like a press release. Neither one alluded to her confinement.

Susannah Verbruggen had died at the age of thirty-seven, under nearly identical circumstances, opening the way for Anne's advancement in 1703. Anne resumed her career as if nothing had happened. But the pregnancy and possible postpartum complications had taken their toll in a small way. "In the Wearing of her Person," Cibber wrote, "she was particularly fortunate; her Figure was always improving until her Thirty-sixth Year."[16] By "figure" he of course meant her appearance in general, and so the reference is not to the plumpness evident in two of the Garrick Club portraits but to a more general change—the vicissitudes of age. To adoring observers, however, she never ceased to give the impression of youth and vitality.

Shortly after her return to the stage, Anne began to rehearse Cibber's new comedy, *The Refusal; or, The Ladies Philosophy*, a free adaptation of Molière's *Les Femmes Savantes*. The title is almost the best thing about the play, which is set during the period of frenzied speculation in South Sea Company stock. ("Refusal" refers not only to stock options but also to the device by which Witling believes he has obtained the "refusal" of Sir Gilbert Wrangle's daughter Charlotte and to her refusal of him.) Anne took the hand-tailored role of Sophronia, Sir Gilbert's elder daughter, an eccentric young lady so caught up in her study of philosophy and the poetry of Milton that she must be wooed in blank verse. The scene of her wooing, and a scene in which Sir Gilbert's wife, Lady Wrangle, chides her maidservant and the cook for using her new translation of the *Passion of Byblis* for waste paper, are amusing, but throughout most of the play, Cibber seemed to be counting on his actors to enliven material that had little inherent sparkle.

The Refusal failed spectacularly, playing to hissing audiences throughout its six-night run. An anti-Cibber cabal, formed by the journalist Nathaniel Mist, was chiefly responsible for disturbances in the theater,[17] but Cibber had also misread the public mood about the recent, disastrous financial crisis, the South Sea Bubble. The "bursting" of the South Sea Bubble not six months earlier, when the company's stock, which had risen as high as one thousand pounds, sank to £124, had ruined thousands of small investors and touched off an investigation that revealed the misdeeds of several government ministers. Cibber's epilogue apologized for evoking painful memories, noting that the play had been written "Before your fair Possessions were betray'd." Anne herself was an investor in the South Sea Company. Two deeds, giving power of attorney for the sale of her stock in the amount of one thousand pounds in 1718, and fifteen hundred pounds in 1723, are preserved in the theater collection of the Garrick Club.[18] They do not indicate the extent of her investment or whether she too suffered in the famous economic disaster.

On April 14, 1721, Margaret Saunders acted for the last time. In *Faithful Memoirs,* Edmund Curll reported that "the Violence of an Asthmatical Indisposition obliged her to leave the Stage."[19] She had

had a respectable career as a supporting actress, being known chiefly for her portrayal of "decayed nurses, widows, and old maids."[20] Her repertoire included Lady Wishfort in the revival of *The Way of the World,* Lady Haughty in *Epicoene,* Lady Fidget in *The Country Wife,* and Aunt Tipkin in *The Tender Husband.* Her position in Anne's household from the Southampton Street days onward is difficult to define, but it can probably be described by the term "dependent"—neither paid servant nor social equal. After her retirement from the stage, she would devote her life to Anne.

A high point of the season of 1721–22 was a revival of Dryden's *Aureng-Zebe,* in which Anne played the captive queen, Indamora, whose beauty provokes rivalry between an aging Mogul emperor and two of his sons. In addition to Anne as Indamora, the cast of this splendid revival—the first performance of the play at Drury Lane since 1713—included Wilks as the noble, ardent Aureng-Zebe, Booth as the brother and rival, Morat, and Porter as the lustful queen, Nourmahal.[21] Once more, a successful revival became a vehicle for Drury Lane's leading actors, showing them to advantage in the face of competition from Anthony Boheme, James Quin, Lacy Ryan, Jane Rogers Bullock, and Anna Maria Seymour—rising stars at Lincoln's Inn Fields.

It would be a year before Anne had another good role, this time in a new play—Steele's *Conscious Lovers.* Steele had been reinstated as coholder of the Drury Lane license in May 1721,[22] but relations between him and the actor-managers were never easy. Financial considerations remained a problem. Booth, Wilks, and Cibber argued, with some justification, that Steele did not shoulder his fair share of managerial responsibilities and that he had failed to provide them with new plays. At last, in the fall of 1722, he presented them with their first new comedy hit in many seasons, and their biggest financial success of any season thus far.[23]

In *The Conscious Lovers* Anne played Indiana, a beautiful orphan wrongly suspected of being the kept mistress of a young gentleman whose father wishes him to marry the daughter of a wealthy merchant. The role required her to play serious emotions absolutely straight, without any playful leavening. (In keeping with the elevated tone, she was paired romantically, this time, with Booth as the honorable lover, Bevil, Jr.) The scene in act 5, in which Indiana is confronted by the merchant Sealand and defends the honor of her lover, knowing that in so doing she must relinquish her claim to him, called for the dignified pathos of Jane Shore with a touch of the distracted Semandra: ". . . if these Actions, Sir, can in a careful Parent's Eye commend him to a Daughter, give yours, Sir, give her to my honest, generous *Bevil*— What have I to do, but sigh, and weep, to rave, run wild, a Lunatick in Chains, or hid in Darkness, mutter in distracted Starts, and broken Accents, my strange, strange Story!"[24]

Indiana is radically different from the comic heroines Anne had played since her apprenticeship days, being neither lively, witty, affected, nor in need of judicious taming. Her appeal is almost wholly in her helplessness, a quality above all others that is difficult to imagine Anne playing. But it is important to remember how attractive she managed to be in the often-colorless roles in her tragic repertoire. Whether or not Steele created Indiana with Anne in mind—he had been working on *The Conscious Lovers,* on and off, for many years— he was apparently confident that she could adapt her tragic style to the more commonplace world of comedy.[25] It is clear that she succeeded admirably, for the emotionally charged reunion of Indiana and Sealand, her long-lost father, was a particular favorite with audiences.

Despite the popularity of the play, Steele felt compelled to defend himself against the critics who objected to a comedy that provoked tears, especially in the stronger sex. "Men ought not to be laugh'd at for weeping, till we are come to a more clear Notion of what is to be imputed to the Hardness of the Head, and the Softness of the Heart; and I think it was very politely said of Mr. Wilks to one who told him there was a *General* weeping for *Indiana,* I'll warrant he'll fight none the worse for that."[26] The general in question has been identified as Charles Churchill, perhaps because the notion of his weeping openly during Anne's performance is so appealing. It should be noted, however, that Churchill was not promoted to brigadier general until 1727. At the premiere of *The Conscious Lovers,* he would have been, at most, a weeping colonel.

In Anne's career, Indiana was merely a side excursion; her next role in a successful new comedy would be the high-spirited Lady Townly, and her popularity in roles of a decidedly amoral cast—Mrs. Brittle, Mrs. Loveit, Laetitia—was undiminished. But she played her part in the success of *The Conscious Lovers,* which is rightly considered a landmark in English comedy. Its combination of pathos and conventional comedy (for Indiana and her tribulations are only a small part of the whole) would be standard by the middle of the eighteenth century. The character of Indiana's lover, Bevil, Jr., would also become a standard figure in mid-century drama, in which strong, attractive representatives of male authority were not only the lovers but the protectors of vulnerable, dependent heroines. A tradition of lively young lovers, well matched in wit, energy, and sexuality, was beginning to give way to early stirrings of benevolent paternalism in male-female relations.

11
Apotheosis

By 1723, when Anne was forty, her professional life had settled into a comfortable pattern, with minor variations from one season to another. She would perform between eighty and one hundred times between mid-September and the end of May or early June; the total number of performances depended in part upon whether she appeared in a successful new play with a long run.[1] Despite her growing fame as a tragic actress, her basic repertoire consisted chiefly of comic characters: Lady Betty Modish, Biddy Tipkin, Lady Heartwell, Mrs. Sullen, Lady Dainty, Estifania, Mrs. Brittle, Mrs. Loveit, Berinthia, the Scornful Lady, Laetitia, Ruth, Caelia, Millamant, and Indiana. Only four tragic roles were performed as frequently: Andromache, Marcia, Jane Shore, and Cleopatra.[2]

An astute manager, she tended her stock of roles carefully, keeping the total about the same from year to year. Room was made for occasional new roles by dropping a few from time to time.[3] Her senior colleagues in the company did the same, partly because it made sense to maintain a manageable repertoire, partly because they enjoyed performing with each other, and partly to cultivate younger members of the company. It is not surprising that they gave up roles from time to time, but that they kept so many. Audiences never tired of seeing them in the same characters year after year.[4] Depending upon a relatively constant stock of roles, the actors fortified themselves against dry spells, such as the seasons of 1723–24 and 1724–25, when Anne did not appear in any successful new plays or revivals.

In the spring of 1725, Anne moved from the Haymarket to an even finer new house, number 59 Grosvenor Street in the parish of St. George, Hanover. Geographically she had come nearly full circle;

lower Grosvenor Street, near New Bond Street, was only a few blocks from her birthplace in Pall Mall. But in other respects, she had moved far beyond the scene of her childhood. Mayfair, as the area is commonly known, takes its name from the annual fair that was held in mid-May in an open tract of land north of Piccadilly. In 1720, the Grosvenor family began to develop their extensive property north of the May Fair site for residential use, hoping to attract fashionable tenants from the more crowded, no longer desirable, districts to the east. With her instinct for fashion, Anne became one of the first residents of Mayfair.[5]

Number 59 Grosvenor Street—later renumbered 60—still stands, but the neighborhood has changed greatly. Once a street of handsome private homes, lower Grosvenor Street has been absorbed into the upmarket commercial district around New Bond Street. Number 60 reflects the change. Its interior was virtually gutted by a fire in 1897; since then, the walls on the west side have been broken through to make a common building with the house next door, and the front half of the ground floor, inside and out, has been radically altered to create a large reception room with great plate glass windows overlooking the street.

The house was said to have cost Anne twenty-two hundred pounds,[6] a considerable sum for 1725, but it was one of the smaller structures in the development: twenty-three feet wide and eighty feet deep.[7] The rooms were correspondingly small. Anne could not afford and did not need an establishment as grand as Baron Walpole's across the street at number 16, or Sir Robert Rich's next door to the west. Her household in 1725 consisted of herself, her five-year-old son, her companion Margaret Saunders, and several servants. Churchill undoubtedly stayed with her much of the time, but, like Maynwaring, he always maintained a separate residence.[8]

The present structure consists of four stories and a garret, but the original house was evidently only three stories high. The sale catalogue of the contents of the house, which were put up for auction four months after Anne's death, refers only to the ground floor, the "first pair of stairs," the "second pair of stairs," and the garret.[9] Each floor had three or four rooms. The second floor, with its higher ceilings, contained the public rooms—two parlors, the dining room, and a tiny "closet" furnished with a settee, several stools, and an "India Japan" tea table, cabinet, and trunk. A room such as this was often the setting of an intimate scene in a comedy.

The third floor consisted of private rooms, including the "Wrought bed-chamber," a relatively large room at the front of the house, which was a true boudoir, furnished with chairs and a tea table, in which one could also entertain intimate friends. Forty-seven auction items are listed for this room, including a number of paintings and two bed-steads. The other second-floor rooms, much more simply furnished, are decribed as the "Chince" bedchamber and the "Yellow damask" bedchamber. The ground floor, as the working part of the house, contained the kitchen, a scullery and laundry room, and a "closet" furnished as a bedchamber, probably for a servant. The rest of the servants slept in the garret.

The inventory of furnishings tells us very little about the lives or relationships of the inhabitants, but it brings us a little closer to the elusive private woman who left no written record of her likes and dislikes. We know that she furnished her home in the fashion of the day, with china dishes and figurines, lacquerware, needlepoint, fine linen and damask, numerous paintings "after" such great masters as Brueghel and Holbein, as well as "antique" statuary, and that her library included a preponderance of recent English literature. The last entry in the auction catalogue bears the stamp of the actress-owner: "Plays in 218 Vol."[10]

The Grosvenor Street house was a place in which to relax and be private, but it can also be viewed as a stage setting for another kind of performance, hinted at by Cibber when he spoke of Anne's conduct "in private Societies, where Women of the best Rank might have borrow'd some part of her Behaviour without the least Diminution of their Sense or Dignity."[11] Cultivating her public image as Churchill's respectable mistress, welcome in the best homes, on speaking terms with the royal family, Anne was almost always on stage. Her "role" in fashionable society was to be petted and patronized.

Behind the image of a gay, fashionable lady, whose dress and mannerisms were said to be widely imitated, was the reality of her working life. She was to be seen riding in her carriage with her friend Lord Hervey, but the same carriage took her to work at Drury Lane several times a week during the season. It was reported that she would often go directly to the theater from the homes of her fashionable friends, wearing the same dress onstage in which she had dined a few hours earlier. Onstage, however, the dress became a costume, an appurtenance of her trade. As a woman of substance, she fulfilled her charitable obligations, pledging two guineas—the standard contribution—to a new charity, Westminster Hospital, in 1724.[12] But as a working woman, half of whose annual income depended upon a well-attended benefit, she was expected to "wait upon" her wealthy and titled friends to sell them tickets for a guinea or more.

She might also be called upon to coach a titled young lady who dabbled in theater. In 1727, the Duchess of Marlborough wrote to Charles Churchill, requesting that Anne instruct her favorite grand-daughter, Lady Diana Spencer, in the role she was to play in an amateur theatrical. Churchill politely begged off, noting that Anne had been ill and that Lady Dye's role was one to which "Mrs. Oldfield is a stranger." But Anne, perhaps mindful that it would not do to refuse the formidable duchess so firmly, asked him to add that she was at Lady Dye's service, although she doubted that her assistance was needed.[13]

By the time she was settled in Mayfair, Anne had attained an enviable degree of wealth, comfort, and social acceptance. But the evidence of her performance schedule indicates that she had no intention of retiring from the stage to enjoy these privileges more fully. Clearly her career remained paramount.

In the season of 1725–26, she acquired two exceptionally fine new roles, the first of which was Calista in a revival of *The Fair Penitent*. Rowe's tragedy had not been a great success at its premiere at Lincoln's Inn Fields in 1703, despite the impressive cast: Barry (Calista), Powell (Lothario), Betterton (Horatio), Verbruggen (Altamont), and Brace-girdle (Lavinia). The last two acts, especially, were not well received.[14] A mishap, which occurred during the first run, did not help the situation. According to the common practice, Powell's dresser "lay in" for him as Lothario's corpse in the last act. One evening Powell, quite drunk backstage by the end of the performance, forgot where his servant was and called out to him for assistance, threatening dire punishments. "Poor Warren" obediently leapt from the bier, entangling poor Mrs. Barry in yards of drapery, and showering her with candlesticks, books, bones, and other props of the charnel-house scene.[15] Even if the play had been better received, memories of the incident would have made it difficult to continue the run.

After 1703, there are no records of performances of *The Fair Penitent* until the reconstitution of the Lincoln's Inn Fields company under John Rich in 1714. But even then, the play remained something of a stepchild in the repertory, performed infrequently and generally by second-rank players. At Drury Lane, it was attempted by the younger players in the summer company in 1720 and 1721.

Part of the reason for the play's failure to take hold lay in Rowe's depiction of the heroine and her situation. It would have been easier for eighteenth-century audiences to feel sympathetic toward a woman who has been seduced and abandoned if she had responded in more conventional fashion—going mad or finding a male champion to avenge her. Calista betrays no such weakness. She scorns the gentle, loving Altamont to whom her father has betrothed her, defies Altamont's virtuous friend Horatio, and remains attracted, however unwillingly, to her callous seducer, Lothario. A critic in 1714 flatly called her a whore, insisting that she was not truly penitent but merely sorry that she has been found out. Samuel Johnson later expressed similar doubts about Calista's penitence, and worried that Lothario "retains too much of the spectator's kindness."[16] The very elements that make *The Fair Penitent* one of the most interesting tragedies of the period created problems for its interpreters.

Yet if readers of the play were sometimes uncomfortable, spectators seemed well pleased with the production that opened at Drury Lane on November 12, 1725. Anne solved the problem of the flaws in Calista's character by ignoring them. Her Calista was so magnificent in her pride, so dignified in her demeanor, as to be admirable in spite of herself. In a famous scene in act 3, in which Horatio confronts Calista with a letter that she has written to Lothario, begging him to meet her secretly, she tears it to shreds, crying:

> To atoms thus,
> Thus let me tear the vile detested falsehood,
> The wicked lying evidence of shame.[17]

Conveniently destroying the evidence of her shameful attraction to Lothario, Calista boldly outfaces Horatio, who, although given to meddling, is clearly a figure to be respected. As Anne played the scene, one saw not the sinfulness but the grandeur of the woman:

> Her excellent clear Voice of Passion, her piercing flaming Eye, with Manner and Action suiting, us'd to make me shrink with Awe, and seem'd to put her monitor *Horatio* into a Mouse-hole.

I almost gave him up for a troublesome Puppy; and though Mr. *Booth* played *Lothario* I could hardly leg him up to the Importance of triumphing over such a finish'd Piece of Perfection, that seemed to be too much dignified to lose her Virtue.[18]

Of course, Calista *has* lost her virtue, and there is no way of ignoring it, since her transgression is the central point of the play. But the 1725 production managed to gloss over this detail. Booth played Lothario as "gallantly gay" rather than as "wickedly wanton," seeming to one observer "in some sort to apologize for the Frailty of the Fair." If Calista had succumbed to "any Jessamy Jackanapes, who had Assurrance enough affectedly to prattle raptured Nonsense to her" we could hardly respect her—but then, what woman could have resisted the graceful, manly, honey-tongued Booth?[19]

The Fair Penitent succeeded in 1725 as a vehicle for its stars perhaps more than for its intrinsic merits. Although Booth performed Lothario for only three seasons before his retirement, the role was often mentioned as one of his greatest achievements. For Anne, the new character became one of her most popular and admired roles. She played Calista at least twice each season until she left the stage and in 1730 chose *The Fair Penitent* for her benefit. The success of the revival gained the play a permanent place in the eighteenth-century repertory.

On January 11, 1726, Anne appeared in Vanbrugh's *Provok'd Wife* (1697), which had never been performed at Drury Lane. Once more, a handsomely produced revival was a resounding success. But it nearly failed to come off. As Cibber tells the story, at the first reading of the play, when parts were to be assigned, he suggested that Wilks leave the role of Lady Brute's would-be lover Constant to another actor, since it was "a Character of less Action than he generally appear'd in," and since Wilks, who had complained about his heavy work load, could use the rest. Wilks's response was predictable. It was one thing for him to complain of being overworked and quite another to be edged out of a role in a major revival that had the backing of the court and "Persons of Quality." Attempts to soothe his wounded feelings only made matters worse, causing Anne at one point to titter behind her fan. At last she spoke, rounding on Cibber with, "Pooh! you are all a Parcel of Fools, to make such a rout about nothing." In this fashion, says Cibber, she removed some of the onus from Wilks, distributing it among the managers. It was an easy matter for her to persuade him to take the part of Constant, removing the last barrier to a successful production.[20] (No suggestion was made that Wilks, then about sixty, was too old to play Lady Brute's ardent suitor.)

As the unhappily married Lady Brute, Anne had an opportunity to employ her full comedic arsenal. Musing upon marital fidelity, fending off (and later nearly succumbing to) her determined admirer, attempting to explain the appearance of Constant and Heartfree in her closet, Lady Brute makes the best of a bad situation by exercising her wits. At the end of the play, she and Sir John do not agree to separate, as do Mr. and Mrs. Sullen in *The Beaux' Stratagem;* the possibility remains that she will eventually make Sir John what he persists in believing he already is—a cuckold. (The text is ambiguous on this point, and much would have depended upon what the actors communicated through gestures and facial expressions.)

While successful new plays of the late 1720s did not contain sexually suggestive scenes, older plays with such scenes—*The Provok'd Wife, The Relapse, The Old Batchelor,* and *The Man of Mode* (to name only a few that were a regular part of Anne's repertoire)—were performed season after season to the evident delight of audiences. Perhaps the lax mores of an earlier age could be appreciated as quaint relics, like outworn styles of dress.

Anne chose *The Provok'd Wife* for her benefit on March 3, an indication both of the success of the revival and of her personal triumph. A little more than three weeks later, Vanbrugh died after a brief illness. It is difficult to imagine Anne's career without him. He had promoted her during the crucial apprenticeship period at Drury Lane by giving her her first leading role, Alinda in *The Pilgrim,* and enlarging the role of Jacinta for her in *The False Friend.* The extent to which he was responsible for the favorable treatment she received at the Haymarket in 1706, which offended Anne Bracegirdle, is less certain, but his influence at the time was considerable. Above all, like George Farquhar he left her an invaluable legacy in his plays.

On November 20, 1727, a gentleman who called himself Richard Savage, son of the late Earl Rivers, got involved in a tavern brawl in which a man was killed. Savage was charged with murder, convicted, and eventually granted a free pardon, owing to the intervention of friends who had influence with Queen Caroline and Robert Walpole. Anne Oldfield is said to have been one of those influential friends. No other legend about Anne is more difficult to sort out than the story of her relationship with Savage. It was recounted by no less estimable a figure than Samuel Johnson, whose justly famous biography, *The Life of Richard Savage, Esq.,* published in 1744, did more than anything else to popularize the story of her benevolence to the poor poet.

In 1718, Savage's first play, *Love in a Veil,* had been produced at Drury Lane. Though it was not deemed worthy of presentation during the regular season it was performed four times in June and July. As a special favor, the author received two benefits. Savage had become something of a cause. He claimed to be the bastard son of the late Earl Rivers, a notorious rake, and the former Countess of Macclesfield, who, after her divorce from the Earl of Macclesfield, had married Cibber's friend Colonel Henry Brett. The story he told of his abandonment in infancy and his mother's refusal to acknowledge him—indeed, her continual persecution of him—seldom failed to touch his listeners. Whatever the truth of his claims, which have never been satisfactorily documented, he was a persuasive advocate on his own behalf. Both Wilks and Steele became early sympathizers, and it is likely that Anne met Savage through them.

In Johnson's account, Anne was so pleased with the young man's conversation and touched by his misfortunes that she granted him a pension of fifty pounds a year. This was, if true, an act of rare generosity, duly noted by Johnson, who did not think much of actors in general. That she was not only an actress but a woman whose "general character" one would prefer not to contemplate made her benevolence all the more triumphant, like the kindness of the good Samaritan.[21]

In 1732, Queen Caroline, having read Savage's poem in honor of her birthday, paid him fifty pounds with the promise of the same amount each year if he were to write an "annual panegyric." By contrast, Johnson observed, Anne Oldfield "was contented with doing good without stipulating for encomiums."[22] In a similar vein, Johnson reported on the failure in 1739 of Savage's friends to raise a fifty-pound annuity sufficient for the poet to live in retirement in Wales. "Savage had a great number to court and to obey for a pension less than that which Mrs. Oldfield paid him without exacting any servilities."[23]

There are, however, discrepancies in the story. On the one hand, Johnson reported that Anne was Savage's constant benefactress, paying him fifty pounds per year from some undetermined date until her death in 1730. Such an amount would surely have been sufficient to relieve his basic needs, if not, perhaps, to enable him to live in a style befitting the "son of the late Earl Rivers." On the other hand, Johnson elsewhere tells of Savage's desperate straits. While he was composing his tragedy, *Sir Thomas Overbury,* produced at Drury Lane in June 1723, "he was without lodging, and often without meat; nor had he any other conveniences for study than the fields or the street allowed him; there he used to walk and form his speeches, and afterwards step into a shop, beg for a few moments the use of the pen and ink, and write down what he had composed, upon paper which he had picked up by accident."[24]

In 1728, after Savage had been given a full pardon and released from prison, he was, according to Johnson, "*as before,* without any other support than accidental favour and uncertain patronage afforded him. . . ."[25] Where, in this, is the fifty-pound annuity from Anne, "which was during her life regularly paid"? The answer must be that Savage was continually revising the story of his life, that Johnson knew this perfectly well, and that he was less interested in reconciling conflicting stories than in developing significant themes. The generous actress was a useful foil for self-interested, tardy, or inadequate benefactors, but her assistance was easily forgotten when it was time to present Savage as a neglected genius.[26]

Is there any basis for the story of the annuity? At least one person who knew both Anne and Savage asserted that there was not. Theophilus Cibber, Colley's son, an actor at Drury Lane in the 1720s, played a leading role in Savage's *Sir Thomas Overbury,* in which the poet himself performed. Despite Savage's attempt, later, to dissociate himself from young Cibber, they were on friendly terms at the time of his imprisonment in 1727. It was to "Dear Theo" that Savage wrote from prison, asking him to deliver a letter to his supposed mother, Mrs. Brett, and adding: "if you can find any decent excuse for shewing it to Mrs. *Oldfield,* do;—for I would have all my friends (and that admirable lady in particular) be satisfied I have done my duty towards her [his mother]."[27] Whether Theo, as requested, found a pretext for showing the letter to Anne is not known, but he later alluded to her appeal to Sir Robert Walpole on Savage's behalf.[28]

In annotating Johnson's *Life* of Savage, young Cibber flatly declared that there was no foundation for the story of the fifty-pound annuity, insisting that she disapproved of Savage greatly, never admitting him to her conversation or her house. Nevertheless, "she, indeed, often relieved him with such donations, as spoke her generous disposition.— But this was on the sollicitation [*sic*] of friends, who frequently set his calamities before her in the most piteous light; and from a principle of humanity, she became not a little instrumental in saving his life."[29] This sounds much nearer the truth than the story of the annuity. Johnson did not consider that fifty pounds a year amounted to nearly a tenth of Anne's income—a goodly tithe—or that there were other, more immediate, demands on her resources.[30]

During her lifetime, Anne was never publicly identified as one of Savage's patrons.[31] After her death, however, she was fair game. Savage told Johnson that he wore mourning for her as he would for a mother. (The allegorical neatness of a mother of two natural sons displacing Savage's "unnatural" mother probably did not escape Johnson's attention.) After 1732, when Anne and Wilks were both dead, Savage asserted that she, not Wilks, had been his principal benefactor.[32] Johnson's biography of Savage elaborated upon this "revised version" of the poet's relations with the Drury Lane actors. No subsequent biographer would dream of omitting the story, and so it was that legend acquired the weight of truth.

In 1943, the transcription of a letter purporting to be from Anne Oldfield to Richard Savage was published in the *Times Literary Supplement*.

Villiers Street
Strand

May 2

Dear Mr Savage

I forward you 10 *l* [£] as a small token of my sympathy for you in your unbounded and unmerited misfortunes. Unnaturel [*sic*] fiend I call her to act so to her own flesh & blood. Be of good cheer. He who watches over us all will yet protect you. I am truly glad that Mr Steele is befriending you. I also will see what Mr Maynwaryng may do for you.

Ever your well wisher

Anne Oldfield[33]

If genuine, the letter would be significant, apart from its text, as the only extant letter in Anne's hand. However, a comparison of the writing with examples of her signature on contracts and other authentic documents indicates that it is not in her hand. There are also several puzzling anomalies. Anne never lived on Villiers Street, although Steele lived there in 1718. More important, Arthur Maynwaring had died long before Savage arrived on the scene. In any case, the letter does nothing more than confirm Theophilus Cibber's claim that Anne made occasional gifts to Savage, "as spoke her generous disposition." In the absence of better evidence, we should remain skeptical about the poet's story of the patronage of a famous, beautiful—and conveniently dead—actress.

With the accession of George II in June 1727, Colonel Charles Churchill was appointed groom of the chamber in the royal household and promoted to brigadier general. The coronation of the new king inspired a burst of patriotic enthusiasm at Drury Lane. The coronation scene in *Henry VIII* was turned into a magnificent spectacle, and after audiences tired of *Henry VIII,* the elaborate pageant was tacked onto succeeding productions—comedies, tragedies, history plays—no matter how irrelevant the subject. By December, however, Anne had begun to rehearse for a production that would compete in popularity with the coronation-year pageantry. *The Provok'd Husband,* which opened on January 10, 1728, provided her with her last and most triumphant comic character.

Lady Townly, a "woman of Quality" whose marriage is endangered by her addiction to gambling, was perfectly tailored for Anne. In completing Vanbrugh's unfinished manuscript, *A Journey to London,* Cibber refashioned (and renamed) the character of Lady Arabella to suit contemporary taste. Vanbrugh had told Cibber that he intended to conclude the play unhappily for Lady Arabella, with her exasperated husband turning her out of the house. But Cibber felt that such a conclusion would be "too severe for comedy."[34] Accordingly, he paved the way for reconciliation by mitigating Lady Arabella's faults and preserving her chastity. He also knew what Anne could do to make the character attractive. We are told that "she slided so gracefully into the foibles, and displayed so humorously the excesses, of a fine woman, too confidant of her power, and led away by her passion for pleasure," that no later actress equaled her in the role, although Peg Woffington came close.[35]

There are echoes of the rattlebrained, pleasure-loving Lady Betty in some of the speeches that Cibber created for Anne, especially the catalogue of "infinite liberties" that a wife may take:

To begin with, in the morning: a married woman may have men at her toilet, invite them to dinner, appoint them a party in a stage box at the play, engross the conversation there, call 'em by their Christian names, talk louder than the players; from thence jaunt into the City, take a frolicsome supper at an India-house, perhaps . . . toast a pretty fellow, then clatter again to this end of town, break with the morning into an assembly, crowd to the hazard table, throw a familiar levant upon some sharp lurching man of quality, and if he demands his money, turn it off with a loud laugh, and cry—you'll owe it to him, to vex him. Ha ha![36]

It is fortunate that a fine observer, the actor Charles Macklin, recorded his impressions of Anne's performance in this scene.

Mrs. Oldfield formed the center of admiration, from her looks, her dress, and her admirable performance. Most of the performers who have played this part since her time . . . had too much *tameness* in their manner, under an idea of its being more *easy* and *well bred;* but Mrs. Oldfield, who was trained in the part by the Author, gave it all the *rage* of fashion and vivacity: She *rushed* upon the stage with full consciousness of youth, beauty, and attraction; and answered all her Lord's questions with such a lively indifference, as to mark the *contrast* as much in their manner of speaking as thinking: but when she came to describe the superior privileges of a married above a single woman, she repeated the whole of that lively speech with a rapidity, and *gaieté de coeur,* that electrified the whole house. Their applause was so unbounded, that when Wilks, who played Lord Townly, answers "Prodigious!" the audience applied that word as a compliment to the actress, and again gave her the shouts of their approbation.[37]

Moral considerations and the desire for a happy ending decreed that Lady Townly undergo a reformation by the end of the play. Cibber set the stage by having her confess, in an aside in act 1, that if she were "weak enough to love this man" she would never get any more money from him. Female submission being the prerequisite of marital harmony, the errant wife acknowledges both her error and her husband's worth in a sentimental reconciliation. There is good fun for the first four acts, however. The audience's satisfaction in seeing Lady Townly tamed was in proportion to its delight in her irrepressible spirits.

On opening night, Cibber's enemies massed for an attack, blaming him rather than Vanbrugh for the coarse humor in the scenes involving Sir Francis Wronghead, his avid wife, and their bumptious children. When Anne stepped forward to recite Cibber's epilogue, she was interrupted by a hiss when she had gone no further than the first seven words. But she had endured worse in the past. Confident of her immense popularity, she calmly fixed the offender in her view, paused for effect, "and spoke the words *poor creature!* loudly enough to be heard by the audience, with such a look of mingled scorn, pity, and contempt, that the most uncommon applause justified her conduct in the particular, and the poor reptile sunk down with fear and trembling."[38] Cibber could not praise her performance highly enough, writing of her many excellences in the role and of the ornaments that she herself provided for Lady Townly—"in all respects the paraphernalia of a woman of quality."[39]

As *The Provok'd Husband* continued to run for a total of thirty-seven performances that season, the actor-managers rewarded Anne with a gift of fifty guineas.[40] They could well afford it. According to Cibber, *The Provok'd Husband* earned greater receipts than any play of the past fifty years, despite competition from *The Beggar's Opera,* which opened at Lincoln's Inn Fields at the end of January and took London by storm.[41] As a special favor to her friend Lady Carteret, who had been absent from London during the first run of the play, Anne appeared in *The Provok'd Husband* on June 13, the last performance of the season. Mrs. Delany, who was present on the occasion, reported to her sister that Anne had "topped her part, and notwithstanding it [the play] deserves criticism in reading, nobody (let them be ever so wise) can see it without being extremely pleased, for it is acted to admiration."[42]

In the spring of 1728, Henry Fielding submitted his first play for production at Drury Lane. Whatever the merits of *Love in Several Masques,* it had the misfortune of appearing in the wake of *The Provok'd Husband* and of suffering in comparison. It lasted for only four performances, earning Fielding one author's benefit. Accepting blame for the inadequacy of the piece, he was full of praise for its performers, especially for Anne, who, "though she had contracted a slight indisposition by her violent fatigue in the part of Lady Townly, was prevailed upon to grace that of Lady Matchless," a lively young widow. Mrs. Oldfield, he assured his readers, had not only exerted herself in the role, but had given him the benefit of her superior experience and judgment in suggesting some corrections. "But the ravishing perfections of this lady," the smitten author continued, "are so much the admiration of every eye and every ear, that they will remain fixed in the memory of many, when these light scenes shall be forgotten."[43]

At about the same time, Anne captivated a visitor from France who left behind an equally glowing account of her attractions. The charm of her voice, appearance, and manner were so great, he wrote, that "she made me love the English theater, for which I had at first but small liking." He studied English so that he might be able to understand her better and never failed to attend plays in which she was appearing, studying the texts beforehand.[44] He was not Voltaire, as is often claimed (although Voltaire was in England at the time), but the novelist and adventurer Abbé Prévost, author of *Manon Lescaut*. He paid tribute to the impression of youth and gaiety that Anne gave on the stage, calling her *"une Fille incomparable."* With Cibber and Fielding, Prévost left a striking portrait of Anne in her mid forties, in an era when women aged less gracefully than they do now. The praise that continued to be heaped upon her helps to explain why she did not retire. The great lady of Grosvenor Street drew luster and sustenance from Lady Townly and from the less successful but most aptly named Lady Matchless.

12
The Actress and Her Legend

Midway through the season of 1727–28, Barton Booth retired. While he was only four years older than Anne, alcoholic excesses in his youth and lifelong gourmandizing had played hob with his digestive system, aging him prematurely. The daily routine of his acting career proved too great a strain. Booth's retirement was the first of what Cibber would call "the unavoidable Accidents that drew on our Dissolution."[1] And indeed, an era seemed to be ending. By the end of 1729, Congreve and Steele, who had supplied the stage with so many popular plays, were dead. After Steele's funeral, a London newspaper reported hearing that "Mrs. Oldfield, the celebrated Comedian, hath obtained a reversionary grant of the Patent of Master of the Theatre-Royal in Drury-lane, granted by his Majesty King George the Ist to the late Sir Richard Steele, Kt. for a certain term of years, which expires in 1732." (The *St. James's Evening* replied, rather nastily: "As Mrs. Oldfield is to be Master, our Author should have informed us, who is to be Mistress.")[2]

The Drury Lane season of 1729–30 has special significance for Anne's story because it was her last, but in most respects it was like any other. The fall schedule of stock pieces began with *The Provok'd Husband* on September 11. In the next few weeks Anne appeared in many of her most popular roles: Andromache, Berinthia, Lady Dainty, Laetitia, Jane Shore (with Wilks now playing Hastings), Lady Brute, Biddy Tipkin, and Ruth (in *The Committee*). On October 24, *The Beaux' Stratagem* was advertised but dismissed, with no reason given. The sudden indisposition of a leading player was usually the cause for a last-minute cancellation rather than the substitution of another play for the one advertised, but if an illness of Anne's was the cause it cannot have been very serious, for she was back onstage a week later.

On November 1, she appeared in a command performance of *The Careless Husband,* with Cibber, Wilks, and Porter. The press noted the presence of the Prince of Wales and his party. The royal family often commanded or attended performances that winter, and on several occasions, perhaps in response to their support, Anne took roles that she seldom played any longer—Indamora in *Aureng-Zebe* and Marcia in *Cato.* By the end of December, in addition to repeating some of the roles already mentioned, she appeared as Indiana, the Scornful Lady, Anna Bullen, Lady Heartwell, Mrs. Loveit, and Calista.

The new year brought a change from the usual round of stock pieces, with three new productions. In the first, James Miller's *Humours of Oxford,* which opened on January 9, Anne—now in her late forties—played the young Clarinda, who, in the guise of a heartless flirt, succeeds in unmasking a fortune hunter. Despite some amusing local types, such as the "Oxford flirt" Kitty, played by a new young member of the company, Catherine Raftor (later Clive), the play was not a success.[3]

The Humours of Oxford was followed soon by the premiere of Benjamin Martyn's tragedy *Timoleon,* in which Anne did not have a part but spoke the epilogue—her last appearance in this popular specialty. She appeared in her customary epilogue persona, mocking the serious pretentions of Martyn's tragedy of tyranny, heroism, rape, and virtuous love. But the piece she spoke was not quite "as it was written by the Author." Someone had made alterations and additions, consisting chiefly of pointed sexual allusions, such as the passage in which the ladies in the audience were asked to consider what they would have done had they been poor Cleone, confronted by her ravisher, Timophanes:

Yet, when from Friends remov'd, all Ears at Distance,
A strong Gallant, much Love, and no Assistance,
Who cou'd have blam'd the Doctrine then of Non-Resistance?[4]

Whoever altered Martyn's original epilogue—Cibber, perhaps—knew well the effects Anne could achieve merely by lingering over a suggestive word or pausing significantly. The play had a successful first run of fourteen performances, attracting the Prince of Wales on the fourth night and bringing Martyn four benefits, but it was not entirely a happy experience for him. In the first edition, published soon afterward, he complained about the inadequate two-week rehearsal time and general managerial indifference and printed both versions of the epilogue so that readers might draw their own conclusions about the liberties that had been taken with his work.

After *Timoleon,* Anne appeared in more stock pieces, including two performances of *The Fair Penitent,* one of which was so well attended that according to the *Daily Courant* of February 23, "several Ladies of the first Rank were excluded for want of room." Interest may have been sparked by the appearance of a newcomer, John Highmore, in Booth's former role, Lothario. She was also rehearsing for her last new role, the title character in James Thomson's *Sophonisba.*

When Thomson, a young Scotsman, had come to London in 1725, eager to make his mark in the literary world, he set off on a binge of theatergoing, beginning at Drury Lane. Writing about his experiences to a friend in Scotland, Thomson confessed that he preferred the actresses to the actors, adding that "perhaps their sex prejudices me in their favour." Sex was certainly on his mind when he described Anne: "[She] has a smiling jolly face acts very well in comedy but best of all, I suppose in bed. She twines her body and leers with her eyes most bewicthingly [*sic*]."[5] Who, upon reading this, would have supposed that he would eventually create the most exalted of all of Anne's tragic heroines?

Thomson's tragedy became notorious for one line, "Oh Sophonisba, Sophonisba, Oh!" spoken by Wilks as Massinissa in act 3. Although Thomson had not invented this rhetorical effusion, which was common in heroic tragedy, audiences in 1730 found it risible and he was afterward plagued with cries of "Oh, Jemmy Thomson, Jemmy Thomson, Oh!"[6] The play was taken seriously, however, and was moderately successful, running for ten performances. The *Daily Post* praised its poetry, "hardly inferior to any Piece the Stage has produced for many years," commented upon the magnificence of the costumes and the scenery, and found Anne's performance "surprising"—no doubt in the sense of "admirable" or "astonishingly wonderful."[7] In his preface to the published text, Thomson paid tribute to Wilks and to Anne, who, in the character of Sophonisba, "excelled what, even in the fondness of an author, I could either wish or imagine."[8]

The play was based upon a popular episode in Livy's history of

Rome, which tells the story of Sophonisba, daughter of the Carthaginian general, Hasdrubal, and wife of Syphax, king of Numidia, at the time of the Second Punic War. When Syphax was defeated by the army of Scipio Africanus, led by the exiled Numidian prince, Massinissa, Sophonisba was to be taken to Rome as a slave. Massinissa offered to marry her to save her from captivity, but Scipio forbade it, whereupon she poisoned herself. With this act, Sophonisba became the famous emblem of female heroism. Her story was familiar in art, literature, and drama before Thomson undertook his own version. His debt to Joseph Addison is clear in several lines, such as "She had a Roman soul; for every one/ Who loves, like her, his country, is a Roman," as well as in his conception of Sophonisba as a female Cato. Superior to the claims of personal affection, she can only love liberty and Carthage.

> I formerly to *Massanissa* thee
> Preferr'd not, nor to thee now *Massanissa*,
> But *Carthage* to you both. And if preferring
> Thousands to one, a whole collected people,
> All Nature's tenderness, whate'er is sacred,
> The liberty, the welfare of a state,
> To one man's frantic happiness, be sham'd,
> Here, *Syphax*, I invoke it on my head![9]

Like Cato, she welcomes death in a lost cause rather than submission to the Romans, and like him, she calmly drinks a bowl of poison, her last thoughts not upon her distracted lover but upon her wretched homeland.

As Booth with Cato, Anne was able to arouse admiration and even some excitement for Thomson's rigidly virtuous heroine. To Chetwood, her performance "went beyond Wonder, to Astonishment!"[10] Tom Davies recorded the sensation she created merely by her delivery of one line in act 3: "In reply to some degrading expression of Massinissa, relating to Carthage, she uttered the following line, 'Not one base word of Carthage, for thy soul!—' with such grandeur in her action and look so tremendous, and in a voice so powerful, that it is said she even astonished Wilks, her Massinissa; it is certain the audience were struck, and expressed their feelings by the most uncommon applause."[11] But Chetwood added ominously, "From that Time her Decay came slowly on, and never left her till it conducted her to eternal

Rest." The implication that Anne's exertions in the role brought on her death made her a martyr to her art like Sophonisba to the cause of liberty.

Anne's benefit performance, *The Fair Penitent,* soon after *Sophonisba* ended, was a splendid occasion with the king, the Prince of Wales, and the three eldest princesses in attendance. Then came the break for Passion Week, and a final month of benefit performances for the principal Drury Lane actors. If she had begun to experience any symptoms of her illness, she kept to an unusually heavy schedule of performances, appearing fifteen times in popular stock roles. Colley Cibber's daughter, Charlotte Charke, recalled that Anne's encouragement gave her "lively Hopes of Success" when she made her stage debut on April 8 as Mademoiselle in *The Provok'd Wife*.[12] One of Anne's last roles in life, then, was that of patroness to an aspiring young actress. Her last appearance on the stage took place in another performance of *The Provok'd Wife,* on April 28, 1730—fully a month before she would normally have ended the season.

Deathbed scenes in the early eighteenth century tended to be stern. The emphasis was upon Christian fortitude. When Addison lay dying in the summer of 1719, he summoned Lord Warwick, "a young man of very irregular life," to his bedside "to see how a Christian can die," in the hope that his spirit of resignation might prove exemplary.[13] Resignation was indeed called for. Despite advances in the diagnosis of disease, medical practitioners could do little, besides alleviate pain, to treat the seriously ill.

Anne's illness is described in harrowing detail in the early memoirs. According to *Authentick Memoirs,* on the advice of physicians she was taken to Hampstead, where she experienced

> such exquisite racking Pains, that 'twas past the Patience of the greatest Stoick, or the Constancy of the greatest Hero, to have born them without complaining, and that loudly, too, of their Sufferings: And indeed, in the Agony of her Pains, they did force such dismal Shrieks and Outcries from her, that the Neighbourhood beginning to be alarm'd at the unusual Noise, 'twas thought proper to remove her to her own House in *Grosvenor-street*.[14]

The disease was never named in so many words. But an unidentified woman friend told Curll about the autopsy results, which confirmed the physicians' diagnosis of "a Malady known by every body to be incident to our Sex although we were Vestals."[15] A disease of the female organs, then, but not venereal. This vague hint, coupled with the reports of great pain and the six months that elapsed between her retirement from the stage and her death, suggests cancer of the reproductive system.

According to Curll she had "for some Years languished under a declining State of Health, tho' not from any Cause which Malice may suggest. . . . many times, when she has been playing a Part, and received the universal Applause of an Audience, the Tears have fallen from her Cheeks with the Anguish of Pain she felt. . . ."[16] But Cibber, who would surely have known, says nothing about her health during the last few years, and the record of her performances suggests that she was generally healthy and vigorous.

On June 27, 1730, two months after her last stage appearance, she made her will. Since she was only forty-seven and might, under ordinary circumstances, be expected to live for many more years, it is likely that she knew she was dying. *Faithful Memoirs* reports that she had asked her doctors "not to flatter her, but to give her their Opinions freely, *what they thought of her Case,*" and that they replied that they "feared the Fatality of it."[17]

She lingered through the summer. The account of her terrible cries while she was staying in Hampstead need not be entirely exaggerated. On September 15, she made a codicil to her will, changing the bequest to her aunt, Jane Gourlaw. At this time, she also declined to accept her salary for the new season, although according to her unwritten articles with the actor-managers she was entitled to receive it as long as the company performed, whether or not she was able to appear.[18] This action, as much as the making and amending of her will, bespoke her acceptance of approaching death.

It was reported that Churchill sat at her bedside for nights without rest, until he himself nearly became ill.[19] Margaret Saunders gave the only firsthand account of this time—couched in the conventional language of the deathbed:

> Her *Funeral* I never heard her once mention, but *Christian Fortitude* she had sufficient; for tho' she had no *Priest,* she did the Office of one to the *Last.*
> When her *Dissolution drew nigh,* and the *Lamp of Life waxed dim;*

she then expressed herself in *broken* Words and *pious* Meditations, in the most *moving* and *strongest* Manner you can imagine.

It may be justly said, she *Prayed without ceasing.* She was all Goodness. The best of Daughters, the best of Mothers, and the best of Friends. O! that I had Words to sound forth her Praise. . . ."[20]

In her last days, the private woman and her feelings remained hidden behind the venerated public figure. She died in the early hours of the morning, October 23, 1730.[21]

Drury Lane was closed not only on the night of her death but on the night of her funeral, October 27.[22] This was a standard tribute to performers of her eminence. Many of her colleagues undoubtedly wished to pay their respects, but she was not interred among her peers in the "actors' church," St. Paul, Covent Garden, and no actors bore her to the grave. Instead, she was buried with great pomp in Westminster Abbey, her pall borne by courtiers and gentlemen.

Churchill saw to it that Anne was buried in a manner befitting her public position. The inspiration may have been Congreve's funeral in January 1729, at which Churchill and his cousin George were both pallbearers. Before his interment in Westminster Abbey, Congreve had lain in state in the Jerusalem Chamber, outside the west entrance. Similar arrangements were made for Anne.[23] Only two actors before her had been honored with burial in Westminster Abbey—the great Restoration actor and manager Thomas Betterton, admired equally for his genius and his respectability, who died in 1710, and his wife Mary, buried beside him in 1712. Voltaire would write about the disparity between the funeral arrangements of England's leading actress and the ignominious burial of the great French actress, Adrienne Lecouvreur, in the same year.[24]

A protectionist law, designed to discourage the importation of linen, called for burial in good English woolen, but it was unthinkable for an actress famous for her elegance in dress to lie in state in plain woolen. In keeping with prevailing custom, a penalty would be paid so her corpse might be dressed more fashionably. "As the Nicety of Dress was her Delight when Living, she was as nicely dressed after her Decease; being by Mrs. *Saunders's* direction thus laid in her Coffin. She had on a very fine *Brussels*-Lace-Head; a Holland Shift with Tucker, and doubled Ruffles of the same Lace; a Pair of New Kid-Gloves, and her Body wrapped up in a Winding Sheet."[25] Alexander Pope would later evoke memories of the elegance of her burial attire in illustrating the "ruling passion" of female vanity:

> "Odious! in woollen! 't would a Saint provoke,"
> (Were the last words that poor Narcissa spoke)
> "No, let a charming Chintz, and Brussels lace
> Wrap my cold limbs, and shade my lifeless face:
> One would not, sure, be frightful when one's dead—
> And—Betty—give this Cheek a little Red."[26]

From Pope's footnote it is clear that the reference to Anne was specifically intended in these lines. However uncomplimentary, even cruel, they are a tribute to her popular identification with the frivolous Narcissa types she played.

Curll himself witnessed the funeral procession, writing that when he saw her corpse approaching the abbey, "the Gloom of the Church, and the faint lights before the Procession, contributed to the melancholy Disposition I was in."[27] The interment took place the next day between ten and eleven o'clock in the evening. Churchill having no official relationship to her, young Arthur Maynwaring led the funeral party as chief mourner. The pallbearers were all friends of Churchill's: John West, Baron De La Warr, a gentleman of the royal bedchamber; George Bubb Dodington, lord-lieutenant of Somerset and a lord of the Treasury; John, Lord Hervey, Vice-Chamberlain of the royal household; Walter Carey, Esq.; a Captain Elliot; and a man identified by Curll as Charles Hedges.[28] And here, at the brink of the grave, a final piece of scandal arises.

The gentleman in question was probably not Charles, but John Hedges, named by Anne as coexecutor of her will with Churchill and Lord Hervey. Although not titled, John Hedges held the important position of treasurer to the Prince of Wales and was very much a part of the social circle in which Churchill, Sir Robert Walpole, and Lord Hervey moved. According to Horace Walpole, Hedges had once composed a charming epigram for Anne's son—

> Give but Cupid's dart to me,
> Another Cupid I shall be;
> No more distinguished from the other,
> Than Venus would be from my mother.[29]

"Scandal," Walpole added, "says Hedges thought the two last [i.e., Venus and Anne] very like; and it says too, that she was not his enemy for thinking so." Without a scrap of additional evidence, a footnote to this passage in the Yale edition of Horace Walpole's letters puts the matter more baldly. Hedges "was the reputed lover of Mrs Oldfield while she was the accepted mistress of Lt–Gen. Churchill." Whether the Hedges who bore Anne's pall was Charles or John, the rumor certainly existed that John Hedges had been her lover. If the rumor was true, the appearance of Hedges in the funeral party was not particularly shocking. It is more difficult to gauge the significance of his nomination as coexecutor of her will alongside Churchill: callous? free spirited? a refutation of "scandal?" Then of course, Walpole can also have been wrong. While such speculation is idle, it is necessary at least to raise the matter in the face of the popular legend of her fidelity to Churchill.

On the subject of Churchill's fidelity to her there is irrefutable evidence—in the person of his illegitimate daughter, Hariett Churchill, born July 23, 1725. The existence of Hariett was apparently unknown to Anne's biographers, but she was no mystery to her contemporaries. As Charles Churchill's daughter, she enjoyed the advantages of his wealth and position in society just as if she had been his legitimate child, and in due course, she married a noted public figure, Sir Everard Fawkener, and lived respectably. Yet there is a mystery of sorts. Who, for example, was her mother? No mention is made of the woman in any family documents, and it may be presumed that she was dead by the time Churchill made his will in 1745, leaving a handsome bequest to "Hariett Churchill, a Minor who was of the age of nineteen years on the Twenty third of July last and is now living with me."[30]

An equally great mystery is the question of whether Anne knew about Hariett. If Hariett's mother had been part of Churchill's immediate social circle, Anne could hardly have been ignorant of the affair and its consequences. It is always possible, of course, that the woman was someone whom Churchill encountered either on one of his many trips abroad or elsewhere in England.[31]

The existence of Hariett Churchill may be an embarrassment to those who sentimentalize Anne's relationship with Churchill, but it need not be taken as evidence of a breach between them. Whether she was unfaithful to him, or knew about Hariett, there is nothing to suggest that he was any less devoted to her, or she to him, to the very end.

Anne's will was proved on November 2, 1730; its contents were published as an appendix to *Faithful Memoirs*[32] in April 1731, and soon became generally known. Immediately after her death, however, there were reports in the London papers of handsome bequests to her mother, to "several poor Relations," to "her Woman" (possibly Margaret Saunders), to her servants, and to her executors, "besides several other charitable Legacies." She was reported to have left large sums to both sons, and the Grosvenor Street house, its furniture, and her jewels ("worth £11,000") to young Churchill.

The actual terms were far less grand, rumor having greatly exaggerated the extent of her wealth. Her first priority had been to ensure the welfare of her sons. This she did by providing young Maynwaring with a legacy of five thousand pounds, of which only the interest was to be paid until his thirtieth birthday, after which he was to receive the principal. Young Churchill, only ten years old, needed no regular income since his father could well afford to care for him; therefore, he was to receive the deed for the Grosvenor Street house. The remainder of her estate and personal effects, "except some small Trifles that I may direct to be given away: and except what is already placed out in the Funds, or on other Publick Securities," was to be liquidated as soon as possible and invested carefully by her executors. In the event of Maynwaring's death before the age of thirty—after which, presumably, it would pass to his own heirs—his legacy was to go to young Churchill; but if her younger son were already dead it was to go to "the Honourable Brigadier General *Charles Churchill.*" Churchill senior was also to receive the Grosvenor Street house and the bulk of the remaining estate in the event of her sons' premature deaths.

Her mother received an immediate bequest of ten guineas and an annuity of sixty pounds. The only other relation mentioned in the will was her aunt, Jane Gourlaw, who, according to the codicil, was to receive an annuity of ten pounds to be paid during the senior Mrs. Oldfield's lifetime, after which it would revert to the estate. Margaret Saunders, provided for with an annuity of ten pounds, is said to have retired to Watford, in Hertfordshire.[33] The small annuity would provide a few extra comforts; it is likely that Anne knew about Margaret's plans when she made the bequest. Small gifts were probably made personally to her servants, as part of the aforementioned "small Trifles that I may direct to be given away." There were no bequests to her executors, who were far wealthier than she.

The will provided finally that "immediately upon, and from, and after, the Deaths of the said *Anne Oldfield* my Mother, the said *Jane Gourlaw* my Aunt, and the said *Margaret Saunders,* and the Death of the Survivor of them," her estate (not including those parts already disposed of) be divided into three equal parts, of which two parts were to be paid to her son Maynwaring and the third to her son Churchill. It was not that she favored one child over the other, but that young Churchill, who stood to inherit his father's considerable estate, had less need of the money. Each was well and sensibly provided for.

It is striking that this document is the only direct evidence we have of Anne's feelings about herself and those close to her. Couched in the legal jargon of the time, it is nevertheless revealing. Since Churchill was not only named executor but residuary legatee, it appears that he still stood high in Anne's affections at the time of her death. By contrast, her mother was comfortably, but not overgenerously provided for. The complex arrangements for the bequests to her sons, and the care with which she determined how her estate was to be managed after her death so that it might increase, bespeak not only a prudent and devoted mother (as her early biographers eulogize her) but a woman proud of what she had achieved, in real terms—not without help, but largely through her own gifts and good sense.

It was not long before poetic tributes of various sorts began to appear in the London papers, and the business of posthumous legend building began. First into the fray was Richard Savage, whose anonymously published "Poem to the Memory of Mrs. Oldfield" was appended to the first edition of *Authentick Memoirs,* published only two days after her funeral. In twelve stanzas of heroic couplets, he celebrated her accomplishments in public and private life, describing her as "the Glory of the *British* Stage, / Pride of her Sex, and Wonder of the Age." The roles he mentioned presumably suggested the range of her artistry, from "*Cleopatra's* Form" to "*Laetitia's* Artifice" and "*Townley's* Ease."

The *Grub Street Journal* of November 5 published the poem in which these often-quoted lines appear:

Gay was the Pit, whenever she was gay.
Coquetts would blush and Jilts would envy bear,
To see themselves so well perform'd in her. . . .

A poem in the *Whitehall Evening Post* of February 11, 1731, had the merit of suggesting the distinctive nature of her charm:

OLDFIELD alone
An Abstract seem'd of Womankind in One.
Delightful smiles enliven'd ev'ry Grace;
And Love itself look'd lovelier on her Face;
Each Passion, heighten'd by her Action, pleas'd,
And with her Transports, our Surprize encreas'd;
Her Mien so graceful, yet so gay her Air,
EXTRAVAGANCE itself was elegant in Her!

With *Authentick Memoirs* running into six editions before the end of 1730 and with outpourings of celebratory verse in the daily press, Anne Oldfield became the first stage star whose death excited great public attention. In 1733, a newspaper advertised the publication of her portrait in miniature, "Fit to be put into a Watch or Snuff-box with ornaments around it,"[34] an early instance of the marketing of a popular stage personality. In part, such celebrity reflects the rapid growth of newspapers and the reading public they served. Not all of the readers of these tributes had seen her perform, but most of them would have known who she was. The attention devoted to her death was not mere puffery. For nearly thirty years, she had been a glamorous and sometimes controversial public figure. The situation might have been different if she had died in old age, after a long retirement. But she did not suffer the indignity of outliving her fame.

Of those close to her who outlived her, young Arthur Maynwaring remains a shadowy figure. The income from his legacy would have enabled him to live comfortably as a military officer, on half pay in peacetime. In 1736, he was appointed captain in Major General Henry Harrison's regiment, the Fifteenth Foot. He was promoted to major sometime during the War of Jenkins' Ear—that ignoble skirmish between England and Spain over trading rights and the slave trade in the Caribbean. Arthur married well, for his wife, Katherine Pyne, was the daughter and coheiress of an Anglo-Irish gentleman. He lived long enough, by not quite two years, to possess the principal of his legacy. In April 1741, he was killed during the disastrous Cartagena campaign, leaving behind a widow and a young daughter, Margaret, who died unmarried in 1767.[35]

General Churchill lived for nearly fifteen years after Anne's death. As far as we know, he never took another mistress. On the whole, he seems to have led a happy, leisurely life. His friendship with Sir Robert

Walpole, nearly as legendary as his romance with Anne, endured for a lifetime, and there are numerous instances of his staunch political allegiance. Such loyalty was, of course, handsomely rewarded. In addition to his position in the royal household, which he retained until death, and his promotion to major general in 1735 and lieutenant general in 1739, Churchill was given a number of sinecures, of which the principal were governor of Plymouth and deputy ranger of St. James's Park.[36] From this he amassed an estate large enough to leave his children handsomely provided for.

Churchill died on May 14, 1745. He had been visiting Bath at the time of his death and was buried quietly, in accordance with the terms of his will, in Bath Abbey. A fine monument near the east end of the north aisle marks the place of his interment. With the death of the older generation, however, the Churchill-Walpole alliance did not come to an end. Indeed, within less than one year, it became more firmly fixed. On February 23, 1746, Lady Mary Walpole, Robert Walpole's natural daughter by his longtime mistress (and eventual wife), Maria Skerrett, married young Charles Churchill.

Upon hearing of his half sister's intentions, in the fall of 1745, Horace Walpole complained to his friend Horace Mann that it was "a foolish match, but I have nothing to do with it." Mann commiserated: "I could have wished it had been to anybody else, though really young Churchil [*sic*] has a great deal of merit. Still, there is an objection; I don't believe his father would have proposed it to yours."[37] Whatever the implication of Mann's comment, a curious provision in Churchill's long, complex will suggests that in 1745 a tie of some kind existed between Lady Mary and the Churchill family. The will, dated March 26, 1745, eight days after Robert Walpole's death, provides that in the event of Hariett Churchill's marriage without consent or a proper settlement, and young Charles Churchill's death without heirs, the amount of twenty thousand pounds would go to Lady Mary Walpole.[38] It is possible, then, that the two fathers had been discussing the eventual marriage of their children and that Churchill felt an obligation to Lady Mary. Or perhaps the provision was merely Churchill's way of giving his blessing to the arrangement, in the form of an implied widow's jointure. Whatever his intentions, the bequest amounted to five thousand pounds more than he provided for his own daughter's dowry.

Apart, perhaps, from his illegitimacy and his mother's low birth and occupation, Charles was a good enough catch. He followed in his father's footsteps as a military officer and member of Parliament, inheriting—in addition to the major portion of his father's estate— the elder Churchill's political allegiances and some of his sinecures. Educated as a young gentleman at Westminster School, he made the obligatory grand tour of Switzerland and Italy in his late teens. In Geneva in 1737, he demonstrated, in a gentlemanly fashion, that he had also inherited some of his mother's talent. The occasion was a series of elaborate amateur theatricals in which he appeared as Abudah in *The Siege of Damascus,* Malcolm in *Macbeth,* and, most notably, Harlequin in a pantomime. "I question if Rich was equal to him, combining grace, action, and agility," noted one of the participants.[39]

Before his marriage, Charles apparently had an affair with a singer, by whom he is supposed to have had an illegitimate daughter.[40] However, with his marriage Charles became (unlike his father and paternal grandfather) a proper paterfamilias. To this he added a new role: country gentleman. In 1755, at the urging of his brother-in-law Horace Walpole, Churchill rebuilt an older estate at Chalfont Park, Buckinghamshire, into a fine example of eighteenth-century Gothic.[41] Walpole's letters refer often to Charles and Lady Mary, their travels, their country home, the births of their children, their visits to his villa— Strawberry Hill—and their busy social life. The marriage produced five sons and two daughters. His daughter Sophia married another Walpole, Horatio, third Baron Walpole of Wolterton, thereby further strengthening—if strengthening were needed—the ties between the two families.

Young Charles Churchill lived to be very old, dying at number 59 Grosvenor Street in his ninety-second year, on April 13, 1812. If he was able to attend the theater in his later years, he would have seen the great Sarah Siddons, whose fame at the end of the eighteenth century eclipsed his mother's.

Anne Oldfield's reputation was kept alive during the eighteenth century by actors, those great transmitters of theatrical tradition, and in the memories of theatergoers. In the nature of the stock system, her roles were played by successive generations of actresses, and her performances remained, for many years, the benchmark to be equaled or exceeded. Thus, Mrs. Delany noted in 1752 that Peg Woffington had performed the part of Lady Townly "better than I have seen it done since Mrs. Oldfield's time.''[42] It was chiefly in roles of the Lady Townly type that she would be remembered.

A century later she was not altogether forgotten; but few of the plays in which she had appeared were still being performed, and the conception of the genteel lady had changed so radically that few readers could have understood the original nature of her appeal. Charles Reade's "Art: A Dramatic Tale,''[43] published in 1857, is a prime example of new legend making. The story tells of a young man's infatuation with Anne Oldfield just as she is about to become queen of the London stage in 1706 and of her good-natured promise to the boy's father to "cure" him and set him on the path of bourgeois respectability. Of course it was not intended to be a truthful account of the actress, and it should not be judged as such. Reade was familiar with a few details of Anne's life and career, probably through tradition rather than reading. Lady Townly, Indiana, and Sophonisba are paid due respect. But he also casts Anne as Belvidera and Lady Macbeth, roles she never played, has her rehearsing the role of Phaedra (instead of Ismena) in 1706, and, in the climactic contest for queen of the stage, has her appearing as Statira opposite Anne Bracegirdle as Roxana in *The Rival Queens*. Maynwaring is relegated to the sidelines as the phonetically spelled "Mannering," a devoted older gentleman who proposes marriage and keeps a respectful distance. The charm of the story, aside from its neat and delightful plot, is the presentation of Anne as the quintessence of that bygone era, "merrie England." But in the process, she is robbed of the qualities that made her a distinctive personality, becoming instead the stereotypical female star, mercurial, sentimental, vain—yet (as Reade saw her) at heart a simple country-born girl. "Nance" Oldfield, darling of the Victorian era, was born.

In 1894, Reade's story was adapted for the stage by Mildred Aldrich under the title *Nance Oldfield,* with starring roles for Ellen Terry and her son Gordon Craig. The piece is usually mentioned only briefly in biographies of Terry, but it was a fine vehicle for her light comic style, as it would have been for Anne herself. Nance's many moods and the manner in which she practices her wiles upon curmudgeonly Nathan Oldsworthy and his lovelorn son must have been a delight to perform and to watch. Like Reade's original story, the play was not intended to be anything more than a harmless fiction, but it contributed never-theless to the late-Victorian picture of Anne. Edward Robins's *Palmy*

Days of Nance Oldfield, published in 1898, was merely one more excursion into the same territory, dignified this time by the name and some of the paraphernalia of biography.

For a long time after the Robins biography was published, it appeared that Anne would be relegated to the status of "filler" for playbills, for it was there that her story would occasionally reappear, embellished from *Palmy Days.* The same few details and anecdotes would be repeated, having becomed ingrained in theatrical lore. "Captain" Oldfield rode with the Guards again, Farquhar discovered her in the Mitre Tavern, she was taken on at Drury Lane only to be ignored for a twelvemonth and then discovered once again in *Sir Courtly Nice,* Maynwaring loved and died, Churchill introduced her to the best families, and Richard Savage enjoyed her bounty.

Then came a curious flurry of interest in her in the mid-1950s. A biographical novel, *Narcissa,* which makes Churchill, not Maynwaring, the great love of her life, was published in 1956. The publication of *Gay Was the Pit,* in 1957, and the continuing popularity of romantic fiction such as *Forever Amber,* inspired another biographical fiction, published originally under the title *The Player Queen,* in 1968, and reissued as a paperback romance, *The Lovely Wanton,* in 1977. From this it would seem that Anne's legend had come a long way from Nance Oldfield. And indeed, in *The Player Queen,* Constance Fecher did not shrink from the subjects of fornication and bastardy. The difference between the fictions of Reade and Fecher is, however, only a choice of popular myth. Fecher recasts Anne as a twentieth-century heroine of romance, in whom the desire for independence clashes with more "womanly" longings. Her Anne, giving her body to other men but her heart only to Maynwaring, is as saintly in her own way as dear Nance, and not nearly such good company.

The legends that lived after Anne Oldfield testify to the lasting interest of her story and to the fascination that unconventional women, and actresses in particular, possess for storytellers in every generation. But legends say very little about the woman and her significance. It would be nice to know how she viewed the choices she made in the course of a long career and two long love affairs. No wonder that fiction has stepped in to fill the many blanks in what might be called the existential record of her life. Still, it is possible to sum up her character and glimpse something of her essential nature.

Single-mindedness and deliberation come instantly to mind. Talent aside, it was these qualities that enabled her to survive and prosper in a competitive profession. Picking an appropriate model for her comic style, elbowing her rivals away when good parts became available, calculating the time to become a tragedienne were all means to the end of a successful stage career. If she did not instigate the rivalry with Anne Bracegirdle, she was willing to go through with it. (Arthur Maynwaring and his friends may have supported her behind the scenes, but it was she who had to face her rival's fans.) On every occasion in which she courted unpopularity, she seems to have kept her sights firmly fixed upon her career and its enhancement. With the possible exception of her involvement in *Three Hours After Marriage,* her judgment was remarkably sound.

The progress from stagestruck child to "sole Empress of the Stage" typically entails personal sacrifice. (In fiction and popular biography, the great female star is often lonely, unloved, and exploited, finding solace in alcohol, casual sex, or drugs.) Anne clearly made choices that affected her personal life to further her career and her position in the world, but whether they can be considered sacrifices—in the sense that she regretted them—is impossible to say. Except for Margaret Saunders, who was not quite on equal footing, she probably had no intimate female friends, for such friendships were rare between actresses and potential rivals, and an indefinable but unbridgeable gulf lay between Anne and the aristocratic ladies she met through Churchill. (It is easier to imagine her letting down her hair with Lord Hervey, mimicking his enemies and laughing at his witticisms, than it is to see her conversing intimately with a female friend. But then, according to Lady Mary Wortley Montagu, there were three sexes: men, women, and Herveys.) As for the other sacrifices that female stars have often made, in fact and fiction, Anne managed to enjoy the benefits of marriage and motherhood without legitimizing them, combining independence and domesticity to a degree that few women in any age have achieved.

There is no way of knowing whether, in the privacy of her boudoir, she often lay down and cried. But we may guess that she was fundamentally a happy as well as a successful woman, not prone to illness or bouts of depression, which would have shown up in frequent absences from the stage. Her life in later years does not strike us as hard driving but evenly paced and generally uneventful. (If anything, during the last decade, it was perhaps too unvarying—did she never tire of repeating Lady Betty's speech about her enchanting new scarf?) But such serenity had been hard earned.

What did her life signify in a more general sense? Surely, more than the sum of her parts. Dr. Johnson spoke of his famous contemporary, David Garrick, as contributing to the store of harmless pleasure. Most actors do that. But the tribute paid to Garrick, Anne Oldfield, and Thomas Betterton by the mere fact of their burial in Westminster Abbey acknowledged that a few actors in each age have also been the bearers of communal consciousness. If we could see Anne as Sopho-nisba or as Lady Betty, we would know, far better than words can tell us, what a lady of her time, great or small, was supposed to be. But, in the end, it is the words of Sophonisba and of Lady Betty that must help us capture those images.

Not one base word of Carthage—for thy Soul!

'Tis all Extravagance both in Mode and Fancy; my Dear, I believe there's Six Thousand Yards of Edging in it.

Appendixes
Abbreviations
Notes
Index

Appendix 1

༄

List of Anne Oldfield's Roles in the Order
in Which She First Played Them

Role	Play	Author
1699–1700		
Candiope (?)	*Secret Love*	John Dryden
SILVIA	*The Grove*	John Oldmixon
ALINDA	*The Pilgrim*	John Fletcher and John Vanbrugh
1700–1701		
AURELIA	*The Perjur'd Husband*	Susanna Centlivre
LUCILIA	*Love at a Loss*	Catherine Trotter
ANN OF BRITTANIE	*The Unhappy Penitent*	Catherine Trotter
MIRANDA	*The Humour of the Age*	Thomas Baker
HELEN	*The Virgin Prophetess*	Elkanah Settle
1701–2		
LADY SHARLOT	*The Funeral*	Richard Steele
CIMENE	*The Generous Conqueror*	Bevil Higgons

Caps = role she originated; R = revival; ? = no cast information available, but she probably began to play the role in this season.

Role	Play	Author
CAMILLA	*The Modish Husband*	William Burnaby
JACINTA	*The False Friend*	John Vanbrugh
1702–3		
LUCIA	*The Old Mode and the New*	Thomas Durfey
LUCIA	*The Fair Example*	Richard Estcourt
BELLIZA	*Love's Contrivance*	Susanna Centlivre
Leonora	*Sir Courtly Nice*	John Crowne
1703–4		
Elvira (?)	*The Spanish Fryar*	John Dryden
Lady Lurewell (?)	*The Constant Couple*	George Farquhar
Narcissa (?)	*Love's Last Shift*	Colley Cibber
Celia (?)	*Volpone*	Ben Jonson
Hellena (?)	*The Rover*	Aphra Behn
Teresia (?)	*The Squire of Alsatia*	Thomas Shadwell
Florella (?)	*Greenwich Park*	William Mountfort
VICTORIA	*The Lying Lover*	Richard Steele
MARY, QUEEN OF SCOTS (?)	*The Albion Queens*	John Banks
Lady Harriet (?)	*The Funeral*	Richard Steele
1704–5		
2d Constantia (?)	*The Chances*	John Fletcher and George Villiers, duke of Buckingham
LADY BETTY MODISH	*The Careless Husband*	Colley Cibber
MARIANA	*Farewell Folly*	Peter Anthony Motteux
BIDDY TIPKIN	*The Tender Husband*	Richard Steele
1705–6		
ARABELLA	*Hampstead Heath*	Thomas Baker

Caps = role she originated; R = revival; ? = no cast information available, but she probably began to play the role in this season.

Role	Play	Author
LADY REVELLER	*The Basset Table*	Susanna Centlivre
IZADORA	*Perolla and Izadora*	Colley Cibber
VILETTA	*The Fashionable Lover*	unknown
SILVIA	*The Recruiting Officer*	George Farquhar
Lucina	*Valentinian*	John Fletcher and John Wilmot, earl of Rochester

1706–7
ISABELLA	*The Platonick Lady*	Susanna Centlivre
Widow	*The Comical Revenge; or, Love in a Tub*	George Etherege
Lady Heartwell (R)	*Wit Without Money*	Francis Beaumont and John Fletcher
Florimell	*Marriage à la Mode; or, The Comical Lovers*	John Dryden and Colley Cibber
MRS. SULLEN	*The Beaux' Stratagem*	George Farquhar
Imoinda	*Oroonoko*	Thomas Southerne
Monimia	*The Orphan*	Thomas Otway
ISMENA	*Phaedra and Hippolytus*	Edmund Smith
Maria	*The Fortune Hunters*	James Carlisle

1707–8
LADY DAINTY	*The Double Gallant*	Colley Cibber
ETHELINDA	*The Royal Convert*	Nicholas Rowe
MRS. CONQUEST	*The Lady's Last Stake*	Colley Cibber
Countess of Nottingham	*The Unhappy Favourite; or, The Earl of Essex*	John Banks
Estifania	*Rule a Wife and Have a Wife*	Francis Beaumont and John Fletcher
Elvira	*Love Makes a Man*	Colley Cibber
Angelica (R)	*Love for Love*	William Congreve
Semandra (R)	*Mithridates*	Nathaniel Lee
Euphronia	*Aesop*	John Vanbrugh

Caps = role she originated; R = revival; ? = no cast information available, but she probably began to play the role in this season.

Role	Play	Author
The Silent Woman	*Epicoene; or, The Silent Woman*	Ben Jonson

1708–9

Role	Play	Author
LADY RODOMONT	*The Fine Lady's Airs*	Thomas Baker
Carolina (R)	*Epsom Wells*	Thomas Shadwell
LUCINDA	*The Rival Fools; or, Wit at Several Weapons*	John Fletcher and Colley Cibber
Mrs. Loveit	*The Man of Mode*	George Etherege

1709–10

Role	Play	Author
Louisa	*Love Makes a Man*	Colley Cibber
Mrs. Brittle	*The Amorous Widow; or, The Wanton Wife*	Thomas Betterton
BELINDA	*The Man's Bewitched*	Susanna Centlivre
Berinthia	*The Relapse*	John Vanbrugh
Scornful Lady	*The Scornful Lady*	John Fletcher
FLORA	*Hob; or, The Country Wake*	Colley Cibber
Laetitia	*The Old Batchelor*	William Congreve
Ruth	*The Committee*	Sir Robert Howard
Countess of Rutland	*The Unhappy Favourite; or, The Earl of Essex*	John Banks

1710–11

Role	Play	Author
OGLE-FIDELIA	*Injur'd Love*	unknown

1711–12

Role	Play	Author
ARABELLA	*The Wife's Relief*	Charles Johnson
Anna Bullen	*Vertue Betray'd; or, Anna Bullen*	John Banks
CAMILLA	*The Perplex'd Lovers*	Susanna Centlivre
Caelia	*The Humourous Lieutenant*	John Fletcher

Caps = role she originated; R = revival; ? = no cast information available, but she probably began to play the role in this season.

Role	Play	Author
ANDROMACHE	*The Distrest Mother*	Ambrose Philips

1712–13

XIMENA	*Ximena; or, The Heroick Daughter*	Colley Cibber
VICTORIA	*The Humours of the Army*	Charles Shadwell
EMILIA	*Cinna's Conspiracy*	unknown
MARCIA	*Cato*	Joseph Addison

1713–14

ERIPHILE	*The Victim*	Charles Johnson
JANE SHORE	*The Tragedy of Jane Shore*	Nicholas Rowe
VIOLANTE	*The Wonder: A Woman Keeps a Secret*	Susanna Centlivre

1714–15

LADY JANE GRAY	*The Tragedy of Lady Jane Gray*	Nicholas Rowe

1715–16

LADY TRUEMAN	*The Drummer*	Joseph Addison

1716–17

Arpasia (R)	*Tamerlane*	Nicholas Rowe
LEONORA	*The Cruel Gift*	Susanna Centlivre
MRS. TOWNLEY	*Three Hours After Marriage*	John Gay, Alexander Pope, and John Arbuthnot
ATALINDA	*The Sultaness*	Charles Johnson
ROSALINDA	*Lucius, The First Christian King of Britain*	Delariviere Manley

Caps = role she originated; R = revival; ? = no cast information available, but she probably began to play the role in this season.

Role	Play	Author

1717–18
MARIA | *The Non-Juror* | Colley Cibber
Millamant (R) | *The Way of the World* | William Congreve

1718–19
Cleopatra (R) | *All for Love* | John Dryden
SOPHRONIA | *The Masquerade* | Charles Johnson
FLORINDA | *Chit Chat* | Thomas Killigrew
MANDANE | *Busiris, King of Egypt* | Edward Young

1719–20
CELONIA | *The Spartan Dame* | Thomas Southerne

1720–21
SOPHRONIA | *The Refusal* | Colley Cibber

1721–22
Indamora (R) | *Aureng-Zebe* | John Dryden
Amestris (R) | *The Ambitious Stepmother* | Nicholas Rowe

1722–23
MRS. WATCHIT | *The Artifice* | Susanna Centlivre
INDIANA | *The Conscious Lovers* | Richard Steele
QUEEN MARGARET | *Humfrey, Duke of Gloster* | Ambrose Philips

1723–24
PRINCESS CATHERINE | *King Henry V* | Aaron Hill
CYLENE | *The Captives* | John Gay

1724–25
CLEOPATRA | *Caesar in Egypt* | Colley Cibber

Caps = role she originated; R = revival; ? = no cast information available, but she probably began to play the role in this season.

Role	Play	Author
1725–26		
Calista (R)	*The Fair Penitent*	Nicholas Rowe
Aurelia (R)	*The Twin Rivals*	George Farquhar
Lady Brute (R)	*The Provok'd Wife*	John Vanbrugh
1726–27		
AMORET	*The Rival Modes*	James Smythe
1727–28		
LADY TOWNLY	*The Provok'd Husband*	John Vanbrugh and Colley Cibber
LADY MATCHLESS	*Love in Several Masques*	Henry Fielding
1728–29		
No new roles		
1729–30		
CLARINDA	*The Humours of Oxford*	James Miller
SOPHONISBA	*Sophonisba*	James Thomson

Total roles: 112
Original roles: 68

Caps = role she originated; R = revival; ? = no cast information available, but she probably began to play the role in this season.

Appendix 2

Anne Oldfield's Complete Repertory, by Season

Season	Candiope, Secret Love	SILVIA, The Grove	ALINDA, The Pilgrim	AURELIA, The Perjur'd Husband	LUCILIA, Love at a Loss	ANN, The Unhappy Penitent	MIRANDA, The Humour of the Age	HELEN, The Virgin Prophetess	LADY SHARLOT, The Funeral	CIMENE, The Generous Conqueror	CAMILLA, The Modish Husband
1699–1700	?	X	*X								
1700–1701			?	X	X	X	X	X			
1701–1702									X	X	X
1702–1703			?				?		?		
1703–1704			?								
1704–1705			?								
1705–1706			X								
1706–1707			X								
1707–1708			X								
1708–1709			X								
1709–1710			X								
1710–1711											
1711–1712											
1712–1713											
1713–1714											
1714–1715											
1715–1716											
1716–1717											
1717–1718											
1718–1719											
1719–1720											
1720–1721											
1721–1722											
1722–1723											
1723–1724											
1724–1725											
1725–1726											
1726–1727											
1727–1728											
1728–1729											
1729–1730											

? = no cast information, but she probably played the role that season
* = she chose the play for her benefit

X = she played the role at least once that season
CAPS = original role

184

	JACINTA, *The False Friend*	LUCIA, *The Old Mode & the New*	LUCIA, *The Fair Example*	BELLIZA, *Love's Contrivance*	Leonora, *Sir Courtly Nice*	Elvira, *The Spanish Fryar*	Lady Lurewell, *The Constant Couple*	Narcissa, *Love's Last Shift*	Celia, *Volpone*	Hellena, *The Rover*	Teresia, *The Squire of Alsatia*
1699–1700											
1700–1701											
1701–1702	X										
1702–1703		X	X	★X	X						
1703–1704					?	?	?	?	?	?	?
1704–1705					?	?	?	?	?	?	?
1705–1706					?	?	?		?	?	?
1706–1707					X	X	X		X		
1707–1708					X	X	X	X		X	X
1708–1709					X	X	X	X		X	X
1709–1710	X				X	X	X	X		X	
1710–1711					X	X	X	X		★X	X
1711–1712					X	X	X	X		X	X
1712–1713					X	X	X			?	
1713–1714						?	X			?	
1714–1715					?	X	X	X		X	
1715–1716					?	X	X	?			
1716–1717					?	X	X	X			
1717–1718						X	X				
1718–1719					X	X	X	X			
1719–1720						X	X	X			
1720–1721						X	X				
1721–1722						X	X	X			
1722–1723						X	X				X
1723–1724											
1724–1725							★X				
1725–1726							X				
1726–1727							X	X			
1727–1728							X				
1728–1729					★X		X				
1729–1730						X	X				

? = no cast information, but she probably played the role that season
★ = she chose the play for her benefit

X = she played the role at least once that season
CAPS = original role

Season	Florella, *Greenwich Park*	VICTORIA, *The Lying Lover*	MARY, QUEEN OF SCOTS, *The Albion Queens*	Lady Harriet, *The Funeral*	2d Constantia, *The Chances*	LADY BETTY MODISH, *The Careless Husband*	MARIANA, *Farewell Folly*	BIDDY TIPKIN, *The Tender Husband*	ARABELLA, *Hampstead Heath*	LADY REVELLER, *The Basset Table*	IZADORA, *Perolla and Izadora*
1699–1700											
1700–1701											
1701–1702											
1702–1703											
1703–1704	?	X	?	?							
1704–1705	?		?		★?	X	X	X			
1705–1706	?			X		X		★X	X	X	X
1706–1707						X		★X			
1707–1708	X			X	X	X		X			
1708–1709	X			X	X	X		X			
1709–1710				X	★X	X		X			
1710–1711			X	X	X	X		X			
1711–1712			X	X	X	X		X			
1712–1713			X		X	X		X			
1713–1714			X		?	X		X			
1714–1715			?		X	X		X			
1715–1716					X	X		?			
1716–1717					X	X		?			
1717–1718					X	X		X			
1718–1719						X		X			
1719–1720						X		X			
1720–1721						X		X			
1721–1722						X		X			
1722–1723			X			X		X			
1723–1724						X		X			
1724–1725						X		X			
1725–1726						X		X			
1726–1727			X			X		X			
1727–1728			X			X		X			
1728–1729			X			X		X			
1729–1730			X			X		X			

? = no cast information, but she probably played the role that season
★ = she chose the play for her benefit

X = she played the role at least once that season
CAPS = original role

	VILETTA, The Fashionable Lover	SILVIA, The Recruiting Officer	Lucina, Valentinian	ISABELLA, The Platonick Lady	Widow, The Comical Revenge; or, Love in a Tub	Lady Heartwell, Wit Without Money	Florimell, Marriage à la Mode; or, The Comical Lovers	MRS. SULLEN, The Beaux' Stratagem	Imoinda, Oroonoko	Monimia, The Orphan	ISMENA, Phaedra and Hippolytus
1699–1700											
1700–1701											
1701–1702											
1702–1703											
1703–1704											
1704–1705											
1705–1706	X	X	X								
1706–1707		X		X	X	X	X	X	X	X	X
1707–1708		X					X	X			
1708–1709		X				X	X	★X			
1709–1710		X				X	X	X	X		
1710–1711		X				X	X	X			
1711–1712		X						X			
1712–1713						?		X			
1713–1714								X			
1714–1715						?		X			
1715–1716						?		X	X		
1716–1717						X		X	X		
1717–1718						?		X	X		
1718–1719								?	X		
1719–1720								X	X		
1720–1721								X			
1721–1722						X		X			
1722–1723						?		X			
1723–1724						X		X			
1724–1725						X		X			
1725–1726						X		X			
1726–1727						X		X			
1727–1728								X			
1728–1729						X		X			
1729–1730						X		X			

? = no cast information, but she probably played the role that season
★ = she chose the play for her benefit

X = she played the role at least once that season
CAPS = original role

	Maria, *The Fortune Hunters*	LADY DAINTY, *The Double Gallant*	ETHELINDA, *The Royal Convert*	MRS. CONQUEST, *The Lady's Last Stake*	Countess of Nottingham, *The Unhappy Favourite; or, The Earl of Essex*	Estifania, *Rule a Wife and Have a Wife*	Elvira, *Love Makes a Man*	Angelica, *Love for Love*	Semandra, *Mithridates*	Euphronia, *Aesop*	*The Silent Woman, Epicoene; or, The Silent Woman*
1699–1700											
1700–1701											
1701–1702											
1702–1703											
1703–1704											
1704–1705											
1705–1706											
1706–1707	X										
1707–1708	X	X	X	X	X	★X	X	X	X	X	X
1708–1709							X	X			
1709–1710	X					X		X			X
1710–1711	X					X		X			X
1711–1712						X		X	X		X
1712–1713		X				X		?			
1713–1714		X				?		X			
1714–1715		X				X		X	X		
1715–1716		?				?		★X	X		X
1716–1717		X				X		★X	?		X
1717–1718		X				X		X	?		X
1718–1719						X		X			X
1719–1720		X				X		X			
1720–1721		X				X			X		X
1721–1722		X				X		X			X
1722–1723		X				X			★X		
1723–1724		X				★X			X		
1724–1725		X				X					
1725–1726		X				X					
1726–1727		X				X		X	X		
1727–1728		X				X			X		
1728–1729		X				X			X		
1729–1730		X				X		X			

? = no cast information, but she probably played the role that season
★ = she chose the play for her benefit

X = she played the role at least once that season
CAPS = original role

	LADY RODOMONT, *The Fine Lady's Airs*	Carolina, *Epsom Wells*	LUCINDA, *The Rival Fools, or, Wit at Several Weapons*	Mrs. Lovett, *The Man of Mode*	Louisa, *Love Makes a Man*	Mrs. Brittle, *The Amorous Widow; or, The Wanton Wife*	BELINDA, *The Man's Bewitched*	Berinthia, *The Relapse*	Scornful Lady, *The Scornful Lady*	FLORA, *Hob; or, The County Wake*	Laetitia, *The Old Batchelor*
1699–1700											
1700–1701											
1701–1702											
1702–1703											
1703–1704											
1704–1705											
1705–1706											
1706–1707											
1707–1708											
1708–1709	X	X	X	X							
1709–1710		X		X	X	X	X	X	X	X	X
1710–1711				X		X			X		X
1711–1712		?		X		X		X	X		X
1712–1713				?		X			X		X
1713–1714				?		X			X		X
1714–1715		X		X		X			★X		X
1715–1716		X		★X		X		X	X		?
1716–1717				X		X		X	X		X
1717–1718				?		X		★X	X		X
1718–1719				X		X		X			X
1719–1720				★X		X		X	X		X
1720–1721				X		X		X	X		X
1721–1722				X		X		X	X		X
1722–1723				X		X		X	X		X
1723–1724				X		X		X	X		X
1724–1725				X		X		X	X		X
1725–1726				X		X		X	X		X
1726–1727				X		★X		X	X		X
1727–1728				X		?		★X	X		X
1728–1729				X		X		X	X		X
1729–1730				X				X	X		X

? = no cast information, but she probably played the role that season
★ = she chose the play for her benefit

X = she played the role at least once that season
CAPS = original role

	Ruth, *The Committee*	Countess of Rutland, *The Unhappy Favourite; or, The Earl of Essex*	OGLE-FIDELIA, *Injur'd Love*	ARABELLA, *The Wife's Relief*	Anna Bullen, *Vertue Betray'd*	CAMILLA, *The Perplex'd Lovers*	Caelia, *The Humourous Lieutenant*	ANDROMACHE, *The Distrest Mother*	XIMENA, *Ximena; or, The Heroick Daughter*	VICTORIA, *The Humours of the Army*	EMILIA, *Cinna's Conspiracy*
1699–1700											
1700–1701											
1701–1702											
1702–1703											
1703–1704											
1704–1705											
1705–1706											
1706–1707											
1707–1708											
1708–1709											
1709–1710	X	X									
1710–1711	X		X								
1711–1712	X			X	X	X	*X	X			
1712–1713					X		X	X	*X	X	X
1713–1714					X		X	X			
1714–1715					X		X	X			
1715–1716		X					?	X			
1716–1717		X					?	X			
1717–1718		X					X	X			
1718–1719							X	?	X		
1719–1720	X						X	?			
1720–1721	X						X				
1721–1722	X	X					X	X			
1722–1723	X						X	X			
1723–1724	X						X	X			
1724–1725	X				X			X			
1725–1726	X				?			X			
1726–1727	X	X			X		X	X			
1727–1728	X	X			X		X	?			
1728–1729	X				X		X	X			
1729–1730	X				X		X	X			

? = no cast information, but she probably played the role that season
★ = she chose the play for her benefit
X = she played the role at least once that season
CAPS = original role

	MARCIA, Cato	ERIPHILE, The Victim	JANE SHORE, Jane Shore	VIOLANTE, The Wonder: a Woman Keeps a Secret	LADY JANE, The Tragedy of Lady Jane Gray	LADY TRUEMAN, The Drummer	Arpasia, Tamerlane	LEONORA, The Cruel Gift	MRS. TOWNLEY, Three Hours After Marriage	ATALINDA, The Sultaness	ROSALINDA, Lucius, The First Christian King of Britain
1699–1700											
1700–1701											
1701–1702											
1702–1703											
1703–1704											
1704–1705											
1705–1706											
1706–1707											
1707–1708											
1708–1709											
1709–1710											
1710–1711											
1711–1712											
1712–1713	X										
1713–1714	X	X	*X	X							
1714–1715	X		X		X						
1715–1716	X		X		X	X					
1716–1717	X		X				X	X	X	X	X
1717–1718	X		X				X				
1718–1719	X		X				X				
1719–1720	X		X				X				
1720–1721			X								
1721–1722	X		X				X				
1722–1723	X		X								
1723–1724	X		X								
1724–1725	X		X								
1725–1726	X										
1726–1727			X								
1727–1728			X								
1728–1729											
1729–1730	X		X								

? = no cast information, but she probably played the role that season
* = she chose the play for her benefit
X = she played the role at least once that season
CAPS = original role

	MARIA, *The Non-Juror*	Millamant, *The Way of The World*	Cleopatra, *All for Love*	SOPHRONIA, *The Masquerade*	FLORINDA, *Chit Chat*	MANDANE, *Busiris, King of Egypt*	CELONIA, *The Spartan Dame*	SOPHRONIA, *The Refusal*	Indamora, *Aureng-Zebe*	Amestris, *The Ambitious Stepmother*	MRS. WATCHIT, *The Artifice*	INDIANA, *The Conscious Lovers*
1699–1700												
1700–1701												
1701–1702												
1702–1703												
1703–1704												
1704–1705												
1705–1706												
1706–1707												
1707–1708												
1708–1709												
1709–1710												
1710–1711												
1711–1712												
1712–1713												
1713–1714												
1714–1715												
1715–1716												
1716–1717												
1717–1718	X	X										
1718–1719		★X	X	X	X	X						
1719–1720		X	X		X		X					
1720–1721		★X	X					X				
1721–1722		★X	X						X	X		
1722–1723		X	X						X		X	X
1723–1724		X	X									X
1724–1725		X	X									X
1725–1726		X	X									X
1726–1727		X								X		X
1727–1728		X	X									X
1728–1729		X	X									
1729–1730		X							X			X

? = no cast information, but she   X = she played the role at least
    probably played the role that season   once that season
★ = she chose the play for her benefit   CAPS = original role

	QUEEN MARGARET, *Humfrey, Duke of Gloster*	PRINCESS CATHERINE, *King Henry V*	CYLENE, *The Captives*	CLEOPATRA, *Caesar in Egypt*	Calista, *The Fair Penitent*	Aurelia, *The Twin Rivals*	Lady Brute, *The Provok'd Wife*	AMORET, *The Rival Modes*	LADY TOWNLY, *The Provok'd Husband*	LADY MATCHLESS, *Love in Several Masques*	CLARINDA, *The Humours of Oxford*	SOPHONISBA, *Sophonisba*
1699–1700												
1700–1701												
1701–1702												
1702–1703												
1703–1704												
1704–1705												
1705–1706												
1706–1707												
1707–1708												
1708–1709												
1709–1710												
1710–1711												
1711–1712												
1712–1713												
1713–1714												
1714–1715												
1715–1716												
1716–1717												
1717–1718												
1718–1719												
1719–1720												
1720–1721												
1721–1722										X		
1722–1723	X											
1723–1724		X	X									
1724–1725				X								
1725–1726					X	X	*X					
1726–1727					X	X	X	X				
1727–1728					X		X			X		
1728–1729					X		X			X		
1729–1730					*X		X			X	X	X

? = no cast information, but she probably played the role that season
★ = she chose the play for her benefit

X = she played the role at least once that season
CAPS = original role

Appendix 3

List of Prologues and Epilogues Spoken by Anne Oldfield

Occasion	Type	Author (if not the playwright)
premiere, *The Perjur'd Husband*	prologue	"by a gentleman"
premiere, *The Unhappy Penitent*	prologue	
premiere, *The False Friend*	epilogue	
premiere, *Perolla and Izadora*	epilogue	Arthur Maynwaring[1]
premiere, *Camilla*★	epilogue	Arthur Maynwaring[2]
premiere, *Phaedra and Hippolytus*	epilogue	Matthew Prior[3]
premiere, *The Royal Convert*	epilogue	
premiere, *The Man's Bewitched*	epilogue	Colley Cibber
premiere, *The Wife's Relief*	epilogue	Arthur Maynwaring[4]
premiere, *The Distrest Mother*	epilogue	Eustace Budgell
premiere, *Ximena*	epilogue	
premiere, *The Victim*	epilogue	Colley Cibber
premiere, *Jane Shore*	epilogue[5]	
benefit, March 5, 1716	epilogue[6]	
premiere, *The Drummer*	epilogue	
premiere, *The Cruel Gift*	epilogue	Nicholas Rowe
premiere, *Three Hours After Marriage*	epilogue	
premiere, *The Non-Juror*	epilogue	
premiere, *The Masquerade*	epilogue	

★ = *play in which Mrs. Oldfield did not appear as a character.*

Occasion	Type	Author (if not the playwright)
premiere, *Busiris*	epilogue	
premiere, *The Invader of His Country* ★	epilogue	Colley Cibber
premiere, *The Artifice*	epilogue	George Sewell
premiere, *The Conscious Lovers*	epilogue	Benjamin Victor[7]
premiere, *Humfrey, Duke of Gloster*	epilogue	
premiere, *King Henry V*	epilogue	
premiere, *The Captives*	epilogue[8]	
premiere, *Caesar in Egypt*	epilogue	
premiere, *The Provok'd Husband*	epilogue	
premiere, *The Double Falsehood* ★	epilogue	
premiere, *Timoleon* ★	epilogue	altered by Cibber?[9]

Key

1. See Henry Snyder, "The Prologues and Epilogues of Arthur Maynwaring," *Philological Quarterly*, 50 (October 1971): 614.

2. Snyder, "Prologues and Epilogues," p. 615.

3. For attribution to Prior, see *Faithful Memoirs*, p. 29.

4. Snyder, "Prologues and Epilogues," p. 619.

5. In the spring of 1717, Pope published an epilogue to *The Tragedy of Jane Shore* in a new collection of his works, titling it "Epilogue for Jane Shore. Design'd for Mrs. Oldfield." It is different from the one she spoke at the premiere, which was published with the first edition of the play, and the assumption has been that Pope's epilogue was rejected, perhaps by Anne Oldfield herself. In that seemingly harmless phrase, "design'd for Mrs. Oldfield," rather than the more common "design'd to be spoken by Mrs. Oldfield," Norman Ault sees a slap at Anne—suggesting that the speaker's designation of herself as a "sister sinner" was "designed to fit" Mrs. Oldfield. See Norman Ault, *New Light on Pope with Some Additions to His Poetry Hitherto Unknown* (London: Methuen, 1949), 6. Malcolm Goldstein, in *Pope and the Augustan Stage* (Stanford: Stanford University Press, 1958), 71, states flatly that Mrs. Oldfield refused to speak Pope's epilogue but offers no clue to her motives. It seems unlikely to me that Pope was insulting her in this roundabout fashion when he published the epilogue, since he was perfectly capable of striking a direct blow.

6. *London Stage*, 2:391–92. At the end of her benefit performance of *The Man of Mode*,

★ = *play in which Mrs. Oldfield did not appear as a character.*

Anne Oldfield spoke a pro-Hanoverian "New Epilogue, recommending the Cause of Liberty to the Beauties of Great Britain." The author is unknown. For text, see chapter 9.

7. For attribution to Benjamin Victor, see Shirley Strum Kenny, ed., *The Conscious Lovers* (Lincoln: University of Nebraska Press, 1968), 99–100.

8. For a discussion of Pope's alleged authorship of this epilogue see John Gay, *Dramatic Works,* ed. John Fuller (Oxford: Clarendon Press, 1983), 1:458–59. Fuller believes that the epilogue is by Gay.

9. For discussion of the epilogue and the playwright's objections to it, see chapter 12.

Note on Abbreviations

The following abbreviations are used for frequently cited works.

Add. MSS — British Library, Additional Manuscripts.

Apology — Colley Cibber, *An Apology for the Life of Mr. Colley Cibber, Written by Himself,* ed. Robert W. Lowe, 2 volumes. (1889; reprint ed., New York: AMS, 1966).

Authentick Memoirs — *Authentick Memoirs of the Life of that Celebrated Actress, Mrs. Ann Oldfield, Containing a Genuine Account of Her Transactions from Her Infancy to the Time of Her Decease,* 2d edition (London: J. Johnson, 1730). Unless otherwise indicated, all references are to this edition.

Biographical Dictionary — Philip H. Highfill, Jr., Kalman A. Burnim, and Edward A. Langhans, *A Biographical Dictionary of Actors, Actresses, Musicians, Dancers, Managers, and Other Stage Personnel in London, 1660–1800,* 16 volumes in progress (Carbondale and Edwardsville: Southern Illinois University Press, 1973—).

Chetwood — W. R. Chetwood, *A General History of the Stage from Its Origin in Greece down to the Present Time* (London: W. Owen, 1749).

Davies, DM — Thomas Davies, *Dramatic Miscellanies: Consisting*

of Critical Observations on Several Plays of
Shakespeare: With a Review of His Principal
Characters, and Those of Various Eminent Writers,
As Represented by Mr. Garrick, and Other
Celebrated Comedians. With Anecdotes of Dramatic
Poets, Actors &c, 3 volumes. (London: printed for
the author, 1783–84).

Faithful Memoirs   Faithful Memoirs of the Life, Amours and
                          Performances of that justly Celebrated, and most
                          Eminent Actress of her Time, Mrs. Anne Oldfield.
                          Interspersed with Several Other Dramatical Memoirs.
                          (London: no publisher [o.p.], 1731).

London Stage   The London Stage, 1660–1800, 5 parts in 11
                          volumes. (Carbondale: Southern Illinois
                          University Press, 1960–68). Part 1, ed. William
                          Van Lennap, Emmett L. Avery, and Arthur H.
                          Scouten (1965); part 2, ed. Emmett L. Avery
                          (1960); part 3, ed. Arthur H. Scouten (1961).

PRO PROB   Public Record Office, Principal Probate Registry.

PRO LC   Public Record Office, Lord Chamberlain's
                          Records.

Survey of London   Survey of London (London: Joint Publishing
                          Committee Representing the London County
                          Council and the London Survey Committee,
                          1900—). Volume 20, part 3 (St. Martin-in-the-
                          Fields); volume 29, part 1 (St. James
                          Westminster); volume 36 (St. Paul, Covent
                          Garden); and volume 39 (Mayfair).

Notes

1. Origins

1. Thomas Campbell, *The Life of Mrs. Siddons* (London: Edward Moxon, 1839), 69. Campbell is not, of course, an authority on the beauty of Mrs. Oldfield, but the perpetuator of a legend.

2. Chetwood, p. 202; Cibber, preface to *The Provok'd Husband* (1728), quoted in *Faithful Memoirs*, p. ix.

3. Davies, DM, 3:433. For Macklin's description of her performance of Lady Townly, see chapter 11.

4. For a discussion of these works, see chapter 12.

5. See chapter 11 for a discussion of the spurious "Richard Savage" letter, which, if genuine, would be the only extant letter in Mrs. Oldfield's hand.

6. The first use of the epithet "Ophelia" that I know of appears in Susanna Centlivre's poem to Mrs. Oldfield on the occasion of her appearance in *Cato*, quoted in *Faithful Memoirs*, pp. 58–59. It may have been commonplace by then.

7. *Faithful Memoirs*, p. 1.

8. *Authentick Memoirs*, p. 13.

9. Poor rate books for the parish of St. Martin-in-the-Fields, Westminster City Library, London, 1670–82. Also in the collection of the Westminster City Library is a scrapbook of clippings, *Inns, Taverns, Alehouses, etc. in and Around London*, collected by D. Foster (c. 1900). Volume 27:330–32 contains newspaper clippings from the 1670s to 1709 on the George Tavern in Pall Mall.

10. *Authentick Memoirs*, p. 14.

11. *The Registers of Marriages of St. Mary le Bone, Middlesex, 1668–1754* (London: The Harleian Society, 1917), 91. This information was supplied to me by Edward Langhans, from the notes for his entry on Mrs. Oldfield in

the *Biographical Dictionary*. Unfortunately, there is no way of knowing whether these are Anne's parents, for just as we do not know her mother's maiden name, we do not know her father's Christian name. But it seems more than coincidental that Anne Oldfield had an aunt named Gourlaw, an uncommon English surname.

12. At the library of The Society of Genealogists in London, I discovered, in one of the "name drawers" (card files arranged by surname), under "Oldfield," the following handwritten, unsigned entry: "Oldfield, Anne, dau of William and Anne, February 25, 1682, Westminster." Since this appeared to be a transcription of a baptismal record, and since the names and dates fit so perfectly—a baptismal date of February 25, 1682 would be 1683, New Style, and she could have been the daughter of William Oldfield and Anne Gourlaw—I returned to the Westminster City Library to recheck the baptismal records for all parishes in Westminster in 1682 and also 1681 and 1683. I also checked Westminster Abbey, although it was unlikely that so humble a person would be baptised there. But no source for the citation could be found. I cannot, therefore, report this information as fact, but I must report the finding of it.

13. *Authentick Memoirs*, p. 15.

14. Two Oldfields, George and Sam, are listed among the commissioned officers in Charles Dalton, ed., *English Army Lists and Commission Registers, 1661–1714* (London: Eyre and Spottiswoode, 1892), volume 2. Both were cornets, the lowest ranking commissioned officer, and both received their commissions during the brief reign of James II. Oldfield is a fairly common surname. My doubts prevail.

15. Colonel Clifford Walton, *History of the British Standing Army* (London: Harrison and Sons, 1894), 647. "Working pay," an additional sixpence at home and eighteen pence abroad, was instituted in 1680.

16. *London Stage*, 2:lvii.

17. *Faithful Memoirs*, p. 2. A "Widdow Vosse" or "Voss" was a ratepayer in St. James's Market from 1692 to 1698, according to the rate books for the Parish of St. James, Piccadilly in the Westminster City Library, but there is no reference to a Mitre Tavern.

18. *Faithful Memoirs*, p. 2.

19. *Authentick Memoirs*, pp. 15–16.

20. *Authentick Memoirs*, 3d edition, p. 16.

21. Chetwood, p. 200.

22. *Faithful Memoirs*, pp. 76–77.

23. Chetwood, p. 201.

24. I infer this from the renewal of her verbal agreement with Christopher Rich on March 20, 1704. Since that was the middle of the season, an

unusual time for making a contract, I have assumed that her first contract with Rich was made in March 1699 and renewed every year, or every few years, at that time. For a more complete discussion of the 1704 contract, see chapter 6.

25. *Authentick Memoirs,* 3d edition, p. 16.

26. For a discussion of actors' salaries see the article by Judith Milhous, "United Company Finances, 1682–1692," *Theatre Research International,* 7 (Winter, 1981/2): 45–50. Comparing actors' salaries with contemporary estimates of salaries of skilled and unskilled wage earners, Milhous concludes that actors were relatively well paid. She notes also (p. 47) that actors were paid more than actresses—as one can see by examining contracts and other playhouse documents in the Lord Chamberlain's records—and that until the establishment of the rebel company at Lincoln's Inn Fields (LIF) in 1695, there were no actress-sharers. This subject will be discussed more fully in chapter 6 in relation to the attempt to include Anne Oldfield among the actor-managers of the Haymarket company in 1709.

2.   *Apprenticeship*

1. *Apology,* 1:305.

2. *Apology,* 1:181. Nothing is said about Anne being an unsalaried probationer, but it is likely that she did not receive the fifteen shillings per week at which she was hired until she had completed a brief probation.

3. Much information about actors and their roles for this period comes from the "Dramatis Personae" in published texts. There are often small parts— chiefly servants—omitted from these cast lists.

4. See *London Stage,* 1:516 for documentation concerning the total number of performances during the season of 1699–1700.

5. The failure rate for new drama was quite high. *Love Without Interest, The Rise and Fall of Massaniello,* and *Achilles* were all failures. Big successes, such as *The Constant Couple,* were rare.

6. Judith Milhous and Robert D. Hume, ed., *Roscius Anglicanus* (London: The Society for Theatre Research, 1987), 106. The popular Restoration actor Charles Hart was often cast opposite Nell Gwynn, as Anne Oldfield was with Robert Wilks.

7. For a detailed account of this episode, see Judith Milhous, *Thomas Betterton and the Management of Lincoln's Inn Fields, 1695–1708* (Carbondale: Southern Illinois University Press, 1979), chapter 3.

8. For the complex history of the ownership of the Drury Lane patent, see Judith Milhous, "Company Management," in *The London Theatre World,*

1660–1800, ed. Robert D. Hume (Carbondale: Southern Illinois University Press, 1980), 6–12.

9. *Apology,* 1:252–53.

10. *Apology,* 1:237–38.

11. *Apology,* 1:239. Powell returned to Drury Lane in 1704, playing Lord Morelove in *The Careless Husband.* Except for a few appearances at the Haymarket and LIF, he remained at Drury Lane until his death in 1714. By 1704, he seems to have managed to coexist with Wilks, whose authority he did not challenge.

12. *Tatler,* number 182, various editions.

13. *Apology,* 1:182.

14. Aaron Hill, *The Prompter,* ed. William Appleton and Kalman A. Burnim (New York: Benjamin Blom, 1966), 24.

15. Davies, DM, 3:456–60. For a more favorable impression of Cibber see Helene Koon, *Colley Cibber: A Biography* (Lexington, Kentucky: The University Press of Kentucky, 1986).

16. Davies, DM, 2:131.

17. Davies, DM, 2:106.

18. Davies, DM, 3:461–62; Chetwood, pp. 196–97, has an earlier, shorter version of the story.

19. Daniel O'Bryan, Esq. [pseud.], *Authentick Memoirs or, The Life and Character of that Most Celebrated Comedian, Mr. Robert Wilks* (London: S. Slow, 1732), 19.

20. O'Bryan, *Authentick Memoirs of Robert Wilks,* p. 19. This is the only source for such stories.

21. Susannah Verbruggen remained at Drury Lane after her husband, John, went to LIF in 1697 because she had not been included among the joint-sharers. See Milhous, *Betterton and the Management of Lincoln's Inn Fields,* pp. 69–70.

22. *Apology,* 1:166.

23. *Apology,* 1:168–69.

24. For an estimate of the seating capacity of Drury Lane see *London Stage,* 2:xxiv–xxv. Edward Langhans, "The Theatres," in *London Theatre World, 1660–1800,* ed. Robert D. Hume, estimates the seating capacity of Drury Lane between 1674 and 1775 as five hundred to one thousand. The smaller figure would be more appropriate for the earlier eighteenth century.

25. *Apology,* 2:84–86.

26. Edward Langhans, in "Players and Playhouses, 1695–1710 and Their Effect On English Comedy," *Theatre Annual,* 29 (1973), speculates that the shortening of the forestage and the replacement of the lower proscenium doors with stage boxes, which caused the actors to retreat further upstage, toward the scenic area, caused a significant change in audience perception,

such that the actors seemed to "belong to the world of illusion that the scenery creates and not to the world of actuality that they inhabit in the house (p. 35)." He sees this change as contributing to a movement "away from the presentational form [of acting] so suitable for comedies of wit and toward a form more appropriate to comedies of character and situation (p. 36)." Peter Holland, *Ornament of Action: Text and Performance in Restoration Comedy* (Cambridge: Cambridge University Press, 1979), 29, argues on the same basis that this "retreat behind the proscenium" resulted in a trend toward sentimental comedy which is acted within the scenic area rather than in front of it. But Langhans, in his later chapter on playhouses in *London Theatre World, 1660–1800,* ed. Robert D. Hume, discusses the evidence that eighteenth-century actors "did not readily relinquish the forestage" (p. 45). I am not persuaded—by evidence from play texts and descriptions of actors and their styles of playing—that the remodeling of Drury Lane resulted in a significant change in the acting style that descended to Anne Oldfield from Nell Gwynn and Susannah Verbruggen.

27. Davies, DM, 3:459. Davies calls the room "the settle," but it is referred to as the "green room" by Jane Rogers in *The Memorial of Jane Rogers Humbly Submitted to the Town* [1712].

28. *Faithful Memoirs,* p. 2. There is no other evidence for this story, but it was obviously part of Mrs. Oldfield's legend by 1731.

29. [Charles Gildon], *The Life of Mr. Thomas Betterton, the Late Eminent Tragedian* (London: Robert Gosling, 1710), pp. 23–24.

30. As Edward Langhans warns us, in *Restoration Promptbooks* (Carbondale: Southern Illinois University Press, 1981), xxiii, what authors indicate in the way of scenery in stage directions, and what they actually got, were not necessarily the same. Very elaborate scenery was sometimes advertised, as part of "the show."

31. *Apology,* 1:305.

32. Chetwood, p. 201. He also states that Vanbrugh revised the play on her account, which accords with other statements that Vanbrugh was promoting her.

33. See *London Stage,* 2:xcvi. The importance of the benefit as an adjunct to an actor's annual income can be seen in the comment, in the *Universal Spectator,* March 8, 1729, that Anne's takings from her benefit that season totalled about five hundred pounds, of which £240 came from regular ticket prices and the rest from "several Persons of Quality, &c. giving five, ten, and twenty Guineas each." Even if this estimate is inflated, her benefit proceeds would have more than equaled her annual salary. It would be many years, of course, before she had a large number of wealthy patrons.

34. *The History of the English Stage from the Restauration to the Present Time*

(London: E. Curll, 1741), 163, quotes Margaret Saunders as asserting that
Vanbrugh was Anne Oldfield's "great friend in the Business of the House."

35. *Faithful Memoirs,* p. 77.
36. *The Perjur'd Husband; or, The Adventures of Venice. A Tragedy* (London:
    Bennet Banbury, 1700).
37. Joseph Wood Krutch, *Comedy and Conscience After the Restoration* (New
    York: Columbia University Press, 1924) contains the most thorough
    discussion of the "onslaught on the stage." See also Calhoun Winton,
    "The London Stage Embattled: 1695–1710," *Tennessee Studies in Literature,*
    19 (1974): 9–19.
38. Krutch, *Comedy and Conscience,* pp. 175–76.
39. Thomas Baker, *The Humour of the Age* (London: B. Lintott, 1701), act 5.
40. Elkanah Settle, *The Virgin Prophetess; or, The Fate of Troy* (London: A.
    Roper, 1701), act 1, scene 1.
41. Candace Brook Katz, in "The Deserted Mistress Motif in Mrs. Manley's
    Lost Lover, 1696," *Restoration and Eighteenth Century Theatre Research,* 16
    (May 1977): 27–39, discusses the treatment of the same theme by a more
    "overtly feminist" playwright, Delariviere Manley. (Manley is commonly
    known by the Christian name Mary, but Constance Clark, in *Three
    Augustan Women Playwrights* [New York: Peter Lang, 1986], 99–100, dis-
    cusses the evidence that neither she nor her contemporaries used the name
    Mary, preferring instead some form of Delariviere.)
42. Cibber, in *Apology,* 1:263, notes that Rich was so pleased with the success
    of *The Funeral* that "he . . . paid us nine Days in one Week."
43. Shirley Strum Kenny, ed., *The Plays of Richard Steele* (Oxford: Clarendon
    Press, 1971), 53.
44. Staring B. Wells, ed., *A Comparison Between the Two Stages* (Princeton:
    Princeton University Press, 1942), 83.
45. May Fair was held around Whitsuntide each year, and since some of the
    actors had booths at the fair, the theaters were usually closed for a week
    or so. After 1709, the theaters no longer closed for May Fair. See *London
    Stage,* 2:xxxvi–vii.
46. Milhous, *Betterton and the Management of Lincoln's Inn Fields,* p. 147.
47. Bonamy Dobree, ed., *The Complete Works of Sir John Vanbrugh* (Blooms-
    bury: Nonesuch Press, 1927–28), 2:187–88.
48. Arthur R. Huseboe, *Sir John Vanbrugh* (Boston: Twayne Publishers, 1976),
    46–47.
49. *London Stage,* 2:28.
50. For a discussion of birth control in the eighteenth century see Lawrence
    Stone, *The Family, Sex and Marriage in England 1500–1800* (New York:
    Harper and Row, 1977), 415–17. The most commonly used method was
    coitus interruptus.

51. Wells, ed., *Comparison Between the Two Stages,* pp. 80–92.

52. There are many ways to define success or failure. For playwrights, a run of six nights would probably be a success even if the play was never performed again, for there would be an author's benefit on the third and the sixth night. For an acting company, a play was a success if it became a stock piece, to be repeated season after season. For an actor, also, a play was a success if it entered the repertory, especially if he or she was particularly associated with a role in it. In judging successes and failures, I have generally considered the actor's point of view. In some instances, a new play in which Anne Oldfield appeared was not a success at Drury Lane during her lifetime but was revived successfully elsewhere, or at a later date. A glance at appendix 2 will indicate the great number of new plays that were performed for only one season.

53. The stage history of *Love's Contrivance,* especially in its truncated version, is somewhat confusing. On the day of Anne's benefit, March 28, 1704, the Centlivre comedy appeared on a bill with Cibber's *The School Boy; or, The Comical Rivals.* No early cast is given for *The School Boy,* but Anne did not appear in it later. I suspect that she played Belliza in the shortened version of *Love's Contrivance* for her benefit in 1704.

54. *Register of the Parish of St. Martin-in-the-Fields,* microfilm, Westminster City Library. This information was supplied to me by Edward Langhans from notes for his entry on Susannah Verbruggen in the *Biographical Dictionary.*

55. *Apology,* 1:306–7. For "mifty" as a Cibberism for "miffed" see *The Oxford English Dictionary* (OED). In short, Anne spoke her lines in a resentful manner.

3.   *Whig and Lover*

1. See "Establishment of Ye Company," PRO LC 7/3, folio 161, for salaries for a proposed company of players; also actors' contracts, PRO LC 7/3, folios 105–22. It should be emphasized that some of the leading actors were real workhorses, appearing in almost all of the productions. This was less true for actresses because there were fewer roles for actresses. But if drawing power is taken into account, the female stars were still relatively underpaid.

2. *Faithful Memoirs,* p. 3.

3. For Mary Lee see *Biographical Dictionary,* 9:200–201. For Elizabeth Bow-tell, see John Harold Wilson, "Biographical Notes on Some Restoration Actresses, *Theatre Notebook,* 18 (Winter, 1963–64): 45–46, and *Biographical Dictionary,* 2:261. Letitia Cross did not act under her married name, Weier,

in part because her marriage was short-lived but chiefly because, as a married woman, she could not negotiate a contract on her own behalf. See Judith Milhous and Robert D. Hume, "Theatrical Politics at Drury Lane: New Light on Letitia Cross, Jane Rogers, and Anne Oldfield," *Bulletin of Research in the Humanities*, 85 (1982): 424–25.

4. For rumors of Bracegirdle's marriage, see *Biographical Dictionary*, 2:277–78. For rumors of Anne Oldfield's marriage, see chapter 9.

5. *Biographical Dictionary*, 1:313–15.

6. Catherine Howells, "The Kit-Cat Club: A Study of Patronage and Influence in Britain, 1696–1720" (Unpublished Ph.D. dissertation, University of California, Los Angeles, 1982), 33–36.

7. Joseph Foster, ed., *Alumni Oxonienses: The Members of the University of Oxford, 1500–1714* (London: n.p., n.d.), 959.

8. Add. MSS 36,707. Letters to James Harrington.

9. [John Oldmixon], *The Life and Posthumous Works of Arthur Maynwaring, Esq.* (London: A. Bell, 1715), 9.

10. Oldmixon, *Life*, p. 8.

11. Harleian MSS, 2,262. This was a splendid income, *if* he actually received it regularly. He did not leave a large estate at his death, owing in part to extravagant habits and, no doubt, to the high-powered company he kept. His poverty, then, should be considered *relative* within his social circle.

12. Oldmixon, *Life*, pp. 22–23.

13. Steele did not become a member until about 1704. For Kit-Cat support of the theater, see Huseboe, *Sir John Vanbrugh*, pp. 41–47, and Howells, "The Kit-Cat Club," pp. 136–45.

14. Robert Gore-Brown gives an account of their meeting in *Gay Was the Pit; The Life and Times of Anne Oldfield* (London: Max Reinhardt, 1957), 48–49, for which there is not a shred of evidence.

15. Oldmixon, *Life*, p. 42.

16. John Harold Wilson, *All the King's Ladies* (Chicago: University of Chicago Press, 1958), 27.

17. [William Cooke], *Memoirs of Charles Macklin, Comedian* (London: James Asperne, 1804), 24–25. Emphasis is in the original. Gore-Brown accepts the story without question and, for good measure, sets it in Bath in 1703; *Gay Was the Pit*, p. 57.

18. Rumors about such an incident must have circulated earlier in the century, for the 3d edition of the *Authentick Memoirs*, pp. 38–39, tells of attentions paid to her by "a certain late Noble Duke," but gives different details and does not mention Maynwaring. The reference may have been to the second Duke of Bedford, who died in 1712, but from what I have learned about his background and his domineering mother, Rachel, Lady Russell, I have doubts about the story.

19. Oldmixon, *Life,* p. 42.
20. Edward Niles Hooker and H. T. Swedenberg, Jr., general editors, *The Works of John Dryden* (Berkeley: University of California Press, 1970), 10:192.
21. See appendix 3 for a list of her prologues and epilogues.
22. Oldmixon, *Life,* p. 44.
23. *Faithful Memoirs,* p. 12.
24. Frank H. Ellis, ed., *Swift vs. Mainwaring: The Examiner and The Medley* (New York and Oxford: Clarendon Press, 1985), li. James Stanley, tenth earl of Derby, was a fervent Whig but not a Kit-Cat. He has been characterized as an important borough patron by Geoffrey Holmes in *British Politics in the Age of Anne* (London: Hambledon Press, revised edition, 1987), 241. Some modern scholars use the "Mainwaring" spelling; I have spelled it the way Maynwaring himself signed his name.
25. Ellis, in *Swift vs. Mainwaring,* pp. lii–liii, notes, however: " . . . his correspondence with the Duchess is also full of very good advice for dealing with the Queen, which the Duchess simply chose to ignore. The truth seems to be that no one could have any influence on the Duchess of Marlborough."
26. Oldmixon, *Life,* p. 349.
27. Oldmixon, *Life,* pp. 43–44.
28. Ellis, *Swift vs. Mainwaring,* p. liii, says that before the fall of the Whig government in 1710, Maynwaring was offered an important post, "presumably treasurer of the Navy," which entailed a seat in the Privy Council, but that "wholly through the interest of the Duchess of Marlborough, the treasurership went to Robert Walpole, whose personal finances were in perilous straits." Maynwaring's liaison with Anne, which made him vulnerable to public attack, and of which the duchess disapproved, may also have been a determining factor.
29. Oldmixon, *Life,* p. 20.

4.   *Lady Betty*

1. Faithful Memoirs, p. 11.
2. *Apology,* 1:309.
3. *Apology,* 1:308.
4. See Judith Milhous, "The Date and Import of the Financial Plan for a United Theatre Company in PRO LC 7/3," *Maske und Kothurn,* 21 (1975): 81–88.
5. Because theatrical records are still very scanty for this period and casts for stock pieces were seldom advertised, I can only surmise that Mrs. Oldfield

fell heir to these roles soon after Susannah Verbruggen's death. She was certainly playing them regularly five years later. It is possible, however, that Frances Knight played Lurewell for a while.

6. Kenny, *Plays of Richard Steele,* p. 105.

7. Kenny, *Plays of Richard Steele,* p. 116.

8. *Apology,* 2:14. Milhous, in *Betterton and the Management of Lincoln's Inn Fields,* p. 180, notes that Drury Lane was careful to advertise the piece in 1704 as "revis'd and amended, with most material and considerable Alterations both in Title and Substance . . . by Her Majesty's Permission."

9. No cast is given for the 1704 production, and Mrs. Oldfield's name does not appear in the cast until 1711. Nevertheless, James J. Devlin, in "The Dramatis Personae and the Dating of *The Albion Queens,*" *Notes and Queries* (June 1963): 213–15, devises a convincing hypothetical cast for the 1704 production, based on the appearance of what appear to be prompt notes in the first quarto. Mrs. Oldfield's name does not appear there, either, but I agree with Devlin that she was probably in the original cast. If Jane Rogers had originally played Mary, Queen of of Scots, the acquisition of the role by Anne Oldfield in 1711 would undoubtedly have been added to Rogers's list of grievances.

10. For a more complete discussion of this contract, see chapter 6. Since the contract was verbal, we have only Rich's word on the details. I am here correcting an error that has been repeated by everyone who discusses this contract. Because Rich gives the date as March 20, 1703, it has been assumed that the contract was signed in the calendar year of 1703, but because the five-year contract was still in effect in early March 1709, it obviously dates from 1704. The confusion over dates has arisen from the custom of beginning the new year on March 25. Many documents of the period express dates between January 1 and March 25 with both years (e.g., March 20, 1703/4), but Rich's "Answer" does not.

11. In the *Apology,* 1:308, Cibber says that he took up *The Careless Husband* again right after Anne's demonstration of her talent at Bath in 1703. "My Doubts were dispell'd, and I had now a new Call to finish it: Accordingly, *The Careless Husband* took its Fate upon the Stage the Winter following, in 1704." I suspect that he did not work on the play again until later in the 1703–4 season, by which time he would have known that Anne's performance at Bath was not a fluke.

12. Maureen Sullivan, ed., *Colley Cibber: Three Sentimental Comedies* (New Haven: Yale University Press, 1973), 22.

13. *Apology,* 1:173.

14. Sullivan, *Colley Cibber,* p. 89. Richard Barker, in *Mr Cibber of Drury Lane* (New York: Columbia University Press, 1939), 49, also notes the similarity between Millamant and Lady Betty Modish. I am surprised that

Ben Ross Schneider, in "The Coquette-Prude as an Actress's Line in Restoration Comedy During the Time of Mrs. Oldfield," *Theatre Notebook*, 22 (1968): 158–59, does not include Millamant in his list of coquette-prude roles.

15. Sullivan, *Colley Cibber*, p. 107.
16. Davies, DM, 2:407.
17. [Cooke], *Memoirs of Charles Macklin*, p. 23.
18. Kenny, *Plays of Richard Steele*, p. 225.
19. Kenny, *Plays of Richard Steele*, pp. 233–34.
20. But see Kenny, *Plays of Richard Steele*, pp. 196–98 for the story of the play's initial poor showing and Steele's financial difficulties with Rich.
21. *Faithful Memoirs*, p. 12.

5. Principal Comedienne

1. For a discussion of Farquhar's professional and financial problems during part of this period, see Robert John Jordan, "George Farquhar's Military Career," *Huntington Library Quarterly*, 37 (1974): 251–64.
2. The new plays in which they were paired were *The Pilgrim* (1700), *The Albion Queens* (1704), *Hampstead Heath* (1705), and *The Basset Table* (1705). The stock pieces were *The Spanish Fryar*, *The Constant Couple*, *The Rover*, and *The Chances*.
3. *The Works of His Grace George Villiers, Duke of Buckingham* (London: T. Evans, 1775), 1:327. Buckingham's adaptation of the Fletcher comedy was one of the most popular stock pieces on the Restoration and early eighteenth-century stage.
4. Michael Shugrue, ed., *The Recruiting Officer* (Lincoln: University of Nebraska Press, 1965), 19. Subsequent page references are to this text.
5. For a discussion of the erotic significance of the breeches role, see Wilson, *All the King's Ladies*, pp. 73–86, and "The Breeches Part," by Pat Rogers, in *Sexuality in Eighteenth-Century Britain*, ed. Paul-Gabriel Boucé (Manchester: Manchester University Press, 1982), 244–58.
6. Shugrue, ed., *The Recruiting Officer*, p. 64.
7. *Apology*, 2:314.
8. In addition to Anne Oldfield, they included Robert Wilks, William Bullock, Colley Cibber, Benjamin Johnson, Theophilus Keen, John Mills, and Henry Norris. Richard Estcourt, Will Pinkethman, George Powell, Letitia Cross (and probably Jane Rogers) remained at Drury Lane. See *London Stage*, 2:129–30.
9. Theatrical records for this period are very scanty, and only one performance of *The Amorous Widow* (advertised by its subtitle, *The Wanton Wife*)

is recorded for the Haymarket season, on Friday, February 7. No offering of any kind is listed for the Haymarket on Thursday, February 6, but there probably was a performance on that date (a normal playing day) and it might—just might—have been the first of the two legendary performances of *The Amorous Widow.*

10. *Authentick Memoirs,* pp. 20–22.
11. Downes, in *Roscius Anglicanus,* ed. Milhous and Hume, p. 65, notes that the actress who originated Mrs. Brittle, Jane Long, performed the role so well "that none Equall'd her but Mrs. *Bracegirdle."* This was written before the role became part of Anne Oldfield's repertoire.
12. *Authentick Memoirs,* p. 22.
13. W. S. Lewis, ed., *Horace Walpole's Correspondence* (New Haven: Yale University Press, 1954), 17:435.
14. *Faithful Memoirs,* p. 31. The following reference to "other Disputes fomented among the Managers," may be an allusion to the contest.
15. PRO LC 7/2, folio 3.
16. *London Stage,* 2:141. The wording of the advertisement suggests that Anne's benefit was a last-minute change.
17. There is some disagreement about her age. Edward Langhans, in the *Biographical Dictionary,* concludes from the age given at the time of her death in 1748—eighty-five years—that she was born in 1663. But I agree with Lucyle Hook, in "Anne Bracegirdle's First Appearance," *Theatre Notebook,* 13 (1959): 133–36, that the evidence of Mrs. Bracegirdle's career indicates that she was born about ten years later and that there was an error about her age at the time of her death. That would make her age at the time of her retirement, in 1707, only thirty-four, and would mean that her departure from the stage was not motivated by a sense that she was past her prime.
18. John Genest, *Some Account of the English Stage from the Restoration in 1660 to 1830* (Bath: n.p., 1832), 2:376.
19. Add. MSS 40,060, folio 67. I am indebted to Catherine Howells for helping me to find this document. She notes that Scarsdale was not a Kit-Cat and that the entire entry is probably facetious. *Biographical Dictionary,* 2:277 mentions the Earl of Scarsdale's bequest of one thousand pounds to Mrs. Bracegirdle in his will, proved early in 1708, which, in addition to the high salaries she had been getting for more than ten years, made her early retirement possible.
20. *Apology,* 1:189.
21. There is the matter, however, of Anne Oldfield playing Monimia in Otway's *The Orphan* on March 1, 1706, only three nights after her benefit. Monimia was one of Barry's most famous roles, and it is hard to understand why Anne played it at this time. The cast of this production, like

many casts in the 1706–7 season, was a mixture of actors from both companies. Keen (Acasto), Wilks (Castalio), Cibber (the chaplain), and Oldfield were from Drury Lane; Booth (Polydore) and Verbruggen (Chamont) from the LIF/Haymarket company. (In the absence of other Drury Lane actresses besides Mrs. Mills, a member of the LIF/Haymarket company must have played Serena.) It is unlikely that Anne had played Monimia before, since *The Orphan* had not been performed very often at Drury Lane and she had appeared in very few tragedies at this time. Because the role was strongly associated with Barry, several possibilities occur: (1) Barry, also piqued by Anne's precedence in the benefit schedule, staged a brief walkout and then thought the better of it; (2) Barry was ill; (3) there was a misprint.

22. Davies, DM, 3:204.

23. PRO LC 7/2, folio 3.

24. Mismated wives in Restoration comedies, especially lively young women married to impotent or otherwise ineffectual older men, often cuckolded their husbands. One of Anne's most popular stock roles was Laetitia in *The Old Batchelor,* who cuckolds her husband, Fondlewife, without a qualm. Reconciliations could therefore be regarded with skepticism.

25. Michael Cordner, ed., *The Beaux' Stratagem* (London: Ernest Benn Limited, 1976), 30. Subsequent page references are to this text.

26. Judith Milhous and Robert D. Hume discuss the implications of this obsession with money in *Producible Interpretation: Eight English Plays, 1675–1707* (Carbondale: Southern Illinois University Press, 1985), chapter 10.

27. Edna Leake Steeves, ed., *The Art of Sinking in Poetry* (New York: Columbia University Press, 1952), 67.

28. Cordner, ed., *The Beaux' Stratagem,* pp. 121–22.

29. See Milhous and Hume, *Producible Interpretation,* pp. 291–95, for a review of the criticism.

30. Chetwood, p. 151, note b. Milhous and Hume, *Producible Interpretation,* p. 293, note 10, express disbelief in the authenticity of the anecdote. I agree, but I find it interesting that the story was told at all.

31. Milhous and Hume, *Producible Interpretation,* pp. 312–16. The authors note that the production history of the play suggests that the latter approach, lighthearted "romp," which is more pleasing to audiences, has generally been the case. See also the essay by Hume in *The Rakish Stage: Studies in English Drama, 1660–1800* (Carbondale: Southern Illinois University Press, 1983), 203, in which he describes the play as "humane comedy at its finest" and adds: "Farquhar indulges in departure from reality, but he is not blind to it."

32. By this time she had exchanged the role of prim Lady Sharlot, in *The*

Funeral, for that of the livelier Lady Harriet, playing opposite Wilks. Jane Rogers exchanged the role of Lady Harriet for the meatier, if less attractive, character of Lady Brumpton, which had been originated by Susannah Verbruggen. It is possible that this change occurred soon after Verbruggen's death and that Anne had been playing Lady Harriet since the fall of 1703—unfortunately there is no information on casts until March 1708. For a discussion of Anne's new, more sophisticated characters, see chapter 7.

33. Oldmixon, *Life,* p. 42.
34. George Stonehill, ed., *The Complete Works of George Farquhar* (London: Nonesuch Press, 1930), 2:325.
35. In the *Biographia Britannica* (London: W. Innys, 1750), 3:1888–89, a man described as "an old officer of the army, who had very well known Mr. Farquhar and some of his youthful gallantries," identified Anne as the Penelope of *Love and Business.* The story was repeated in the introduction to a late eighteenth-century edition of Farquhar's works and has gained currency simply by being repeated so often. Eric Rothstein, in *George Farquhar* (New York: Twayne Publishers, 1967), 106, notes a number of discrepancies between the letters and the real life circumstances of Farquhar and Oldfield, concluding: "Given these facts, it would be wiser to avoid miring onself in unsubstantial hypotheses, and to assume that the 'Farquhar' . . . of the letters represents a fictional *persona.*"
36. Stonehill, ed., *Complete Works of George Farquhar,* 2:316–17.
37. Anne has also been identified by Stonehill as the character of Chloe in *Letters of Wit, Politicks and Morality,* to which Farquhar was a contributor. See Stonehill, ed., *Complete Works of George Farquhar,* 2:256. Shirley Strum Kenny has examined the problem of the authorship of the "Celadon-Astrea" letters, in which Chloe appears. Despite the inclusion of what seem to be biographical details from Farquhar's life, including a reference to Chloe that may allude to the story of his discovery of Anne Oldfield, she concludes that the letters in the Celadon-Astrea sequence are not Farquhar's. Shirley Strum Kenny, ed., *The Works of George Farquhar* (Oxford: Clarendon Press, 1988), 2:416–20.
38. *Faithful Memoirs,* p. 69.

6. *Mrs. Oldfield Complains*

1. The complex issues underlying the events of this chapter are lucidly and thoroughly discussed by Judith Milhous and Robert D. Hume in "The Silencing of Drury Lane in 1709," *Theatre Journal,* 32 (December 1980): 427–47. They argue that a plot was engineered by a group of actors at

Drury Lane, in cahoots with the Lord Chamberlain, to put Rich out of business. I am, of course, chiefly interested in the events as they involve Mrs. Oldfield.

2. *Apology*, 2:8; 1:334–35.

3. Judith Milhous and Robert D. Hume, ed., *Vice Chamberlain Coke's Theatrical Papers, 1706–1715* (Carbondale: Southern Illinois University Press, 1982), 49–50.

4. PRO LC 7/2, folios 102–3.

5. James Boswell, *The Life of Samuel Johnson, LL.D.* (London: Macmillan and Company, 1929), 57, note 1, recounts the story that the famous "Steinkirk scene" in *The Careless Husband,* in which Lady Easy discovers her sleeping husband in compromising circumstances with her maid and covers his bare head with her kerchief, was inspired by an incident in the domestic life of the Bretts.

6. See appendix 2.

7. She later played the pathetic Countess of Rutland in the same play, but the role was not a major addition to her repertory.

8. Chetwood, p. 201.

9. George Colman, *Epicoene; or, The Silent Woman* (London: T. Becket, 1776), 74. This was, of course, a reversal of the more common situation in which a woman dressed in boy's clothes is revealed, at the end, as a woman.

10. Davies, DM, 2:406–7.

11. *The Laureat: or, The Right Side of Colley Cibber, Esq.* (London: J. Roberts, 1740), 56.

12. The plays were William Burnaby's *Reform'd Wife* and *The Ladies' Visiting Day,* and Susanna Centlivre's *Love at a Venture;* Cibber had rejected the Centlivre play upon her submission of it several seasons earlier.

13. Burnaby's play had capitalized upon the interest aroused by the visit of Peter the Great to London in 1698.

14. Colley Cibber, *The Dramatic Works of Colley Cibber, Esq.* (London: C. Hitch and L. Hawes, 1760), 3:106.

15. *Apology*, 2:2–3.

16. Emmett L. Avery, *Congreve's Plays on the Eighteenth-Century Stage* (New York: Modern Language Association, 1951), 37.

17. Reprinted in Percy Fitzgerald, *A New History of the Stage* (London: Tinsley Brothers, 1882), 2:445.

18. *Apology*, 2:68.

19. Figures taken from "Rich's Answer," PRO LC 7/3, folio 175, and from Zachary Baggs, *Advertisement Concerning the Poor Actors, Who Under Pretence of Hard Usage from the Patentees, Are About to Desert Their Service* [1709], 2.

20. PRO LC 7/3, folio 104.
21. "Rich's Answer."
22. *Apology,* 2:71. The Lord Chamberlain's order, PRO LC 5/154.
23. The contracts, duly signed and witnessed in the Lord Chamberlain's Office, are in PRO LC 7/3, folios 105–20. Most were signed in March, April, and May, before the Lord Chamberlain acted against Rich.
24. PRO LC 7/3, folios 111–12. The provision that allowed her not to act before September 10 or after June 10 was not a special favor but a standard feature of contracts, since these dates typically represented the beginning and the end of the season. An examination of her performance schedule over the years indicates that she usually acted between these dates, sometimes ending the season a little earlier—by the end of May.
25. As a holdover, perhaps, from the days of all-male companies, after women began to act professionally in 1660 they were not admitted to the elite ranks of actor-sharers, who shared in the profits. Actresses retained the lower status of salaried players even after they had become well established.
26. See Milhous, *Betterton and the Management of Lincoln's Inn Fields,* pp. 162–63.
27. *Apology,* 2:69–71.
28. *Apology,* 2:68.
29. Baggs, *Advertisement Concerning the Poor Actors,* p. 2.
30. *Apology,* 2:72.
31. *Survey of London,* 36:205–9.
32. Deed in the Greater London Record Office. "Peppercorn rent" for the first two years of a lease is a standard provision, intended to encourage development of property.
33. See *Survey of London,* 36:232. Plate 48b shows Covent Garden in the eighteenth century, and one can almost see Mrs. Oldfield's house, just off the plaza in the upper left corner.
34. *Survey of London,* 36:211.
35. Add. MSS 61,459, folios 29–30. Undated letter, placed from internal evidence among his correspondence in the spring of 1708.
36. Baggs, *Advertisement Concerning the Poor Actors,* pp. 2–3.
37. *Faithful Memoirs,* p. 49.
38. Curll, *History of the English Stage,* p. 163.
39. *Registers of St. Bene't and St. Peter, Paul's Wharf* (London: Harleian Society, 1911), 102.
40. Information on young Maynwaring's military career is in Charles Dalton, *George the First's Army, 1714–1727* (London: Eyre and Spottiswoode, 1912), 2:218–19. He is described in a footnote (p. 219) as "an illegitimate son of Anne Oldfield the famous actress."

41. Lady Llanover, ed., *The Autobiography and Correspondence of Mary Granville, Mrs. Delany* (London: R. Bentley, 1861–62), 1:2.
42. PRO PROB 11 (1711), folio 522.
43. *Authentick Memoirs*, pp. 27–28.
44. Oldmixon, *Life*, p. 345.

7.   The Distrest Mother

1. *Faithful Memoirs*, p. 31, describes her as "Sole Empress of the Stage," which was not technically true until Elizabeth Barry retired permanently at the end of the season of 1709–10. Barry had left the stage temporarily in the season of 1708–9.
2. MS collection of wardrobe and property bills, Drury Lane, in the Folger Shakespeare Library.
3. The Countess of Cork and Orrery, ed., *The Orrery Papers* (London: Duckworth and Company, 1903), 1:67.
4. See *Biographical Dictionary*, 9:58–60, for the roles played by Frances Knight. At Drury Lane, she played many of the leading roles that Barry played at LIF but she was not a star in terms of salary or reputation.
5. See Barker, *Mr Cibber of Drury Lane*, pp. 82–83; Milhous and Hume, "Silencing of Drury Lane," pp. 440–41.
6. Milhous and Hume, ed., *Vice Chamberlain Coke's Theatrical Papers*, pp. 130–31 and note 2. Milhous and Hume think that Swiney intended to include Mrs. Oldfield in a reorganized partnership. See also document 81, pp. 132–33.
7. *Apology*, 2:92–93, and note.
8. *Apology*, 2:94–95.
9. David Green, *Sarah Duchess of Marlborough* (New York: Charles Scribner's Sons, 1967), 154.
10. *London in 1710. From the Travels of Zacharias Conrad von Uffenbach*, trans. and ed. by W. H. Quarrell and Margaret Mare (London: Faber, 1934), 138–39.
11. She seems to have returned on May 24 as Hellena in *The Rover*, but was replaced again, on June 9, in *Epicoene* (advertised by its subtitle, *The Silent Woman*) and then finished up the season. Judith Milhous and Robert D. Hume, in "Theatrical Politics at Drury Lane: New Light on Letitia Cross, Jane Rogers, and Anne Oldfield," *Bulletin of Research in the Humanities*, 85 (1982): 421, note that from about March 9 until June 29, Mrs. Oldfield was mentioned in only one advertisement and that plays in which Jane Rogers appeared were featured. They suspect that Oldfield was ill or pregnant (or perhaps ill from pregnancy). But there is too little information

available to draw any definite conclusions. Very few casts were advertised during these months; we cannot assume that Oldfield was not appearing in plays that were in her repertoire simply because her name does not appear. She was clearly absent in May and part of June, when substitutes were announced for her roles.

12. Barker, *Mr Cibber of Drury Lane,* pp. 81–82.

13. See Henry L. Snyder, "Arthur Maynwaring and the Whig Press, 1710–1712," *Literatur als Kritik des Lebens: Festschrift zum 65. Geburtstag von Ludwig Borinski,* ed. Rudolf Haas, Heinz-Joachim Müllenbrock, and Claus Uhlig (Heidelberg: Quelle and Meyer, 1975), 120–36, for a discussion of Maynwaring's journalistic endeavors; also, Ellis, *Swift vs Mainwaring,* pp. liv–lxiii.

14. Add. MSS 61,461, folio 89. Letter dated Monday, November 6, 1710.

15. He did, however, continue to receive rent for costumes and properties taken from the Haymarket. See Milhous and Hume, *Vice Chamberlain Coke's Theatrical Papers,* pp. 175–76.

16. *Apology,* 2:70.

17. Add. MSS 57,861. Letters to Lord Coningsby, dated March 13, 1711 and June 5, 1711.

18. At the end of this season, she resigned the role of Alinda to young Mary Willis. Within the next three years, she dropped several other comic roles: Maria (*Fortune Hunters*), Florimell, and Silvia. Florimell was taken up at Drury Lane by Susannah Mountfort; *The Comical Lovers* was performed infrequently after 1710–11; after Anne gave up the role of Silvia, *The Recruiting Officer* was also performed infrequently at Drury Lane, but it became a popular stock piece at LIF after 1715, with Margaret Bicknell as Silvia. Eventually the play returned to the Drury Lane repertory, where it continued to be popular. For the popularity of Farquhar's plays, see Shirley Strum Kenny, "Perennial Favorites: Congreve, Vanbrugh, Cibber, Farquhar, and Steele," *Modern Philology,* 73, No. 4, Part 2 [Friedman Festschrift] (1976), S4–S11.

19. Milhous and Hume, *Vice Chamberlain Coke's Theatrical Papers,* p. 170.

20. Milhous and Hume, "Theatrical Politics at Drury Lane," p. 425. The *Biographical Dictionary,* 3:64, says that the managers "apparently refused to let her act but had put it about that the refusal had come from her." She did not appear on the London stage again until the formation of a new company at LIF in 1714.

21. Chetwood, p. 201.

22. The *Biographical Dictionary,* 2:211, gives the year of his birth as 1679 or 1681.

23. [Benjamin Victor], *Memoirs of the Life of Barton Booth, Esq.* (London: John Watts, 1733), 29.

24. Theophilus Cibber, *The Lives and Characters of the Most Eminent Actors and Actresses of Great Britain and Ireland, from Shakespear to the Present Time* (London: R. Griffiths, 1753), 50.

25. *London Stage,* 2:263. Kenny, in "Perennial Favorites," makes the point that comedy declined noticeably after 1710, when Congreve, Vanbrugh, Cibber, Farquhar, and Steele were no longer writing for the stage (pp. S5–S6).

26. [Gildon], *Life of Betterton,* p. 40.

27. Snyder, "Prologues and Epilogues," pp. 627–28.

28. Susanna Centlivre, *Works* (1760–61; rpt. as *Dramatic Works,* London: John Pearson, 1872), 2:252.

29. *Faithful Memoirs,* p. 32.

30. A unique copy of this document is in the Harvard Theatre Collection. The following account is taken from this document, unless otherwise indicated.

31. The import of the last sentence is not clear. Was Mrs. Oldfield threatening to walk out, period? Or was she refusing to play another role, Hermione, in the same play? Since it is unlikely that she was cast as Hermione, I suspect that she was threatening to quit altogether.

32. R. Jordan, "Richard Norton and the Theatre at Southwick," *Theatre Notebook,* 38 (1984): 114, note 26. This is probably the incident referred to by Cibber (*Apology,* 2:166) in which a dispute between two actresses over "the chief Part in a new Tragedy" caused such a disturbance that the managers were "forced to dismiss an Audience of a hundred and fifty Pounds." I am very grateful for Jordan's discovery of the letter to Norton, for until this document came to light there was no corroborating evidence for Mrs. Rogers's dismissal and for the disturbance at Mrs. Oldfield's benefit.

33. A transcription of this document is in the article by Milhous and Hume, "Theatrical Politics at Drury Lane," pp. 420–22. Subsequent quotations are from this transcription. In a note they identify Dr. Wall as a "pock-doctor"—a specialist in the treatment of venereal disease (p. 421).

34. A scabrous ballad about Robert Harley and Abigail Masham (who replaced Sarah Churchill as the queen's favorite), attributed to Maynwaring, is in Frank H. Ellis, ed., *Poems on Affairs of State* (New Haven: Yale University Press, 1975), 7:317–21.

35. So I interpret the phrase, "Mrs. *Rogers,* an Actress, who in her Turn, had made a considerable Figure on the Stage," in *Faithful Memoirs,* p. 32.

36. She may also have appeared in *Oroonoko* on May 20, *The Funeral* on May 30, and *The Recruiting Officer* on June 10.

37. *Apology,* 1:311. For a dissenting opinion about Anne in her later years, see the comment by Catherine Clive that a later actress, Fanny Abington,

playing Lady Townly, "is Mrs. Oldfield, that is, the vainest Monster that ever trod the stage." Letter in the Folger Shakespeare Library manuscript collection.

38. Ambrose Philips, *The Distrest Mother* (London: S. Buckley, 1712).

39. In the April 1, 1712 issue of the *Spectator,* Budgell insisted that it was not inappropriate for a tragedy such as *The Distrest Mother* to conclude with a comical epilogue: "The Moment the Play ends, Mrs. *Oldfield* is no more *Andromache,* but Mrs. *Oldfield;* and tho' the Poet had left *Andromache stone-dead upon the Stage* . . . Mrs. *Oldfield* might still have spoken a merry Epilogue." He was probably referring to Gwynn's famous epilogue at the end of *Tyrannick Love.* Epilogues were often dropped after the third night of the first run, but Mary E. Knapp, in *Prologues and Epilogues of the Eighteenth Century* (New Haven: Yale University Press, 1961), 23, quotes a number of playbills that advertise prologues and epilogues, evidently because they had become popular in themselves. This one was popular enough that the play was sometimes advertised, in later seasons, "with the original epilogue."

40. Chetwood, p. 92.

41. Reprinted at the end of *Faithful Memoirs,* pp. 201–2. Davies, DM, 3:242.

42. Add. MSS 64,461, folio 164. Letter tentatively dated July 1712.

43. Add. MSS 61,461, folio 166.

44. Add. MSS 61,461, folio 169.

45. Add. MSS 61,461, folio 165. Unsigned, dated only "Saterday six a clock [*sic*]." In 1980, I was able to identify the handwriting as that of Margaret Saunders, from her signature on Mrs. Oldfield's contract with Swiney in 1709. Dr. Frances Harris, who had indexed the Duchess of Marlborough's papers in the British Library manuscript collection, confirms the identification. (The signature contains eleven different letters, and their size and shape correspond to the same letters in words in the unsigned document.) It is interesting to see how nearly illiterate Mrs. Saunders was, when we read her elegantly written letters in *Faithful Memoirs* and Curll's *History of the English Stage.*

46. Add. MSS 61,461, folio 186. Within a few weeks Godolphin himself was dead—a terrible shock to the Churchills, whose devoted friend he had been for many years.

47. Portland Papers, Longleat House, 4: folio 182.

48. Oldmixon, *Life,* p. 343.

49. Reprinted in *Faithful Memoirs,* appendix 1, pp. 1–3. Checked against the copy in the Public Record Office.

50. "Consumption" was an all-embracing and very imprecise diagnosis at that time, covering a wide range of symptoms including violent fevers. It did not refer specifically to lung disease. It has often been said that Maynwaring

died of tuberculosis, but in the accounts of his illness in the summer of 1712, there is no reference whatever to coughing, to spitting blood, or to any weakness of the lungs—merely to high fever, chills, and delirium. Maynwaring's recurring fevers between 1710 and 1712, high enough to cause temporary deafness, resemble malaria. The "headake" to which he refers in his letter to the duchess in July 1712 is a classical symptom of the onset of a malarial attack. Malaria was endemic in England at this time; indeed, it was particularly prevalent in Hertfordshire, where the Marlborough estate at St. Albans was located, and it is ironic that at one point Maynwaring went there to recuperate.

51. Oldmixon, *Life,* pp. 350–51.

8. *Tragedienne*

1. *Authentick Memoirs,* p. 30. Her first performance after Maynwaring's death happened to be as Andromache in *The Distrest Mother.*
2. Preface to *Ximena; or, The Heroick Daughter,* in *Dramatic Works* (1760), 3:113–14.
3. Oldmixon, *Life,* p. 357.
4. *Authentick Memoirs,* 3d edition, p. 30, adds a mildly scandalous anecdote, reporting that she had an affair with a married man, a "Mr. F——e," who is said to have had "a very considerable place in his [*sic?*] Majesty's Customs." As it happens, a man named Henry Ferne held a position in the customs office at the time of Maynwaring's death, and he is probably the same Henry Ferne who, according to the poor rate books for the parish of St. Paul, Covent Garden, lived around the corner from Anne on Henrietta Street. There is nothing, however, to connect him with the statement in the *Flying-Post.* And indeed, from the context, it is doubtful that a specific person was referred to. Rather, the sense seems to be: We have it on good authority that any lover she may have must be a Whig.
5. *Apology,* 2:129–30.
6. Peter Smithers, *The Life of Joseph Addison* (Oxford: Clarendon Press, 1968), 260; John Oldmixon, *An Essay on Criticism* (1728; rpt. Los Angeles: Augustan Reprint Society, 1964), 5–6.
7. Smithers, *Life of Addison,* p. 260. Smithers suggests, and I agree, that the success of *The Distrest Mother,* an "edifying and correct tragedy," probably encouraged Addison to think that audiences would be receptive to *Cato.* See also *Apology,* 2:128.
8. Robert Halsband, "Addison's *Cato* and Lady Mary Wortley Montagu," *Publications of the Modern Language Association,* 65 (1950): 1122–29.
9. *Apology,* 2:128.

10. Lady Mary Wortley Montagu, *Essays and Poems,* ed. Robert Halsband (Oxford: Clarendon Press, 1977), 67.

11. Benjamin Rand, ed., *The Correspondence of George Berkeley and Sir John Percival* (Cambridge: Cambridge University Press, 1941), 112.

12. Harold Williams, ed., *Journal to Stella* (Oxford: Clarendon Press, 1948), 2:654.

13. Joseph Spence, *Anecdotes, Observations and Characters of Books and Men* (Carbondale: Southern Illinois University Press, 1964), 107.

14. Rand, *Correspondence of Berkeley and Percival,* p. 113. See also Steele's dedication to Addison's *The Drummer* (London: J. Darby and T. Combes, 1722).

15. George Sherburn, ed., *The Correspondence of Alexander Pope* (Oxford: Clarendon Press, 1956), 2:175.

16. Sherburn, ed., *Correspondence of Alexander Pope,* 2:175. Another version of the incident is given in the *Apology,* 2:130.

17. *Apology,* 2:130.

18. Rand, *Correspondence of Berkeley and Percival,* pp. 115–16.

19. *Apology,* 2:135–36. See also the article by Sybil Rosenfeld, "Some Notes on the Players in Oxford, 1661–1713," *Review of English Studies,* 19 (October 1943): 372–74. Reynardson, in "The Stage," reprinted in *Faithful Memoirs,* observes in a footnote (p. 201): "The Players last summer [i.e., 1711] were expected to play at Oxford, but were order'd away." If that was true, it is good to think that their behavior was so highly commended in 1713.

20. For details of the complex legal situation, see Barker, *Mr Cibber of Drury Lane,* pp. 90–96, which is based upon Cibber's own account in the *Apology,* 2:140–50. In two very interesting letters, transcribed in Milhous and Hume, *Vice Chamberlain Coke's Theatrical Papers,* pp. 194–97, Booth describes the economic disadvantages under which he had labored for so many years. Especially noteworthy is his claim (p. 197) that Cibber, Wilks, and Doggett had "by their shares for these two years past . . . receiv'd more money, than I have by my Salary, *since I was first an Actor"* [emphasis added].

21. MS collection of wardrobe and property bills, Drury Lane, in the Folger Shakespeare Library.

22. Barker, *Mr Cibber of Drury Lane,* p. 99.

23. Charles Johnson, *The Victim* (London: F. Burleigh, 1714).

24. J. R. Sutherland, *Three Plays by Nicholas Rowe* (London: Scholartis Press, 1929), 11. See also H. W. Pedicord, ed., *The Tragedy of Jane Shore* (Lincoln: University of Nebraska Press, 1974), xviii–xix.

25. Pedicord, ed., *The Tragedy of Jane Shore,* pp. xxi–xxii.

26. [Charles Gildon], *A New Rehearsal; or, Bays the Younger* (London: J. Roberts, 1714), 74.

27. Downes, *Roscius Anglicanus,* p. 95. See also the discussion in chapter 11.

28. Pedicord, ed., *The Tragedy of Jane Shore,* p. 49.

29. J. Douglas Canfield, in *Nicholas Rowe and Christian Tragedy* (Gainesville: University of Florida Press, 1977), 150, points out that Rowe followed the lead of Thomas Heywood in *Edward IV* in making the Shore marriage a happy one, broken only when Jane is compelled to become the king's mistress. Canfield's discussion of Christian imagery, which locates the play in the homiletic tradition, explains the power of much of the language. While I agree that human forgiveness is "emblematic of the divine" (p. 167), I believe it is especially significant that the husband pronounces redemption.

30. I discuss this development at length in my unpublished Ph.D. dissertation, "The Domestication of English Tragedy, 1700–1760," University of California, Berkeley (1974), 179–272.

31. Judith Milhous, in "The First Production of Rowe's *Jane Shore,*" *Theatre Journal,* 5 (October 1986): 314–15, analyzes the wardrobe bills (in the Folger Shakespeare Library collection) for this period and concludes that Anne wore two costumes—white satin with silk trim for the first four acts and a white calico gown, which could, presumably, be dirtied to convey the impression of Jane's wretched condition, for the fifth act. Nothing in these documents indicates whether Rowe's desire for historical costuming was realized. Cibber apparently wore the robes that he had worn in his adaptation of *Richard III* (Milhous, p. 318).

32. Jonathan Richardson, Jr., *Richardsoniana: or, Occasional Reflections on the Moral Nature of Man* (London: J. Dodsley, 1776), 77. This is a collection of miscellaneous reflections by the son of the artist who painted two portraits of Anne Oldfield.

33. [Edmund Curll], *The Life of That Eminent Comedian, Robert Wilks, Esq.* (London: E. Curll, 1733), 30.

34. Davies, DM, 3:469.

35. Victor, *The History of the Theatres of London and Dublin, from the Year 1730 to the Present Time* (Dublin: G. Faulkner & J. Exshaw, 1761), 2:57.

36. See my unpublished Ph.D. dissertation, pp. 457–62, 477–506.

37. Davies, DM, 3:464–65.

38. See appendix 2.

39. R. Warwick Bond, ed., *The Works of Francis Beaumont and John Fletcher* (London: George Bell and Sons and A. H. Bullen, 1905), 2:562.

40. Nell Gwynn and Susannah Verbruggen, neither of whom played tragedy (or played it well), were two predecessors in the role. Anne Bracegirdle probably played Caelia in productions at LIF—no cast information is available.

9. *Soldier and Courtier*

1. John Strype, *A Survey of the Cities of London and Westminster* (London: A. Churchill, 1720), 4:68. Henry B. Wheatley, in *London Past and Present: Its History, Associations, and Traditions* (London: John Murray, 1891), 2:198, adds the information, taken from rate books, that her house was "seven doors from the top."
2. [John Breval], *The Confederates* (London: R. Burleigh, 1717), 14.
3. In Charlotte Erikson's novel, *Narcissa; The Story of Nance Oldfield* (London: Hutchinson, 1956), Churchill, not Maynwaring, is Anne's great love. But most biographers and novelists have portrayed her as brokenhearted and bereft after Maynwaring's death.
4. J. H. Plumb, *Sir Robert Walpole: The King's Minister* (Boston: Houghton Mifflin, 1961), 42.
5. W. S. Lewis, ed., *Horace Walpole's Correspondence*, 30:42n. I can testify to the difficulty of reading Churchill's handwriting, having given up on one document that did not seem to have anything to do with Mrs. Oldfield, and plowed painfully through another that did. But the connection between bad handwriting and semiliteracy has not been established.
6. F. H. Blackburne Daniell, ed., *Calendar of State Papers, Domestic Series, for the Reign of Charles II, Preserved in the Public Record Office* (London: HMSO, 1904).
7. A. L. Rowse, *The Early Churchills: An English Family* (New York: Harper and Brothers, 1956), 319.
8. PRO PROB 12/115, folio 164.
9. The Churchills' sister Arabella had been James II's mistress many years earlier and had borne him four children, all of whom went into exile with the king in 1689. Despite their unswerving allegiance to Protestantism and the Hanoverian succession, the Churchills maintained connections with their Jacobite relations.
10. Charles Hanbury Williams, *The Works of the Right Honourable Sir Chas. Hanbury Williams* (London: E. Jeffrey and Son, 1822), 1:75.
11. Advertisement for a lost dog, in the *Daily Courant*, April 21, 1713.
12. *Faithful Memoirs*, p. 121.
13. Thomas Wentworth, Earl of Strafford, *The Wentworth Papers, 1705–1739* (London: Wyman and Sons, 1883), 442.
14. Robert Halsband, *Lord Hervey, Eighteenth-Century Courtier* (Oxford: Clarendon Press, 1973), 21.
15. John Hervey, Earl of Bristol, *Letter Books of John Hervey, First Earl of Bristol* (Wells: Ernest Jackson, 1894), 2:23.
16. John Loftis, *Steele at Drury Lane* (Berkeley: University of California Press, 1952), 37.

17. *Biographical Dictionary,* 2:285.
18. They included Mary Kent and Henrietta Moore, as well as Letitia Cross, returning to the London stage for the first time since her run-in with the actor-managers in 1711.
19. She had played Imoinda once before, but that was at the Haymarket during the season of 1706–7, when Jane Rogers was not in the company. As long as she and Rogers were performing together she did not attempt Imoinda. Likewise, she had played Berinthia twice at the Haymarket in the season of 1709–10, when Frances Knight was at Drury Lane, and once in the season of 1711–12. After Knight left Drury Lane, Anne played Berinthia three or four times each season and twice chose the role for her benefit.
20. Sir John Vanbrugh, *The Relapse,* ed. Curt A. Zimansky (Lincoln: University of Nebraska Press, 1970), 94.
21. For Churchill's part in the campaign see J. W. Fortescue, *A History of the British Army* (London: Macmillan and Company, 1899), 2:5–7.
22. Preface to the first edition, Nicholas Rowe, *The Tragedy of Lady Jane Gray* (London: B. Lintott, 1715).
23. Rowe, *The Tragedy of Lady Jane Gray,* pp. 36–37.
24. *Diary of Dudley Ryder, 1715–16,* edited and transcribed by William Matthews (London: Metheun, 1939), 181.
25. *An Epilogue Recommending the Cause of Liberty to the Beauties of Great Britain.* Second edition (London: Bernard Lintott, [1716]).
26. *Diary of Dudley Ryder,* p. 195.
27. *Diary of Dudley Ryder,* p. 359.
28. Edward Robins, *The Palmy Days of Nance Oldfield* (London: William Heinemann, 1898), 145–46. In *Gay Was the Pit,* p. 148, Gore-Brown repeats the story with his own alterations. The source for the story is Tom Davies, DM, 3:434.
29. Peter Quennell, *Caroline of England: An Augustan Portrait* (New York: Viking Press, 1940), 54–55.
30. Davies, DM, 3:434.
31. Manley, a playwright, novelist, journalist, and generally controversial figure in the early eighteenth century, was one of several people who took over the editing of the Tory *Examiner* after Swift gave it up in 1711. This circumstance led Gore-Brown to identify Manley as the author of the nasty posthumous attack upon Maynwaring in the *Examiner* in the spring of 1713 and to assume a relationship of enmity between the two women (*Gay Was the Pit,* pp. 123–24). Richard B. Kline, in "Anne Oldfield and Mary De La Riviere Manley: The Unnoticed Reconciliation," *Restoration and Eighteenth-Century Theatre Research* 14 (1975): 53–56, casts serious doubt upon this story. It is certainly true that Anne appeared in Manley's play in May 1717 without apparent reluctance, that Manley tried to make

amends to some of her former Whig enemies, and that in 1720 she wrote to Matthew Prior that on the occasion of a revival for her benefit, "gracious Mrs. Oldfield" had agreed to speak Prior's original epilogue (Kline, p. 55).

32. Among the candidates for Phoebe Clinkett are the Countess of Winchelsea, Susanna Centlivre, and the Duchess of Newcastle. See the discussion by John Fuller, editor of John Gay, *Dramatic Works* (Oxford: Clarendon Press, 1983), 1:440–42.

33. Fuller, in Gay, *Dramatic Works,* p. 442, refers to the "more speculative realm of satire through mimicry." It is true that we cannot be certain that the incidents described in *The Confederates* took place, but the effectiveness of such satirical pieces depended in part upon their basis in truth.

34. Richard Morton and William M. Peterson, ed., *Three Hours After Marriage, with* The Confederates *and the* Two Keys (Plainsville, Ohio: Lake Erie College Press, 1961), 88.

35. A helpful footnote to *A Key to the New Comedy,* in *Three Hours After Marriage,* ed. Morton and Peterson, explains that the "fat Baroness" is "Lady M—n." Metrical clues ("M—n" is a one-syllable name) and such telling details as her age, her fatness, and her red cheeks identified her further as Lady Mohun, widow of the notorious Baron Mohun. The "ill-judging Beauties (tho' of high Degree)" would easily be identified as three of Princess Caroline's maids of honor, who are supposed to have patronized the production.

36. Morton and Peterson, *Three Hours After Marriage,* p. 102.

37. Morton and Peterson, *Three Hours After Marriage,* p. 111.

10.   *The Patent Company*

1. *London Stage,* 2:475.

2. For a description of the theater, which was torn down at the end of the eighteenth century, see Graham Barlow, "Hampton Court Theatre, 1718," *Theatre Notebook,* 37 (1983): 54–63.

3. The play had been performed at court in 1704 with a cast chiefly from LIF and with Wilks from Drury Lane as Dollabella, the role he played again in 1718. It had also been performed at Drury Lane in 1709 with a cast of second-rank players, except for Powell.

4. Chetwood, p. 201, speaks of her "Majestical Dignity" as Cleopatra; the comment upon this scene in act 2 is from Davies, DM, 2:369. In the same passage, Davies remarks upon Anne Oldfield's "harmonious and powerful voice," "fine person," and "grace and elegance of gesture." Milhous and Hume, *Producible Interpretation,* p. 134, surmise that Anne Oldfield and

Elizabeth Barry would have played Dryden's Cleopatra in a "much more energetic and aggressive style, more overtly sensual and passionate" than the role's originator, Elizabeth Bowtell. It should be emphasized, however, that *no* contemporary commentator ever described Anne Oldfield's tragic style as sensual or passionate—quite the opposite. That she brought some of these qualities to such colorless roles as Marcia, Andromache, and Sophonisba is only a guess, based upon knowledge of her very energetic and sexy comic style. The fact remains that commentators invariably stressed her dignity, grace, elegance, and decorum in tragic roles.

5. Downes, *Roscius Anglicanus*, pp. 94–95.

6. *London Stage*, 2:477. Davies, DM, 3:373, comments that as Millamant, "Oldfield's fine figure, attractive manner, harmonious voice, and elegance in dress, in which she excelled all her predecessors and successors except Mrs. [Fanny] Abington, left her without a rival."

7. Loftis, *Steele at Drury Lane*, pp. 55, 84–85.

8. *The Correspondence of John Hughes* (Dublin: T. Ewing, 1773), 1:135.

9. The most frequently performed Shakespeare comedy during Anne Oldfield's career was *The Merry Wives of Windsor. Measure for Measure, The Tempest, The Taming of the Shrew,* and *The Jew of Venice,* also popular, were greatly adapted from the original. *Much Ado About Nothing* was performed only once. These comedies were performed chiefly at LIF; for reasons that are not clear, the tragedies and history plays were chiefly performed at Drury Lane.

10. For the details of Steele's enmity with Newcastle see Loftis, *Steele at Drury Lane*, pp. 121–24. See also Calhoun Winton, *Sir Richard Steele, M.P.: The Later Career* (Baltimore: Johns Hopkins Press, 1970), 141–46.

11. Barker, *Mr Cibber of Drury Lane*, pp. 121–22.

12. John Dennis, *The Invader of His Country; or, The Fatal Resentment* (London: J. Pemberton and J. Watts, 1720), "Advertisement."

13. Barker, *Mr Cibber of Drury Lane*, p. 123.

14. PRO LC 5/157, folio 284.

15. For Horton's career, see the *Biographical Dictionary*, 5:419. She was a famous beauty—though not as celebrated as Anne Oldfield—and after Anne's death she inherited such roles as Millamant, Lurewell, Mrs. Sullen, Andromache, Lady Dainty, Berinthia, and Lady Townly. Thurmond, who joined the company in 1718, also became one of Drury Lane's leading actresses after Anne's death and inherited some of her roles: Angelica, Imoinda, Leonora, Narcissa, the Silent Woman, Silvia, Jane Shore, and Berinthia. There was no single successor to Anne's roles—no one new star who would become "the finisht copy of Mrs. Oldfield."

16. *Apology*, 1:310.

17. Barker, *Mr Cibber of Drury Lane*, p. 127.

18. Garrick Club Library, C. B. Smith's "Scrapbook of Original Letters," 1:123; 2:125.
19. *Faithful Memoirs,* p. 142.
20. Davies, DM, 3:436.
21. Indamora had been Jane Rogers's role at Drury Lane, but when she moved to LIF, she gave the role to her daughter, taking Nourmahal for herself. The play was not revived at Drury Lane until well after the death of Rogers in 1718.
22. Winton, *Sir Richard Steele, M.P.,* p. 199.
23. Kenny, *Plays of Richard Steele,* pp. 282–83.
24. Kenny, *Plays of Richard Steele,* p. 375.
25. Kenny, in *Plays of Richard Steele,* pp. 380–81, reprints an epilogue by Leonard Welsted, "Intended to be spoken by *Indiana.*" In it, Mrs. Oldfield makes it quite clear that Indiana is a radical departure from her usual comic role. The lines:

     With more Respect I'm entertain'd To-night:
     Our Author thinks, I can with Ease delight.
     My Artless Looks while modest Graces arm,
     He says, I need but to appear; and charm.

     seem to confirm the notion that Mrs. Oldfield's charms were depended upon to make the exemplary character a success.
26. Kenny, *Plays of Richard Steele,* pp. 299–300.

11.   *Apotheosis*

1. She maintained this pace until overtaken by illness in 1730; the chief difference between these years and the earlier years of her career is that she added fewer new roles. See appendix 1.
2. Beginning with the season of 1719–20 she began to play the lively and resourceful Ruth, in Robert Howard's popular comedy *The Committee,* several times each season. She had played it a few times from 1709–10 to 1711–12, but the role seems to have belonged to Susannah Verbruggen's daughter, Susannah Mountfort. Mountfort died in 1720, which may explain why Oldfield took up the role again at that time. Other tragic roles that she performed were Indamora, Anna Bullen, in Banks's sentimentalized historical tragedy *Vertue Betray'd; or, Anna Bullen,* Semandra, and Mary, Queen of of Scots.
3. See appendix 2.
4. In one famous instance of the tyranny of popularity, at the end of the

season of 1722–23 Wilks announced that he was giving up Sir Harry Wildair in *The Constant Couple*. But he was so popularly associated with the role that the play could not be given without him, and after one season in which it was not performed at all, the play was reinstated in the repertory—with Wilks, who played Sir Harry until his death.

5. The invaluable source for information on the history of Mayfair as a residential development is *Survey of London*, 39, see especially chapter 2. In 1977, the assistant editors, John Greenacombe and Victor Belcher, graciously provided me with unpublished material relating to the deed and the subsequent history of the house, as well as a ground plan for the lower floor of the house as it was in 1812, when Anne's son died. In 1980, I was able to walk through the building, which now houses the offices of Octopus Press.

6. *Authentick Memoirs*, p. 29. According to Mr. Greenacombe and Mr. Belcher, this amount was more than a house of that size usually fetched, but it is possible that she had the builder put in some expensive extra features. Over the years, her salary was raised, and by 1725 she was probably earning three hundred guineas per year. *Apology*, 2:71.

7. Dimensions taken from the ground plan for 1812. On the ground plan there is also a stable yard and stables, but whether they existed when Anne Oldfield lived there is not certain. See note 12 for a reference to her coach.

8. *Survey of London*, 39:180–83.

9. *A Catalogue of ALL the Rich Furniture of Mrs. OLDFIELD, deceas'd* [1731?]. Copy in the Folger Shakespeare Library. I am indebted to Edward Langhans for supplying me with a copy of this fascinating document.

10. After Mrs. Oldfield's death, Queen Caroline is said to have purchased this collection of plays for 120 guineas. *Notes and Queries*, second series, 11:123.

11. *Apology*, 1:309.

12. Westminster City Library, Buckingham Palace Road; Westminster Collection number 10/343: Roll of Charitable Subscribers to Westminster Hospital between 1719 and 1733. It was Mrs. Delany who saw Lord Hervey riding in Anne's coach: *Autobiography and Correspondence of Mrs. Delany*, 1:171.

13. Add. MSS 61,450, folio 230. I am particularly grateful to Dr. Frances Harris for locating this document in the Duchess of Marlborough's papers.

14. Downes, *Roscius Anglicanus*, p. 95.

15. Chetwood, pp. 253–54.

16. Samuel Johnson, *Lives of the English Poets* (London: Oxford University Press, 1906; rpt. 1964), 1:390–91. I wonder how Johnson could have failed to notice Calista's repentence in the harrowing scene in the last act, especially if he saw the role performed by Susanna Cibber, probably the first actress to portray Calista as a "fond, believing maid." His judgment

must have been based upon reading, rather than seeing the play—though Calista's change is also there for the reader to see. The critic who called Calista a whore was Charles Gildon, supposed author of *The New Rehearsal; or, Bays the Younger,* p. 59.

17. Malcolm Goldstein, ed., *The Fair Penitent* (Lincoln: University of Nebraska Press, 1969), 38.

18. Chetwood, pp. 201–2. Calista's sin is a little more palatable because her seduction occurs before the action of the play begins, although Lothario—the eponymous Lothario—describes it in luscious detail. In the course of the play her chief sin is filial disobedience.

19. Theophilus Cibber, *Lives and Characters of the Most Eminent Actors and Actresses of Great Britain and Ireland,* pp. 54–56.

20. *Apology,* 2:234–37. Cibber was pleased with the outcome, for the point was not to replace Wilks in the role but to make him see that his hard work for the company (never in dispute) did not set him above his fellow managers.

21. Dr. Marian Ury called to my attention that the poor reputation of Samaritans generally made the *good* Samaritan's act of charity all the more remarkable.

22. Johnson, *Lives of the Poets,* 2:139.

23. Johnson, *Lives of the Poets,* 2:164–65.

24. Johnson, *Lives of the Poets,* 2:105.

25. Johnson, *Lives of the Poets,* 2:117 [emphasis added].

26. For a discussion of Savage as a reviser of his life and of Johnson's approach to the biography of Savage, see Robert Folkenflik, *Samuel Johnson, Biographer* (Ithaca: Cornell University Press, 1978), especially chapter 9.

27. Leonard Howard, D.D., *A Collection of Letters and State Papers from the Original Manuscripts* (London: printed for the author, 1756), 2:676.

28. Footnote to "The Life of Richard Savage, Esq."—Johnson's biography—in Theophilus Cibber's edition of *Lives of the English Poets* (London: R. Griffiths, 1753), 5:44. Johnson himself does not mention Anne's role in procuring the pardon.

29. T. Cibber, ed., *Lives of the English Poets,* 5:33.

30. Bequests to her mother and her aunt, in her will, were probably a continuation of annuities that she paid them during her lifetime. *Faithful Memoirs,* appendix 2, pp. 6–7.

31. Savage's patrons assisted him by subscribing to the first edition of *Miscellaneous Poems and Translations by Several Hands* (London: Samuel Chapman, 1726), which included poems by Savage, Aaron Hill, William Popple, and William Colepepper. They included Sir Richard Steele (who had a falling-out with Savage six years earlier but was evidently sufficiently reconciled to be listed as a subscriber), and two of Anne's colleagues at Drury Lane—

Theophilus Cibber and Barton Booth. Booth subscribed for two books. But Wilks did not subscribe, nor did Anne Oldfield, although the book contained a poem by Savage in praise of her performance of Cleopatra in *All for Love*.

32. "As for the obligations he [the author of an anonymous biography of 1727] talks of from me to Mr. Wilks, he is again in error; I did subsist at that time on such obligations as he mentions, but they came from Mrs. Oldfield, not from Mr. Wilks." Letter dated May 10, 1739, in Montagu Pennington, *Memoirs of the Life of Mrs. Elizabeth Carter* (London: F. C. and J. Rivington, 1808), 1:60.

33. This is my own transcription from a photocopy of the original letter in the collection of the Loyola University of Chicago library. It differs in one important respect from the transcription published by Reverend Edward Carrigan, S.J., in the *Times Literary Supplement*, 42, no. 2,173 (September 25, 1943): 463. Father Carrigan transcribed the address as "Bliss Street." But there is no such street in the Strand or elsewhere in London. Upon closer examination, I saw that it was "Villiers Street," a street in the Strand where Steele was living at the time of his first acquaintance with Savage. Clarence Tracy, in *The Artificial Bastard: A Biography of Richard Savage* (Cambridge, Massachusetts: Harvard University Press, 1943), 46, repeats Carrigan's error. The "unnatural fiend" would be Savage's putative mother, Mrs. Brett, whose behavior—including the story that she pleaded against clemency for him after his murder trial—could certainly be termed unnatural, if she *was* his mother. "Mr Maynwaryng" is a key slipup in the letter, and it will not do to suggest that the reference is to Anne Oldfield's son. Young Arthur Maynwaring was a boy of nine when she first met Savage. Thus, even if he *had* a considerable amount of money in 1720, when Tracy believes the letter was written, it would not have been at his disposal, nor is it likely that Mrs. Oldfield would have referred to her young son as "Mr. Maynwaring." More irresponsible is Tracy's flat assertion (pp. 46–47) that the friendship between Oldfield and Savage existed, and his further insinuation that Anne may have been Savage's mistress— when she was not busy with the Prince of Wales! As evidence for the affair with Savage, he cites Savage's assertions to the contrary, arguing that the poet was "protesting too much." Tracy's evidence for the affair with the Prince of Wales is the use of the epithet "Ophelia" for Anne Oldfield, by Savage and others, for Tracy assumes that the Shakespeare character was understood to be the mistress of Hamlet, the heir to the Danish throne. But Mrs. Oldfield had been called Ophelia as early as 1713 (*Faithful Memoirs*, p. 59), before the advent of the Prince of Wales. This was, as noted in chapter 1, an obvious play on the pronunciation of "Oldfield." The play on words is certainly all that was meant by the coy introductory

remarks of the author of "Ophelia: or, The Lover's Day," published in *Faithful Memoirs*, p. 156, which Tracy cites. Perhaps the matter will rest here?

34. Peter Dixon, ed., *The Provoked Husband* (Lincoln: University of Nebraska Press, 1973), 5.

35. Davies, DM, 3:438–39.

36. Dixon, ed., *The Provoked Husband* pp. 16–17.

37. [William Cooke], *Memoirs of Charles Macklin*, pp. 23–24.

38. Davies, DM, 3:438.

39. Preface to *The Provoked Husband*, ed. Peter Dixon, p. 8.

40. *Apology*, 1:310.

41. *Apology*, 2:191.

42. *Autobiography and Correspondence of Mrs. Delany*, 1:175.

43. Preface to Henry Fielding, *Love in Several Masques*, in *The Complete Works of Henry Fielding, Esq.* (London: William Heinemann, 1903), 1:7–8. It is always possible, of course, that Fielding was flattering Mrs. Oldfield, with an eye to obtaining her support for his work, but I am inclined to believe that he was truly dazzled by her.

44. Abbé Prévost, *Mémoires et aventures d'un homme de qualité qui s'est retiré du monde*, ed. Mysie E. I. Robertson (Paris: T. V. Champion, 1927), 5:67. The events of volume five of *Mémoires* are set in 1716, but they are based upon Prévost's experiences in London from 1728 to 1730. This translation is my own. Chetwood's more free translation, in *General History*, p. 204, often quoted, has been mistakenly attributed to Voltaire. "It must be owned, she is an incomparable sweet Girl! She reconciled me to the English stage. Her Voice, her Shape, and all her Actions, so charm'd me, that I made the more Haste to learn the Language, that I might understand her." Chetwood (pp. 203–4) also repeats Prévost's apocryphal story about the wooing of Anne Oldfield by Sir Roger Mostyn.

12.   *The Actress and Her Legend*

1. *Apology*, 2:253. In addition to the retirement of Booth in 1728, these "accidents" included the death of Anne Oldfield in 1730; the injury of Mary Porter in 1731, which caused her temporary retirement from the stage; and the death of Wilks in 1732. Although Cibber lived until 1757, after 1733, he ceased his active participation in the affairs of Drury Lane.

2. British Library, R. J. Smith Collection, "History of the Stage," volume 4. Item (possibly from the *Grub Street Journal*) dated May 7, 1730. There is no indication that such a disposition was ever made. Steele's share of the patent, as part of his estate until three years after his death, passed to

his orphan daughters, who badly needed the income. See Loftis, *Steele at Drury Lane,* pp. 229–30.

3. There is a story that Anne had particularly encouraged Miller in his playwriting career, commissioning a comedy based on characters from *The Tatler;* she was to play opposite Wilks—"but the deaths of the two former occasioned its being laid aside." David Erskine Baker, *Biographia Dramatica* (New York: AMS Press, 1966), 1:515.

4. Benjamin Martyn, *Timoleon. A Tragedy* (London: J. Watts, 1730). "Non-resistance" was, of course, a punning reference to the doctrine of nonresistance, or passive obedience, to the established Church.

5. James Thomson, *Letters and Documents,* ed. Alan Dugald McKillup (Lawrence: University of Kansas Press, 1958), 7–9.

6. Johnson, *Lives of the Poets,* 2:351–52.

7. This is undoubtedly the usage—now obsolete—of "surprising" that was intended. (See OED, definitions 2a and 2b.) Gore-Brown, *Gay Was the Pit,* p. 182, infers that "perhaps the critics had guessed her state of health." If so, they were remarkably perceptive, for she continued throughout the remainder of the season at a brisk pace.

8. James Thomson, *Sophonisba* (London: A. Millar, 1730), preface.

9. Thomson, *Sophonisba,* p. 48. Thomson spells the name of the Numidian prince "Massanissa," but the standard spelling is "Massinissa."

10. Chetwood, p. 202.

11. Davies, DM, 3:436–37.

12. [Charlotte Charke], *A Narrative of the Life of Mrs. Charlotte Charke* (London: W. Reeve, A. Dodd, and E. Cook, 1755), 55.

13. Johnson, *Lives of the Poets,* 1:422–23. Johnson comments: "What effect this awful scene had on the earl I know not; he likewise died himself in a short time."

14. *Authentick Memoirs,* pp. 33–34. Laudanum, an opium derivative, was in use at this time as a painkiller, and it may have been used in Anne Oldfield's case. But drugs were not always used, then or later, in such cases; when they were used, relief was not always complete. See Doris Langley Moore, *Ada, Countess of Lovelace: Byron's Legitimate Daughter* (London: John Murray, 1977), 302–3, 313–16, 321–22. Clearly, readers of sensational pieces like *Authentick Memoirs* expected to hear the gory details.

15. *Faithful Memoirs,* p. 147. I am indebted to Risa Kagan, M.D., and Jeffrey L. Wolf, M.D., for suggesting the possibility that the condition was cervical cancer. They inform me that cervical cancer is the most painful of the cancers of the female reproductive system and that the illness, untreated, typically runs a course of about six months after the first symptoms appear.

16. *Faithful Memoirs,* p. 141.

17. *Faithful Memoirs*, p. 141.
18. *Apology*, 1:311–12.
19. *Authentick Memoirs*, p. 34.
20. *Faithful Memoirs*, p. 143. The conventional language and the good grammar and spelling suggest either that this passage was very much altered from Margaret Saunders's original letter or that the words were attributed to her. I suspect the latter. Whatever the source, this eulogy represents what people wished to believe of the actress on her deathbed.
21. *Daily Courant*, October 24, 1730: "Yesterday Morning, about Four o'clock, died the celebrated Mrs. Oldfield, after a long indisposition, at her House in Grosvenor-street." *Daily Post*, October 24, 1730: "Yesterday at One o'clock in the Morning died at her House in Grosvenor-street, that Celebrated Actress, Mrs. Oldfield."
22. *London Stage*, 3:86, 87.
23. Churchill later attempted to have a monument erected near the place of her burial, but his application was denied. Arthur Penrhyn Stanley, ed., *Historical Memorials of Westminster Abbey* (London: J. Murray, 1882), 284–85.
24. Voltaire, *Letters to England*, translated and with an introduction by Leonard Tatlock (Harmondsworth, Middlesex: Penguin Books, 1980), 112.
25. *Faithful Memoirs*, p. 144.
26. John Butt, ed., *The Poems of Alexander Pope* (London: Methuen, 1961), 3:36.
27. *Faithful Memoirs*, pp. 149–50.
28. *Faithful Memoirs*, p. 144.
29. Lewis, ed., *Horace Walpole's Correspondence*, 13:183.
30. PRO PROB 11/740, folio 138. For information about Hariett Churchill's adult life see Norma Perry, *Sir Everard Fawkener, Friend and Correspondent of Voltaire* (Banbury, Oxfordshire: Voltaire Foundation, 1975).
31. Henrietta Tayler, *The Jacobite Court at Rome in 1719, Scottish History Society Publications*, 3d series, 31 (Edinburgh: Scottish Historical Society, 1938), 208. Letter from James Murray to Mrs. Hay, dated April 17, 1721, mentions that "Churchill on his return from Vienna came to his house when he arrived at Paris and gallanted the Dutchess [of Mar] to the Opera." (The Duchess of Mar, Lady Mary Wortley Montagu's sister, was married to an exiled Jacobite peer. Churchill, in part because of his family connections, was able to spy on Jacobite activities for Robert Walpole.) A letter from Lady Mary Wortley Montagu to her sister, dated July 1722, also speaks of seeing and talking to Charles Churchill in Paris at the Opera. Robert Halsband, ed., *The Complete Letters of Lady Mary Wortley Montagu* (Oxford: Oxford University Press, 1965), 2:19.
32. Appendix 2, pp. 4–10. All references are to this will. Checked against the

memorial, PRO PROB 12/100, folio 312. All references are to the published text.

33. *Faithful Memoirs,* p. 142.

34. British Library, R. J. Smith collection, volume 4.

35. Information about the daughter and her death comes from Katherine Maynwaring's will, PRO PROB 11/1069, folios 101–2.

36. Romney Sedgwick, *The House of Commons 1715–1754* (London: Published for the History of Parliament Trust by HMSO, 1970), 1:551.

37. Lewis, ed., *Horace Walpole's Correspondence,* 19:104, 132.

38. PRO PROB 11/740, folio 141.

39. Obituary of Charles Churchill (Mrs. Oldfield's son), *Gentleman's Magazine* 82, no. 1 (1812): 398. The "Rich" referred to is Christopher Rich's son John, manager of Covent Garden and for many years the most famous Harlequin on the English stage.

40. Lewis, ed., *Horace Walpole's Correspondence,* 36:8. The singer was Giulia Frasi. The child seems to have died sometime in 1744.

41. For pictorial and other information about the history of Chalfont Park, I am grateful to William James Taylor and Norman Keen of British Alcan, who took time from their work to talk to me when I visited Chalfont Park, which now houses the Research and Development division of British Alcan, in the summer of 1985.

42. *Autobiography and Correspondence of Mrs. Delany,* 3:79. Tate Wilkinson, in *Memoirs of His Own Life* (London: printed for the author, 1790), 4:84, wrote: "I . . . venture to affirm, against many judgments of stage opinions of a modern green-room, that the celebrated Mrs. Oldfield's Lady Townly &c would now be pronounced excellent." (The reasons he adduces have mostly to do with her elegance of dress and manner.)

43. Charles Reade, "Art: A Dramatic Tale," in *The Course of True Love Never Did Run Smooth* (London: Richard Bentley, 1857), 64–149.

Index

*J*oanne Lafler lives in Oakland, California. At present she is a Research Associate in Dramatic Art at the University of California, Berkeley, where she received her Ph.D. She is also affiliated with the Institute for Historical Study in San Francisco, of which she is a founding member and past president.